HOW TO ROCKET
YOUR PRIVATE INVESTIGATION BUSINESS:
THE COMPLETE SERIES!

John A Hoda

CLI, CFE

How to Rocket Your Private Investigation Business: The Complete Series

Copyright John A. Hoda (2019)

All rights reserved. No part of this publication may be reproduced, stored in a retrieval system, or transmitted in any form or by any means with the prior written permission of the publisher.

ISBN:978-0-9890201-7-6

Requests to publish work from this book should be sent to john@JohnHoda.com.

Cover and Interior Illustrations, Titling, and Interior Layout: Creative Jay (creativejay.com)

HOW TO ROCKET YOUR PRIVATE INVESTIGATION BUSINESS

THE COMPLETE SERIES

John A Hoda
CLI, CFE

BOOK ONE

HOW TO

LAUNCH
YOUR
PRIVATE INVESTIGATION
BUSINESS

90 DAYS TO LIFT OFF!

INTRODUCTION

JOHN A. HODA

This book is written by a person who considered himself an investigator first and a business person second. It took a long time to blend those roles seamlessly to run a successful private investigation business. Understand that being a great investigator doesn't guarantee you will have a tremendous private investigation business. Some will argue that your investigative mindset may get in the way of your operational skills and your business creativity. There is an axiom that says the great bricklayer with average business skills will make less money than the average bricklayer with excellent business skills. You may be able to find anyone but to help anyone see you, you must think like a marketer.

I am not an MBA or a business coach with a good grasp of generic business principles, applying a multipurpose plan to a private investigations business no differently than to a pest control company or a pizza restaurant. I am speaking as a private investigator to private investigators. My goal is to help you avoid the minefields and chart a course for greater success. I know where the mines are hidden, just below the surface. I almost sailed into a few.

INTRODUCTION

The other thing to remember is that you are a professional, in most states, a licensed professional, and that you provide a service. The more your service is specialized, and the more unique your approach is, the less the consumer will view your services as a commodity. More money for you, and you stand above the herd.

As a working investigator, I know what it's like to have an investigator's mindset. I remember thinking like an investigator can sometimes get in the way of making business decisions as they relate to your time management and how you may want to approach new ventures. My experiences through the last twenty-one years have come from some hard-knock lessons and near disasters but, through it all, I was able to forge ahead and have stayed profitable for 84-plus quarters. I've been able to meet all of my financial obligations and have created a retirement plan that will allow me to retire at a date earlier than I had initially projected.

Before we get much further into the introduction, I want to share a personal anecdote with you—one of many to come but let me start with this one.

A few months ago, I was riding with a friend. He was a long-time private investigator and had many years under his belt before I even started back in 1997.

He asked me, "John if you had to do it all over again, would you do it?"

I surprised him with my answer. I told him, knowing what I know now, I would not have leaped. That caused him to raise an eyebrow. I said to him that at the time I decided to go in business for myself, I had a very comfortable position as a well-respected senior special investigator for a significant property & casualty insurance company and was being interviewed for management positions at other special investigations units. I had a very steep mortgage and was paying for both daycares and saving for college education for my two children. My wife had a good job, a steady income, and excellent benefits. After a financial scare nine years earlier, we had set aside six months of gross income, so there was somewhat of a cushion; however, the income that I would have to replace from my job with my new venture was quite a bit. I would have to make that up within seven or eight months of the start-up, or I would have to bail out.

I told my long-time friend that I did not fully appreciate the risk I was about to undertake. I had excellent investigative skills. I was at the top of my game and was hoping to ply my trade doing precisely the same type of work as a private investigator instead of as a salaried employee. That didn't mean I had the business acumen to be able to run a business effectively. I didn't know how to market, and I thought cash flow was what you had in the checkbook at the end of the month. However, I did tell my friend that, having made that leap over twenty-one years ago and having succeeded through all these years, I have very few regrets.

Not only was I able to work in the area of my expertise, insurance fraud investigations, but I was also able to learn how to conduct investigations in the field of forensic genealogy and missing heir research. I also learned how to transfer my criminal investigative skills to that of a criminal defense investigator.

More importantly, I think this is the best part, and I was able to train investigators in my techniques and in the way I went about my investigations. Watching them apply those investigative skill sets to their cases was most gratifying, but more importantly, how they blossomed as investigators.

Does this story surprise you? I hope that, during the course of this book and this series, I will continue to surprise you and challenge some of your assumptions and beliefs. I hope to help you understand why some things are more comfortable than they seem and why some things are harder than they appear.

INTRODUCTION

Primarily, you'll learn which is which, without having to spend much time, money, and effort.

In a nutshell, I want to tell you about all those things I didn't know then and that I had to learn the hard way. These lessons are what I want to share with you here. I want to make your path a little easier and a little straighter, so you can get to your goals quicker and with less anxiety, make more money in your business and, at the same time, enjoy the work you love.

It would be unfair to try to have everyone fit into my mold of how I did things. That's why I've created three characters whom you can compare and contrast. Hopefully, you can learn from these different characters as they approach their liftoff.

First, I will introduce you to **Tony Russo**. He is about to retire from the New York City Police Department as a Detective Sergeant. He's looking to go into PI business where he'll work mostly in Queens, New York, and eastern Long Island.

Beth Clark is a two-tour veteran of the United States Army, with experience in Intelligence from her days in the sandbox of Afghanistan. She relocated to Austin, Texas. A single woman of color, looking to use her smarts and skills and to go into business for herself. She wants to see what she can do without having to deal with the layers of management or bureaucracy between her and the customer. She wants to build a business that will eventually run without her in its daily operations.

Finally, there is **my personal story** of getting prepared for my September 1997 launch date where I was looking to create a business to serve property & casualty insurance companies. My goal was to sell my business to my employees and retire wealthy and early.

We will explore the paths being taken by Tony, looking to work with professionals, Beth, looking to work with the consumers, and John, looking to leverage his specialized skills with specific businesses that would require them.

After I introduce you more fully to Tony, Beth, and John, we will look ahead to the book's sections and then, dive into the hard questions.

Trust me; you'll be glad I asked these hard questions in the beginning. I intend to save you time effort and money with the questions, exercises, and checklists.

INTRODUCTION

Tony Russo is about ready to pull the pin, as they say in police work. He's been on the job for twenty-seven years and is tired of all the bureaucracy and having to supervise a group of detectives who seem to be less interested in the profession than the benefits. He's itching to get out and work some cases on his own again and to simplify his life. This PI business for him is a lifestyle choice. He is looking to augment his pension and work on cases that interest him.

He has decided he wants to work with lawyers, accountants, and small business owners in the borough of Queens in New York City and possibly expand into neighboring Nassau County on Long Island. Combined, both have a population base of over two million people. It would certainly give him enough opportunities to do what he wants in a somewhat condensed geographic area.

Beth Clark is formerly from the Twin Cities of Minneapolis and St. Paul, Minnesota. Upon graduation from high school, she enlisted in the Army and served two tours in Afghanistan as part of an Intelligence unit. Beth is smart and ambitious. Now living in Austin, Texas, she's looking to start her business in that city providing services for regular people. Her business model is business-to-consumer or B2C. She does not have any role models for creating a company and is looking to start from scratch. She is presently working for an armed guard security service that allows her to schedule herself to work available hours while she methodically launches her business.

INTRODUCTION

John is 43 years old. He has been a police officer and has worked his way up in the insurance business to become a claims manager. He also was a Special Agent and Area Supervisor for the Insurance Crime Prevention Institute, providing fraud investigation services to the property and casualty insurance industry. Before launching his business, he was a senior special investigator and quality control SIU manager for different insurance companies. It is the year 1997, at the dawn of the internet. John has a young family and is looking to go out on his own. He wants to scratch the entrepreneurial itch and thinks his investigative methods can be replicated. He wants to grow a regional private investigations company providing insurance fraud investigation and complex investigations for property & casualty insurance companies in a territory from Bangor, Maine to Baltimore, Maryland.

DISCLAIMER

PLEASE READ

I have done my best to give you useful and accurate information in this book, but I cannot guarantee that the information is correct or will be appropriate for your particular situation. Law, procedures, and regulations change frequently and are subject to differing interpretations. It is your responsibility to verify all the information and the laws discussed in this book before relying on them. Noting in this book can substitute for legal advice and cannot be considered as making it unnecessary to obtain such advice. In all situations involving local, state and federal law, especially as it relates to PI regulations and carrying weapons, receive specific information from the appropriate government agency.

OVERVIEW OF THIS BOOK

WHAT TO EXPECT

Section One: Red Light / Green Light (Page 17)

We will talk about:

- The most common reasons for failure and the most common reasons for success and the impact of state licensing on your decision.
- How you're going to talk with your significant others or persons of influence to get buy-in on your decision.
- How to start thinking about beginning your business with the end in mind.

Section One ends with ten fundamental red light/green light questions that will help you determine whether or not you should even go further into the process of expending time and capital to build your business.

OVERVIEW OF THIS BOOK

Section Two: How Not To Get Poor (Page 39)

We will talk about:

- How not to get poor in your business venture.
- How not to drive yourself into a severe debt or worse, bankruptcy.
- How to understand your full list of expenses and see what your true debts are.
- How to determine, in everyday layman's terms, what your savings and equity are.
- Calculating expenses for Tony, Beth, and John
- How to create your chart of monthly expenses

Section Three: Balance Sheet? (Page 49)

We will talk about:

- Income, and the difference between income and revenue.
- Bookkeeping best practices.
- Remaining mindful of what your business is about.
- The impact of taxes, and implication of taxes, on your business.
- Creating a spreadsheet of expenses for Tony, Beth, John, and yourself.
- What revenue you need to break even after covering your business and personal expenses.

Section Four: Forget Mission, Vision, and Value Statements (Page 65)

We will talk about:

- Simon Sinek's TEDx talk on Why, How and What (18 minute YouTube video).
- Charting a Why, How, and What exercise for Tony, Beth, John, and yourself.

Section Five: Needs Analysis (Page 75)

We will talk about:

- Your customer's needs and how to meet those needs with existing or newly learned skill sets.
- Understanding the difference between the user and your ultimate buyer.
- Deciding what business you will be in B2B, P2P, B2C, or a hybrid.
- Who the target audience for Tony, Beth and John are, and determine your own target audience.
- John's story of the International Missing Heir Finders as an example of the above.
- Determining how much to charge per hour.
- Calculating your critical number, which is the most important number to track regularly.

Section Six: What's In A Name (Page 91)

We will talk about

- Naming your business
- Domain names
- Website hosting services

OVERVIEW OF THIS BOOK

- WordPress platform and themes
- Home page
- About page
- Services page
- FAQ page
- Maximizing your SEO for your target audience
- Email capture
- e-Commerce
- Sales Funnels
- Autoresponders
- Checklist

Section Seven: Marketing For The Investigator (Page 107)

We will talk about:

- How to get into the flow of marketing
- Generating Leads
- Qualifying your prospects
- Offering assurances
- Clarifying their questions
- Overcoming objections
- Getting the assignments
- Agreeing on price
- Up-sell strategies
- The importance of communicating with your client
- Testimonials or Customer Satisfaction Surveys
- Referrals
- Creating a one-page marketing plan

Section Eight: The Business Of Your Business (Page 127)

We will talk about:

- Business entities: sole proprietorship, a single member LLC, or an S or C Corporation
- Licensing, Bonding, and Insurance
- Methods to use to maintain your assignments
- Assignment logs
- Client reporting
- CRM or customer relationship management software
- Time management methods
- Accounting software
- Using a checklist during your 90 days to lift off

Section Nine: Countdown Summary (Page 145)

We will talk about:

- Putting all the pieces together in the building block fashion
- Tony's Sample plan
- Beth's Sample Plan
- John's Sample Plan
- The tasks that need to be done and where to put them on the launch schedule.

Section Ten: Bonus Story (Page 163)

- John's launch of Elm City Detectives, 9-21-12 to 1-1-13

SECTION ONE:
RED LIGHT / GREEN LIGHT

(you will thank me later)

SOBERING STATISTICS

What is the real cost of failure? One of my mentors Jimmie Mesis, the former owner and editor of *PI Magazine*, once told me 85% of all private investigators do not renew their licenses after two years. That is an astounding failure rate.

Similarly, statistics from the Small Business Administration say that after five years, 85% of all small businesses fail. Additionally, in the next five years, of those remaining 15%, another 85% of those businesses fail. So essentially, after ten years, only 3% of small businesses will still be in business.

I'm sure the statistics for private investigation businesses are very similar. You have to ask yourself why.

We will get into those reasons in a few minutes, but for now, let's talk about the real cost of failure. Let's talk about crushed dreams, lost capital, drained bank accounts, maxed out credit cards. Worse, how about those who took out a second mortgage and then had to file for bankruptcy?

SECTION ONE: RED LIGHT / GREEN LIGHT

Then there's the emotional factor of having to reenter the job force and explain to a prospective employer where you were for the last year or year and a half?

What about having to take calls from the aggressive collection agencies or angry creditors; people who trusted you enough to do business with you? All this has an emotional toll on your psyche.

How could this have been avoided? How could you have changed things? What could you have done differently? These are all questions that could go through your mind.

In a book titled *How To Launch Your Private Investigation Business: 90 Days To Lift Off,* you're wondering why the first section has to do with sobering statistics of failure. Well, it's because we've all seen lots of grainy television footage and movie footage of rocket ships that exploded on liftoff or while still in our atmosphere. A few of these, unfortunately, were human-crewed spaceflights.

The reality is that many rocket ship failures occur before rocket ships are launched successfully. There is a learning-from-failure principle here that the scientists gain knowledge from. My hope is you can build a business by learning from my failures and those of others, so you can avoid the hardship of becoming one of those failure statistics.

Most Common Reasons For Failure:

- You didn't want to be in business for yourself, and you're more comfortable working for someone else.
- Running out of money.
- Lack of paying customers.
- Not having a clear business plan (round peg - square hole)
- Not bothering to work the plan you made
- Squandering your time
- Chasing "bright shiny objects' or in other words, changing direction without a solid business case or reason to do so
- Not spending enough money on the proper equipment.
- Not allocating enough money for marketing (at least 10% of your expense budget)
- Biggest cause: not spending enough time on marketing your business.

Traits For Success:

- Burning desire to overcome all obstacles
- Positive attitude when dealing with problematic circumstances or people
- Preserving cash and understanding that "cash is king."
- Executing your game plan on a quarterly, monthly, weekly, and daily basis
- Understanding what the most important numbers for your business success are
- Exceeding customer expectations; Are you a problem solver?
- Consistently tweaking your plan to attract prospects and convert them into customers in a replicable and scalable manner
- Streamlined processes for the delivery of products or services to your clients
- Seamless integration of back-office processes that allow for the delivery of all products or services in an efficient manner

State Licensing–Do Not Pass Go If...

In a cursory check of state licensing requirements—and I am no expert, I expect you to check very carefully what your state requires in order to have a license—we see several states do not require any licenses such as Idaho and South Dakota.

Some states require licensing in towns if you wish to work in a particular city.

Then there is the question of what are the *requirements* to become licensed. They go from Alaska having no requirements, to Delaware having to have five years of investigative experience. In Arkansas, there is a need of two years of working with a PI in either Arkansas, Tennessee, Oklahoma, or Louisiana, and then passing an exam.

Some states require a college education; most don't, however, and you can substitute years of experience by having either an Associate's degree, Bachelor's degree, or even a Master's degree.

Some states require passing an examination (Nevada, Montana, and New York) and attending a 40-hour class (Louisiana).

This is a cursory review and is by no means advice on whether or not your state has a license requirement that you must meet.

Generally speaking, people come into the private investigation business from law enforcement, where their years of education and investigative experience qualifies them to apply for a license.

Other persons come into the investigative business by working for a private investigator or private investigations firm, from an apprentice role to a full-time employee status that allows them to secure their license.

The application process sometimes requires a background check, such as credit reports, driver histories, criminal checks, and fingerprinting which are all geared to protect the consumer from unscrupulous business practices.

SECTION ONE: RED LIGHT / GREEN LIGHT

A few states allow reciprocity between states and you should check the reciprocity agreements between states before thinking about crossing state lines.

I needed to secure a state license in New York, New Jersey, Connecticut, Massachusetts, Vermont, New Hampshire, and Maine, and town licensing in Rhode Island.

In the Commonwealth of Pennsylvania, you have to go before a county judge to be granted a license.

Almost all states require bonding; that is a performance bond. A performance bond is a *surety* bond and offers some compensation to aggrieved clients who have not received the services rendered. They can claim your bond.

Most states also require errors and omissions coverage. My state, Connecticut, requires a one-million-dollar policy and I have a two-million-dollar aggregate.

Some states also require a professional liability insurance.

Carrying a gun has its own rules and regulations. If you wish to carry a concealed weapon as a private investigator, you have to know your private investigator's code inside and out before even considering it. Understand a concealed carry license will increase your premium for your liability insurance and failing to disclose that you carry a gun as a regular part of your business would be grounds for your insurance company to deny coverage in the event your gun is involved in a claim being made against you.

Part of your homework, at this time, is to understand all the licensing requirements for the states where you wish to work, and whether bonding and insurance are required. You must especially understand the laws governing the carrying of the weapons or concealed weapons.

Personal Experience On Deciding To Take The Plunge

Back in 1996 and 1997, John had a young family and a steep mortgage. He and his wife were both paying for daycare and setting aside money for college for their two children, at the same time as funding their retirement accounts. They had created a budget for their combined expense. They were both in their early earning years when raises and promotions were regularly occurring. They were able to keep up on the necessary costs and had some money to go on occasional travel vacations.

Shortly after moving to Connecticut on a job promotion, the then-Governor instituted a personal income tax where there had not been one before. For the next two years, his family did not go on any vacations because the money that had been earmarked for vacations had to pay for the newly created personal income taxes. Thank you, Lowell Weicker.

When he began talking about going out on his own, his wife astutely pointed out that there was no one in his immediate family, and no one in her immediate family, who had any experience running a successful solo business, and neither of them had the business acumen to do so. She was also concerned about the loss of income during the time it would take to build the business up to where it would become profitable. These were very valid concerns, and those concerns were voiced both logically and emotionally. He spent much time, during the planning stages before liftoff, to assuage her fears he would be able to not only return his family to its standard of living but also would increase it.

It is at this time you have to think about having "the talk" with your loved ones and significant others about the changes self-employment will have on the family dynamic. You might have gone to a job location every day, and now you'll be working at home. Even working at home has its issues, as it relates to your workspace, time management, and how you're going to go about your business when house chores are calling.

Will you need to tighten the belt and explain to your family they may have to forgo some of their extravagances during the time it takes to ramp up your business? Are they willing to sacrifice financially now for the long-term benefit?

These are all questions to ponder at this time for one fundamental reason: you need to have allies during this significant time. It can be a very lonely time, especially in the private investigation business, to go out on your own. You will strive to launch a business by pitching prospects for the investigative services you wish to provide them. You will be met with your self-doubt when some prospects turn you down.

It is an uphill battle to try to launch a business without having the support of family and your closest friends. So, keep this in the back of your mind as you go through the next couple sections. Right now, it's okay to talk about the idea of wanting to go out on your own, but you need to have a little bit more understanding of the complexity of that decision before you talk with any family members or friends about doing so.

Begin With The End In Mind

This is one of the most important pieces of advice I wish I had received when I started out. Generally, I had an idea that I wanted to create a business I would be able to sell to my employees once we reached our goal of becoming a regional investigations firm covering the mid-Atlantic and New England states.

I didn't plan on having to learn the skill sets necessary to accomplish that goal. I thought my small team project management skills were sufficient. I was viewing the business through the eyes of an investigator and not through the lens of a business person. I failed to consider all the steps necessary to create a vibrant business that could operate competitively in ten mid-Atlantic and New England states. In the twenty-one years of self-employment, I observed other Private Investigators also fail to begin with the end in mind of what they hoped to accomplish and how did they foresee their business reaching its final stages.

For some, they just want to work for X number of years, then tell their clients that they're going to stop taking on new cases. When they reached their last case, they would turn off the lights and close the door behind them.

For others, it is creating a partnership and selling their share to the remaining partners as a part of a buyout.

A few want to eventually sell the business to a buyer with generous upfront terms or, more effectively, selling the company over time to their employees, which would give them a guaranteed income on a gradual buyout (more of that later in the series).

You have to begin with the end in mind, and you have to see the arc of your business clearly and where it's going to be at various stages in your life. The skills you have now may not be the skills you will need later to accomplish your end goal. Please keep this in mind as we proceed.

Abort! Abort! Abort!

Now it is time for a difficult discussion. I'm talking about what to do when things don't work out the way you thought they would.

Were there circumstances beyond your control, or circumstances that you didn't even contemplate, which sabotaged your launch? You have to outline specific criteria that will mean it's time to pull the plug. You must pick a date by which, if you are not making X dollars a week or month, regularly, you need to abort the mission. You need to know that it is much better to amputate the limb than bleed out and lose the body.

I knew too many people in the private investigation business that put a second mortgage on their house, maxed out their credit cards, and began robbing Peter to pay Paul to keep a leaky boat afloat. They would have been better off getting into the lifeboats and scuttling the ship. They would still have some money, some creditworthiness, and the ability to move back into the industry, without leaving much flotsam in the water.

I repeat it here: a serious discussion has to be held as part of "the talk" with the people important to you. Explain to them that, if by date certain, you have not reached X for your revenue, then the **exit plan** has to be activated.

So, as part of beginning with the end in mind, you need to know how you want your business to prosper—define what success looks like for you—and have an exit strategy, should various factors force you to abandon your self-employment goals for now.

Plan B: The Pivot

Besides ending your business on a profitable note or aborting it to retain what little capital you have left and returning to the workforce, the third option is called Plan B.

In the latest Silicon Valley start-up parlance, it is called a pivot. That is when you realize the direction in which you first sought to generate leads, prospects, and customers were faulty and, with your time and remaining resources, begin searching for different customers and/or customer acquisition methods to scale and replicate.

You might be still going after the same customer base but doing so in a different fashion, emphasizing a different skill set in meeting their needs or learning a new skill.

The pivot happens when you start listening to customers' wants and needs and pivot from what you *thought* they wanted.

RED LIGHT / GREEN LIGHT CHECKLIST

Ten Yes / No Questions

1. Do you have a burning desire?
2. Are you willing to work significantly longer hours than at present? Only a lifestyle business in retirement is the exception here.
3. Are you willing to work on some of the more mundane tasks of running a business consistently?
4. Are you willing to learn enough about bookkeeping, accounting, marketing, and sales to keep your fanny out of the fire?
5. If your business model requires you to be available for your customers on nights, weekends, or holidays, will you able to answer the bell as often as needed?
6. Are you or your family willing to tighten the belt during lean times or periods of protracted low cash flow?
7. Are you willing to learn new investigative skill sets to round out your services to your customers or clients?
8. Are you optimistic you will have the support of family and friends to launch your private investigation business?

SECTION ONE: RED LIGHT / GREEN LIGHT

9. Do you think you have sufficient capital to be able to afford your launch?
10. Have you successfully overcome adversity in the past?

This checklist should be reviewed now and looked at again later if you decide to go on. It would help if you revisited this checklist when you have a better grasp on what it is you're going to do, how you're going to do it, and the money you're going to need to keep your business above water. Keep in mind; this checklist is predicated on the fact you will be capable of procuring the license in the states you wish to operate in.

Tony had to access his feelings. It was not always easy for a thinking man's detective at the NYPD. Cops and detectives have a way of burying feelings as they face the daily onslaught of murder, mayhem, and utter disregard for human life and private property. He had not thought about these red light/green light questions. He had seen a few of his colleagues go out on their own. Most ended up pulling private security details when they came up. Some made up bull when the going got tough and quit before heading to Myrtle Beach or Florida to play golf and take it easy.

Was he burned out? Would he pack it in when the going got tough? No, he wanted to get out from under the NYPD's rules and bureaucracy and work on his own. He missed working the street and wanted to pick and choose his caseload. Nothing else was fatal here. With his pension assured and with his wife's salary and backing, he didn't see any other show-stoppers. He could do this on his terms and at his own pace.

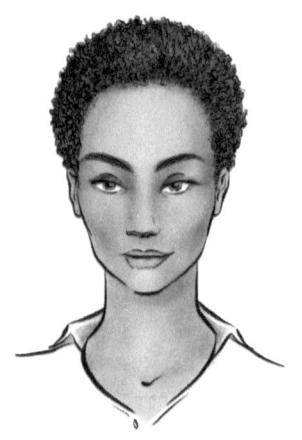 The red light/green light questions for Beth weren't even a speed bump on her road to launch. Years of taking orders in the Army and mining someone else's gold in the armed guard security business had her chomping at the bit. Yes, she needed to learn about business, but she would attack that like a six-miler through the rolling hills of Austin as the sun was rising. One thing the Army taught her in Afghanistan is that things change, and she had to always be on the look-out. Mistakes could get good people killed. She had a knack for breaking complex problems down into digestible parts even when the intel was sketchy. She had stayed friendly with some Army buds on Facebook and made some friends in Austin, and they were all gung-ho for her.

She knew she had to bootstrap this puppy from scratch. It had to be a soft launch.

CONGRATULATIONS!

After completing this checklist, you've decided to either move forward or to shelve your plans to launch your private investigation business.

I'm saying congratulations to the reader that decides to shelve their plans. By taking a few minutes now on the front end to do a gut check, you are saving yourself a lot of heartache, trouble, and expense later on, when one or more of these reasons could become the cause for your business failure.

For those readers wishing to go forward, again, congratulations! You've taken the time necessary to think about the business of your business, and this is going to become much more critical as you go forward.

"The first rule of entrepreneurship is not how to get rich. It's how not to get poor."

—Cliff Ennico, Attorney-at-Law

SECTION TWO: HOW NOT TO GET POOR

YOUR EXPENSES

In this section, we are going to talk about your expenses, your taxes, and what you have set aside for savings and equity. Don't be scared off by the word equity. After you make your last car payment, what is your car worth if you put a sales sign on it? If you had to sell your home right now, after expenses and paying off your mortgage note, what do you have left over? That is equity.

Do you really know your expenses?

A quick review of your checkbook register and credit card statement is not enough to know all of your expenses. You need to sit down and look at least twelve months and make a spreadsheet of the usual and recurring expenses. This will help you with the exercise below.

You will also have to think about what you'd be paying for health insurance, not just what is being deducted from your paycheck. What are all your other payroll deductions that, if you were to leave your employer, you would have to pay for yourself? If you think about it, each of your expenses is what goes out of your pocket after payroll deductions and taxes

What do you have left at the end of the month? Some people are in a negative cash position. They are not able to live on their paycheck and have to rely on paying exorbitant interest rates on larger and larger credit card balances. They keep kicking the can down the road. Eventually, the credit cards will have to be paid off.

How much debt are you carrying?

Mortgage? Car Loans? Furniture? Home Equity Line? Credit cards? Recreational vehicles? Timeshares? Tax repayments?

What are your savings and equity?

Savings are all monies you have set aside, separate from your operating accounts. I'm a little hesitant to call certificates of deposits or CDs 'savings' because of their lack of liquidity, in that you're not able to get your hands on that money right away (although you may be able to take a cash loan against the certificate of deposit at a hefty fee). You think of savings as your retirement accounts. Again, there are penalties for early withdrawal and tax consequences. Also, consider all your stocks and bonds and other financial instruments which can be converted to cash relatively quickly.

I think in terms of liquidity, with savings, as any financial instrument you can turn readily to cash within a short period.

Examples:

Tony, Beth, and John are looking to start their businesses within 90 days. They are looking at their expenses to see how much money they must earn to cover their necessary living expenses.

Keep in mind; this doesn't include what will be their one-time or short-term business expenses related to the formation and operating of their businesses.

YOUR EXPENSES

Lastly, do not forget the tax consequence of their earnings and how much money they have to set aside for federal, state, and local taxes. Pay stubs will give you a ballpark idea, **but you should consult with an accountant about your set apart for your quarterly estimates.**

Expenses	Tony	Beth	John*	You
Mortgage/Rent	$1,750	$1,150	$1,475	
Car Expenses	$900	$275	$600	
Health Care/Co-Pays/Deductibles	$600	$620	$200	
Child Care/College Savings	$0	$0	$1,100	
Clothing	$100	$20	$75	
Food	$1,000	$400	$600	
Entertainment	$500	$154	$200	
Utilities	$325	$200	$300	
Loans	$500	$750	$0	
Credit Cards	$2,254	$500	$775	
Telephone	$54	$100	$300	
Household Repairs and Maintenance	$200	$20	$300	
Gym	$0	$20	$300	
Vacation	$200	$100	$200	
Gifts	$200	$34	$200	
Retirement Accounts	$200	$200	$200	
Total	$8,783	$4,502	$6,579	

*John's startup was in 1997, so for purposes of this writing, the numbers are inflated to equal values at the time of publishing.

SUMMARY

These expense items are not a totality of possible expenses you may be facing. They don't take into account such things as elder care, one-time expenses, emergencies, and so on. This exercise is to get you thinking of what your family unit's real spending is.

"Ouch," Tony thinks. "That hurt."

He and Mary had been living the good life. Even though she was an excellent cook and baker, they spent a ton of money eating out. They spared no expense on their vacations. "Need it? Put it on the credit card." "Want it? Put it on the credit card."

As their property value rebounded following the '08-'09 housing collapse, they remortgaged their house and cleaned up all of their credit card balances, only to let that insidious debt creep up again. He and Mary stared at the spreadsheet in disbelief, then in resignation. How did two smart, hard-working people allow this to happen *twice*?

Now he has to work and make more money than to replace his income. He has to get the credit cards paid off if they want to have any equity in the house they bought years ago and should have paid off by now.

He and Mary agree to cut back on the restaurants and upscale vacations. The car leases were lavish. Today's cars can last ten years, at the rate they put mileage on them. All across the board, the couple decides to tighten their belts and make the adjustments needed to spend less than they earn. Financial freedom becomes a new mantra.

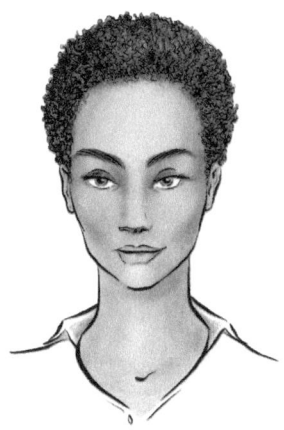

Looking at the numbers, Beth has two choices: Take on a second job or invest in her business and continue to float her debt until she can get into a positive cash-flow.

Co-signing the loans for a family member had been a mistake. They stopped paying on them, leaving her to face that nut every month now, and for the next three years. It was already refinanced down to the lowest interest rate she could get.

She is paying an average rent for a nice unit in a well-kept complex between the airport and downtown Austin. After years of living in spartan Army barracks, this is her only "extra."

Otherwise, she keeps a tight ship. Or so she thinks until she sees her spending on Starbucks and the independent coffee houses in the area. She lives on caffeine, and if she could hang a drip from the top of the Armored vehicles she rode in, she would. Those lattes and artisan drinks make up a whopping $210 a month.

The next day, after swallowing her nitro-infused cold brew, she buys a plain-vanilla drip coffee-maker and a hefty thermos. That saved money can go into the business.

SECTION THREE: BALANCE SHEET?

YOU DON'T NEED NO STINKING BALANCE SHEET.

BALANCE SHEET ACCOUNTS

The balance sheet has the simple but maddening equation:

Assets = Liabilities + Equity

Try to understand what your accountant is saying when he does a trial balance at the end of the year. Thank him for explaining it to you again. Nod your head enthusiastically and say, "Wow!"

I found that the most essential items to be watching are on your income statement or what is called your profit and loss statement (P&L). Later on, I will give you a Cash Flow Snapshot that you calculate on the 15th and the 30th of every month.

Mostly, if you run out of money, you either have to take out loans to pump up the business or factor your receivables or do something drastic to stay in business. So you have to concentrate less on the static Balance Sheet and more on the profit and loss statement along with the cash flow snapshot as a way of maintaining your fiscal health with your business. Your profit and loss statement is made up of income items and expense items that are a little bit more simpler to understand.

Knowing some basics of bookkeeping include the need to discuss debits and credits, knowing what accounts can be debited and credited and why and how what journal entries are made to your general ledger. These are all words that you may not be familiar with, but in concise order, you'll have to get a general idea of what they all mean to understand the basics of running a business.

Bookkeeping Tips

The Internet has made it so much easier to find information on any topic—at least for learning its nomenclature. Go to YouTube and search for 'basic bookkeeping' or 'basic accounting,' and you'll see some paid advertising that will give short tutorials explaining the basics. The most important decision you're going to make, as it relates to how to keep your records, is whether or not you'll use an accountant and a bookkeeper or some combination thereof.

I do not recommend doing your own accounting. My experience is that you should have a professional, preferably a certified public accountant (CPA), look over your books. At tax time, you don't want to be David without his slingshot standing up against the Goliath of your Federal Government (IRS) or your State's Department of Revenue Services.

Most importantly you want to separate your deposits and the check writing functions and keep them away from either your accountant and your bookkeeper. I would recommend in the first years, you handle the checkbook yourself and either make the electronic payments or write out the checks yourself. Delegate the separation of the bookkeeping from the bill paying so that no one person has complete control over your checkbook other than yourself.

We will talk about the way to choose an accountant later in this book; however, the critical point to know when you are choosing an accountant is what the accountant's preferred method of keeping your books will be.

The big daddy of accounting software is QuickBooks by Intuit, and there are other outstanding and less expensive computer software options to ease and facilitate entering all your information and handling online banking as it pertains to your business.

I use QuickBooks because my accountant uses QuickBooks. I also have firsthand knowledge of FreshBooks and Wave and can recommend either one of them. There are other, cheaper, options and yes, there's even a manual ledger system you can utilize if your business is small enough. As long as you keep your receipts and track all your payments and income, a paper system could work as effectively. However, when you want to compare one year to another or one quarter to a previous quarter, the electronic systems can provide reporting tools that make them a definite advantage over paper records.

I suggest you look at some of the tutorials on YouTube for whichever accounting and bookkeeping software you and your accountant decide to use, to familiarize yourself with their user interface.

Over the last four years, I've learned how to work as my own bookkeeper, but I also work with a Certified Public Accountant four times a year, to make sure my entries are not off the rails. I keep scrupulous paper copy records of all my transactions, so we can go back to the source document if I've created a problem or if I made a mistake.

SECTION THREE: BALANCE SHEET

I will repeat this often throughout the course of this book: you are in the business of private investigations. Whether it's running a pizza shop, pest control business, or private investigations company, certain universal things go into your books. How you make your bookkeeping entries, how you keep your books, what accounting method you utilize, what accounting software you use—these are all decisions universal to any business whether you're selling a product, goods, or services.

As a business person, I cannot stress enough the importance of understanding the primary language of bookkeeping and accounting to understand your business better.

Later on, we'll talk about how to set up your budget and how to compare that budget against your actuals. You'll be able to measure the growth or decline of your business on a monthly, quarterly, and yearly basis. You will also be able to compare said growth or decline against last year's numbers for the same periods.

You have to understand how these numbers are generated, so when you look at some outliers or variances, you will be able to deduce where they came from intelligently. Some figures look somewhat out of place because they are either too large or too small.

As a glaring example of understanding cash flow, imagine taking on a new client who promises you a ton of work. You ramp up your operation and hire new people. You spend time training and equipping them. You insure them and make sure the appropriate taxes are taken out for them with your payroll service. You make this new client a priority and stop marketing to other clients and possibly neglect your other steady clients. You do lots of work for the client and do a satisfactory job, maybe even an excellent job. You have paid out many expenses and payroll before you send them a large invoice. You can see where this is going.

Had you been watching the numbers, you would know how dangerous this is, because when this client decides not to pay, or that they want to negotiate your bill, what is your leverage? The work is done, and payroll is looming.

They are negotiating from a position of strength, and they could put you out of business because you failed to foresee the impact of that client's work on the overall health of your business.

Don't Forget Taxes, Ever!

As part of your business, you will be hopefully earning an income. With that income, you'll have income taxes. Depending on where you live, you may have both Federal and State income taxes. Some municipalities even have an additional income tax on top of that. Some states tax Private Detective services, so you have to make sure to keep track of your sales tax if you work in those jurisdictions. Then, you either pay them on a monthly or quarterly basis. In any event, you have to make sure to have enough money set aside to pay your taxes at the end of the year or, as I do, quarterly.

My accountant helps me determine how much money I made the previous year and we estimate how much money my business is going to make in the upcoming year, and he provides me with a breakdown as to what I have to pay quarterly to both the Feds and the State. So, as income comes in during the course of each month, I set aside money—I usually do so in a separate account—to pay the quarterly estimated income taxes and the monthly Sales Tax.

In December, my accountant comes in with me, and we look at the books and see how things are shaping up. He does a trial balance. We went over the books in July, so there should be no surprises there. He comes in again after the year closes and we sit down and finalize the books of the year. By doing so, he's able to give me an estimate of what I'm going to be paying for my taxes in the following year, and we set aside that amount. Now, if I'm doing much better than anticipated, I will spend much more in taxes and have to increase my set-asides. Conversely, if I am not doing as well as we planned, then I may be able to ease off the pedal a little bit on setting aside money for taxes.

The way I look at this is: if I've set aside more money in taxes than I needed to, I can either apply the overage to the first quarter of the following year, or I can supplement my IRA and even lower my taxes further for this year.

However, it is essential that you never forget taxes, I can't stress that enough. I recall in my second or third year of business, my first accountant had done my trial balance in the middle of December and said I set aside more than enough money for all my taxes and I could expect to receive a refund. On the day the taxes were due, he called me up to tell me that he had made a mistake in the calculation of my taxes and I had to come up with $4,500 by midnight. I utilized an interest-free credit card advance to meet the deficit. I then had to add a $400 monthly payment essentially to the following year's expenses, which made it more difficult to see an accurate profit and loss for the following year.

Needless to say, I fired that accountant, and I've been with the same accountant now for almost 20 years.

Business Expenses

Just as we performed an exercise on your personal expenses, now we are going to concentrate on business expenses to give you an idea of what costs to budget for your first year of business.

You need to understand what your expenses are for running this business, as well as what your personal costs are. You also have to remember to set aside money to cover your taxes as well.

Business Expenses	Tony	Beth	John	You
Subcontractors	$100	$200	$200	
Database Usage	$100	$200	$200	
Transcription	$0	$0	$0	
Insurance: Life, Health, Disability	$950	$1600	$1325	
Car: Payments, Gas, Insurance, Maintenance, Repairs	$995	$275	$675	
Computer & IT	$50	$450	$200	
Equipment	$100	$200	$100	
Payroll & Payroll Expenses	$0	$1,050	$1,100	
Professional Services, Accounting, Bookkeeping, etc.	$300	$300	$300	
Marketing	$200	$400	$300	
Travel & Meals	$100	$150	$125	
Meals & Entertainment	$50	$50	$50	
Bank Charges	$7.50	$12.50	$5.50	
Dues & Subscriptions	$25	$30	$30	
Miscellaneous	$20	$20	$20	
Office Expenses	$15	$20	$20	
Monthly Total	$3,015.50	$4,957.50	$4,650.00	
Yearly Total	$36,186.00	$59,490.00	$55,806.00	

This list of expenses is by no means complete. It doesn't include offices outside of the home or Internet costs. I would instead provide a representative sample than have your eyes glaze over with every possible expense related to your business. Some expenses were lumped into categories.

SECTION THREE: BALANCE SHEET

What are your annual expenses related to the running of your business? Tony, Beth, John, and you may each be in different areas of the country, doing different types of work, serving different types of customers, using different kinds of business models. As a result, your expenses may vary widely.

I tried to estimate what the monthly expenses for Beth would be in the business-to-consumer (B2C) world. She is also is younger and has no spouse to lean on for health benefits. On the other hand, she has a higher life premium and disability premium than Tony or John. Beth is relying more on Internet marketing and digital advertising and, as such, requires the services of an Internet-savvy technical person whose services fall under the IT category. Tony, Beth, and John can each deduct their actual mileage using their personal vehicles used for business travel, per IRS regulations.

There will be balance sheet adjustments made by your accountant as it relates to depreciation for your vehicle. You have to give an honest estimate as to how much of your vehicle you use for business use versus personal use (if you track your business mileage, divide that by your car's total mileage for the year). In Beth's case, she's going to buy a tricked-out van with tinted windows and, given the heat in Austin, Texas, install additional silent air conditioning. Because she only uses the van for her business use, it is entirely a business expense. Tony, on the other hand, is utilizing his personal vehicle for business which includes a bumper-to-bumper maintenance plan. He has a higher lease payment than both Beth and John.

Tony's professional to professional business requires half of the marketing expense that John does in the business-to-business and Beth spends more in the business to consumer business model than either one of them.

You have to see what your business model is and determine how much of marketing will be involved to generate leads for your business. If you don't have an idea how to put together this budget at present, I would gently suggest to you that for each line item, you add up Tony, Beth and John's expense then divide by three. Make that your line item expense, unless you know that there's a specific expense that is going to be greater or less based upon your existing equipment and situation. You can make the changes accordingly.

From the previous section, you see that Beth has a monthly personal expense of $4502. Add her business expense of $4,957.50, and **she needs at least $9,459.50 each month to break even after taxes.**

John's personal expenses are $6,579. When splitting that in half, because his spouse is responsible for half, his personal expense costs total $3,289.50. Add that to his business expenses of $4,650. To break even, **John has to earn at least $7,939.50 each month after taxes.**

In Tony's situation, we will assume his wife is responsible for 25% of their income, his pension is 25% of their income, and his business paying 50% of their remaining $8,783 personal expenses, leaving him $4,391.50 personal expenses added to his business expenses of $3,015.50. **Tony needs to make $7,407 to breakeven after taxes.**

> What is the amount of money that you have to make per month to break even?

At this point you might say to me, "John, how am I supposed to know what my business expenses might be given that there are other categories you didn't mention?"

I understand your concern. However, you have to start somewhere, and your projected budget is precisely that. You'll have to extrapolate from this information given to you by a veteran PI business owner telling you what his expenses are every month, annually amortized for any given year, and from the hypothetical expenses for two other investigators based upon their unique situations. It should give you a basis from which you can make a decision.

Of course, you might try to look at some of those expenses and see how you can do away with them, or how you can lower them. Bootstrapping your business is a beautiful way to get started. On the other hand, there might be some additional expenses that you or I did think about.

Over time, a pattern will emerge from your regular expenses as well as the occasional one-time expense which you can annualize; however, it's important to realize that by getting a hold of your personal expenses and making an honest projection of your business expenses, you'll have an idea of how much money you need to make after taxes.

Note: this would be a good time to revisit the red light green light checklist questions. You will thank me later.

Tony is breathing a little easier. He survived his fifteen-rounder with his personal expenses. Having a sharp pencil and a template to follow, he determined his life-style business was easier to maintain than other business models that are reliant on a robust website and employees. A spare bedroom, a good car, decent laptop, and the other necessities were less daunting to calculate than the bloated personal expenses he and his wife were supporting.

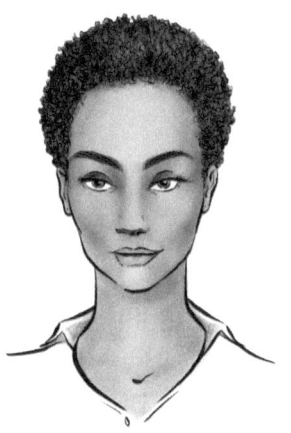

Staring at the numbers, Beth kept working them and working them. She knew that if she wanted to build a company where she would eventually move out of fulfillment and back-room operations, she had to build it from the ground up with that end in mind. Health benefits for her employees were poking her hard in the ribs. Going from the Army to an established company with generous benefits left her shaking her head. She was tri-athlete healthy, but she was also pragmatic. What if some joker was texting while driving by her on her bicycle? What if some of the chemicals she was exposed to back in the Sandbox were to manifest themselves in the form of cancer? She needed to have a rock-solid disability plan to go with her veterans insurance.

This was no place to cut corners. She struggled with how to set up her website. Luckily for her, she was invited out to tacos with some of the good folks at locally based AppSumo. One of their Austin-based 'Sumo-lings' agreed to work with her to build a world-class website. They were intrigued by her business model and wanted to apply their tools to a start-up PI business. These people had serious creds, and she knew not to trust this critical aspect of her marketing to somebody that could disappear with her passwords and hold her website hostage.

SECTION THREE: BALANCE SHEET

John went about bootstrapping his business slightly differently. He created an affiliation with a surveillance company that worked exclusively for insurance companies. He referred them his customers with surveillance while working their customers' investigative needs. John worked the weekends and holidays as a surveillance operative at above-average sub-contractor rates for most of 1997 to pay his one-time-only start-up costs. He had no debt on his Labor Day launch date.

BALANCE SHEET ACCOUNTS

SECTION FOUR: FORGET MISSION, VISION, AND VALUE STATEMENTS

LET'S TALK ABOUT YOUR WHY, HOW, AND WHAT

START WITH THE WHY...

> YouTube search: **TedX Simon SINEK Start with the why...**
> It's 18 minutes long and worth the viewing. I'll be here waiting.

Bankers and lenders will tell you that you have to make a business plan and that you have to toil over a mission, vision, and values statement. They love to go to great lengths expounding upon the necessity for this. The statements are meant to give your company culture the proper grounding from which all decisions are made, from the CEO on down to the boiler-room service reps.

Of course, the latest Mission, Vision, and Value statements are brought in by the new CEO replacing the Mission, Vision, and Value statements of the previous CEO.

All the C suite executives go off to a retreat center, preferably in a very expensive and idyllic setting, where a high-priced facilitator guides them in team-building and trust-building exercises. It's comical to see the CEO fall backward into the arms of his COO, CIO, and CFO. Miraculously, they don't drop him. (That's the most heavy-lifting they have done in a while.)

SECTION FOUR: FORGET MISSION, VISION, AND VALUE STATEMENTS

At the end of the retreat, after word-smithing every word, every comma, phrase, sentence, and paragraph to death, they are excited to return to headquarters with a new vision and a mission, along with a value statement to clarify the most important values of the Corporation. Then, with much fanfare, it gets transmitted down to the Directors, then to the managerial staff, then down to the supervisory ranks, then finally to the line employees where the plaque covers a tear in the break room wallpaper next to the clock.

Needless to say, after several years of disappointing quarters, when the earnings and return on investment is less than what they would have earned in Treasury Bills, that CEO is let go with a buyout package of more money than you or I make in a lifetime, and a new team is assembled and the same process repeats.

As you can see, I am not exactly a big fan of the way mission, vision, and value statements are created in publicly held corporations. I certainly don't see the necessity of them for a business plan of a person looking to launch a private investigation business with one employee (themselves).

Having said that, I'm glad you had a chance to listen to and watch the straightforward message of Simon Sinek as he related to you **Why, How, and What.**

I can wax poetic and say the **Why** is your true North and is what you should be thinking about every morning when you start your business day.

The **How** and the **What** should be your work. Does your work align with your true North? Do the **How** and **What** provide a clear roadmap to your goals?

There are two reasons to talk about the **why, how, and what** in this section of the book after you've done the exercises regarding your true personal expenses and your estimated business expenses.

First, what are you passionate about and second, how will you generate revenue doing what you love? It is in this intersection where you begin to formulate your ideas on how to create revenue to be successful enough to be able to meet your expenses on a weekly, monthly and yearly basis.

Tony is looking to work professional to professional (P2P). He wants to target attorneys, certified public accountants, and property management firms for professional services, along with small to medium sizes businesses.

His **why** is to be on his own and out from underneath the entrenched bureaucracy of the NYPD so he can provide his clients who really care about the outcome with the **what**, i.e., the best possible investigation he can put together on their behalf.

His **how** is to execute all of the investigative objectives, based upon the best information made available to him and by expertly communicating his findings.

His **what** is combining the latest Internet and social media search tools with excellent interviewing skills and 27 years' worth of contacts to secure evidence and facts his clients will eventually use in court.

SECTION FOUR: FORGET MISSION, VISION, AND VALUE STATEMENTS

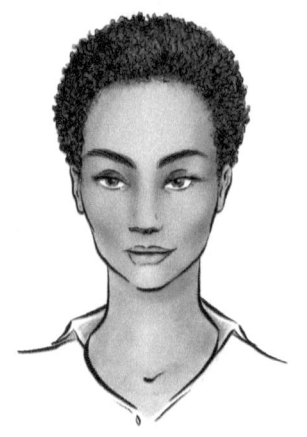

For Beth, who is looking to work in the business to consumer world (B2C), her **why** is to build a private investigations business she can eventually sell to a larger competitor, allowing her to adventure travel. She chafes after years of army life and now, working in a multi-layered Armed Guard company. She will escape to freedom by creating a replicable and scalable lead generation strategy to convert prospects into customers (**how**). These customers are individuals who suspect their significant other of infidelity.

Her **what** is doing surveillance, database searches, and social media searches.

John's **why**, how, and what has the benefit of hindsight. John's why was the need to validate his investigative methodology could be replicated, and a high level of expertise could be transmitted to motivated individuals.

How, he did that by rigorous recruiting, hiring, training, supervision, and evaluation methods he created. He was going to prove his concepts with his initial investigators, then replicate and scale those methods as the business expanded outside of Southern New England and New York.

The **what** would be providing high-end insurance fraud investigative services for special investigation units and insurance fraud, as well as complex investigations on behalf of property and casualty companies.

Now I'm sure there is a way to shoehorn these three different investigators' **why, how, and what** statements into a business plan with a mission, vision, and value statement; however, I think you would agree a thought-out why, how, and what statement is much more focused and serves as a better framework to help you make every business decision.

In John's case, the **why** became more obvious in retrospect when considering the amount of time and effort John put into creating his team of insurance fraud investigators, and how he replicated his training methods and sold the investigators on his methods.

It was also obvious in the way John supervised the investigators and reviewed their reporting. It was a great satisfaction to John to be able to create a cadre of investigators who performed at

SECTION FOUR: FORGET MISSION, VISION, AND VALUE STATEMENTS

a high level daily and learned the time management skills to maintain a heavy caseload while doing so.

Think of the why, how, and what as both the emotional drivers for yourself as well as how you will meet the emotional needs of your clients with the work that you will perform and how well you will do it.

After you write out your why, how, and what, let it sit for a day or two, then ask yourself the question: Is this "Hell yeah"?

If not, revise it until you can say "Hell yeah!" If you can't, then this is gut check time.

> If your answer is not "Hell, yeah," do you really want to take on this risk of time, effort, and capital?
> How does your plan resonate with you, now that you've looked at your personal expenses and projected your business expenses? Is it still a "Hell, yeah"?

If so, now is the time to have 'the talk' with the people whose support you are counting on. You can verbalize **why** you want to take this risk, **how** you are going to provide services to your specific target audience with your skills and tools, and **what** their desired outcome will be. You will be able to show your break-even analysis after intelligently calculating your personal and projected business expenses.

I personally find the **why, how, and what** exercise to be much more fulfilling and meaningful than trying to create a lofty mission, vision, and values statement. I also think that if you keep **why, how, and what** front and center, it will have more meaning to you as you go about planning your weekly and daily tasks. However, that's just my opinion.

SECTION FIVE:
NEEDS ANALYSIS

"GAPS"

YOU'RE FILLING GAPS

Sylvester Stallone's portrayal of Rocky in 1976—which won him the Academy Award for best picture—has a scene where he's talking to his future brother-in-law, Paulie.

> Paulie asks, "Hey, Rock, what do you see in my sister [Adrian]?"
> Rocky replied, "Gaps."
> "Gaps?"
> "Yeah, we fill gaps. She fills my gaps. I fill her gaps."

When you really think about it, you're providing a service for individuals or businesses. You're filling gaps. When you're in a private investigation business, you're filling the gap between what the client knows or suspects and what they need to know. Your job is all about meeting those needs of filling gaps.

SECTION FIVE: NEEDS ANALYSIS

Aligning Customer Needs With Your Skill Sets Or Learning New Ones

A criminal defense attorney has a client who insists he is innocent of any wrongdoing. How do you meet their needs? What investigation has to be undertaken to allow them to go into court and create reasonable doubt?

A wife suspects her husband of cheating and wants to get the proof of his infidelity.

A landlord has to locate a deadbeat renter that skipped out and owes thousands of dollars for back rent.

An insurance company suspects a policyholder of torching their car.

Each of the customers has different needs, and each investigation requires different skill sets.

As investigators firstly, we are sometimes hammers always looking for nails. That's how we find our customers and find our niches. However, as business people, is it better to chase the skill or the customer?

Look at Beth's situation as she builds a business with consumers on fidelity investigations. Her surveillance skills are easily transferable to workers compensation and disability insurance companies. The hammer is apparently searching for other nails, but the search takes her away from her preferred customer base. Her branding and website are for consumers, not businesses.

Instead, what if she learned new skills sets for her existing customer base? She is filling their other gaps. For example, she could invest the time to learn how to locate missing teens quickly for frantic parents when Law Enforcement gives them a cold shoulder. Does Beth want to take on a myriad of general investigations to be able to service her clientele more completely?

Would it be better for Beth to subcontract out some cases so far afield from her skill set, to keep the customer happy while taking a referral fee from the subcontractor?

I don't often recommend books for investigators; however, there is a section in *What Color Is Your Parachute?* by Richard Bolles. In it, he speaks eloquently on how skill sets can translate into other similar skills, or those that are very close, by comparison, that would be easy to bring to proficiency with a little effort.

In Tony, Beth and John's situation, all of their clients need to undertake asset checks on the person they are investigating. The reasons for each customer stem from a different business need, but the skill set is the same. If you don't know how to do asset checks, do you learn how to do them legally, in compliance with the Federal Credit Reporting Act and the Graham Leach Bliley Act?

Is it lucrative enough for you to learn how to create a scalable and repeatable process around asset checks that can give your clients the answers they seek?

If you choose not to learn the skills to meet this need, do you offer another solution for your client, or do you send them elsewhere on a referral? Don't tell me you will tell your customer you don't do that type of search and refuse to help them fill their need.

Another customer need could be that of an SIU investigator or a criminal defense attorney to do a background check on the subject of the investigation or the alleged victim.

Not to make your head spin anymore, but there's also the question of who is the buyer and who is the user? What the buyer wants and what the user needs are sometimes not the same. For example, the gap is seen usually between what the individual consumer thinks they need and what their lawyer has to bring to court in the form of facts or evidence.

Another example is the property and casualty insurance industry, where the buyer may be the highest echelon in the claims department, and the user is the claims adjustor with a sticky claim to deal with. The special investigation unit investigator or the claims adjuster would be the user of the investigation that you provide. However, the payer (buyer) for that investigation is their employer. How are the buyer's needs different from the user's needs, and how do you align them in your marketing and investigative processes?

The buyers', users', and attorneys' needs all have to be juggled by the investigator.

What Business Are You In?

Business-to-Business (B2B): User may not be the buyer. Multiple decision-makers in the process. Contracts, purchase orders, and retainers are usual. Budgets are set, and pricing is subject to volume discounting.

- Professional-to-Professional (P2P): I've not seen this phrase elsewhere, so I'm going to take ownership of it. You, as a licensed professional investigator, are reaching out to other professionals such as Attorneys, Property Managers, Certified Public Accountants, Certified Financial Planners, or anyone that has a professional designation as determined by their schooling and their licensing. They spell out the investigative objective for their clients. A retainer is taken if their client is the buyer and not them. Flat rate pricing for simple cases may replace the usual hourly arrangements.

- Business-to-Consumer (B2C): Think of when you, as a consumer, Google for goods or services to be rendered. You find businesses that will offer their goods or services. You go to their websites and get into their sales funnel to purchase a product or service. An individual walking can do the same in a retail establishment. As this applies to your business, the client is a private individual, and you're dealing with their personal checkbook. Their need affects them personally as opposed to a business decision being made. You are the business they are reaching out to. You could be a solo investigator, or you could have a team working with you. You could work with other associates, but the C part of the equation is more important. Your focus is all on the consumer, the private individual.

- Hybrid: For example, you are an expert. Anybody who needs your expertise comes to you. You market to the highest paying users/buyers. On the other end of the spectrum, you are the only guy or gal in a remote section of the state. You are the only game in that county. You market to other Private Investigators around the world to let them know you are the best solution in that zip code. Your website is optimized for people to find you when they search for your geographical area.

Whether you deal with businesses, professionals, or consumers, everything in your marketing is about them. Each requires different handling and different branding. Each requires their needs to be the focus of your website, your printed materials, and your offers.

It always surprises me when I see other investigators at a lawyer conference who have a booth, signage, and website geared for dealing with consumers. They are clearly in the B2C market, yet they're trying to market in the B2B world or, even more ridiculously, in the P2P world of professional to professional.

Everything from their website and all their leave behinds, brochures and flyers and all the services they render are for private individuals and have **nothing to do with the specific needs of the target audience** they are trying to attract at that conference.

What's worse, in my opinion, is the investigative company that attempts to be a jack of all trades and a master of none. They don't even know if they are B2B, B2C or P2P. They are not a hybrid, because they're trying to do everything for everyone instead of focusing on their specialized knowledge or their geographical exclusivity.

SECTION FIVE: NEEDS ANALYSIS

There is a place for the generalist as I mentioned above. I believe the generalist can be competent when they're the only game in town or are in an out of the way place without much competition. By the sheer fact that they are in an inaccessible area, they can take on all comers. They will be able to take on criminal defense work. They will do skip tracing. They will do cheating wives and husbands, and all the surveillance work for insurance companies because there is no one else in that area to do that work. If that's the case for you, it may make sense to be a hybrid because your competitive advantage is that no one else is there to do the same work as you.

In reality, the only place to go wide with your net of prospects is when you're in the B2C market. You're trying to capture every person in your geographic area with a potential need for a private investigator.

Otherwise, you want to drill very deep into your niche, whether you are B2B or P2P. You want to make sure you are the person they want to come to and that you have the necessary skill sets to be able to meet their needs and to answer their questions.

Tony's Target Audience

Tony has decided to go into the P2P business and is looking to market exclusively to attorneys, certified public accountants, small business owners, and financial planners. Everyone in his target audience can be attracted by his twenty-seven years of expertise in investigations and the ability to understand what the investigative objective is. He has to rely heavily on his NYPD career and contacts. So, his decision to go P2P is also a lifestyle choice of not working nights, weekends or holidays in essentially the Borough of Queens.

Beth's Target Audience

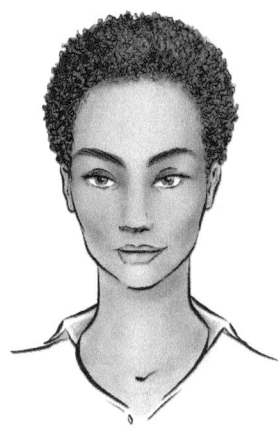

Beth is looking to go to throw a wide net in the B2C ocean. She's looking to provide surveillance services and investigative services as they relate to family law.

She's attempting to attract the private individual before any divorce action is filed or the private individuals looking to modify their custody agreements based upon the miscreant behaviors of their ex-spouse.

She's looking to be a high-volume, low-cost provider to individuals. She will take credit cards and PayPal. She's hoping to scale her business through an excellent website presence and attendance at Chamber of Commerce events. She will institute a referral program from Gyms, Hair, Beauty, Wellness and Nail Salons.

SECTION FIVE: NEEDS ANALYSIS

John's Target Audience

John's B2B business, Independent Special Investigations, LLC was created to meet the needs of the growing community of Special Investigation Units of the property and casualty insurance industry in 1997, as well as the litigation departments of all the casualty claims units of both personal and commercial insurance carriers.

John was very clear that he wanted to work with property and casualty insurance industry and maximize his contacts in his Rolodex to grow his business regionally in the Northeast and Mid-Atlantic states.

Your Target Audience

Who is going to be the end-user as well as the buyer for the services you're going to offer? Are you B2B, P2P or B2C? Keep in mind your 'why' and what gaps that are you filling, as Rocky said. Find some lined paper or create a new document file and fill out as much detail as you can.

A Business with No Customers

This is a story about International Missing Heir Finders, LLC, a business that didn't have customers per se.
"How can that be?" you ask.
Well, John started it as a paying hobby. Eventually, he created a national business named International Missing Heir Finders, LLC. The concept was straightforward. He found probate estates that were recently opened throughout the United States where not all of the rightful heirs had been located. John then went

about determining those rightful heirs and advised them that they were the rightful heirs in an estate of a person who had died and, as an heir, they may be entitled to a portion of the money from that estate. Those heirs then signed a contract before they were advised of who died and where the estate was probated. John also then provided an attorney for them. The heir would pay no expenses. Upon receipt of the funds from the probate court, the attorney would, by contractual agreement, pay International Missing Heir Finders a percentage of the heir's inheritance and the attorney would take their fee from John's share.

You might say the *heirs* were the customers, but they did not come to International Missing Heir Finders asking, "Can you find an estate where I'm entitled to money?" Instead, IMHF came to them, and for a percentage of the inheritance, they would connect the person to that estate and also pay for their legal fees. So in a sense, they were not customers.

John had to sell the heirs on the agreement that they would receive monies from an estate they did not know about. John had to convince Tracers throughout the United States to go out and locate those estates in their local probate courts regularly in exchange for a percentage of the estate when the estate finally settled out. John and his team would do the Forensic Genealogy to locate the heirs. John then had to follow the progress of the estate until the final payout. It was a sweet gig while it lasted, but the business model proved to be too volatile with a high cash burn while waiting for a payout that may or may not happen.

SECTION FIVE: NEEDS ANALYSIS

How to Price Your Services

Regardless of whether you charge clients a fixed budget, flat rate, special offer, discount rate, or by the hour, for purposes of this exercise, you will need to convert them to a per hour rate. If it takes you usually two hours to perform a $500 asset check, your hourly rate is $250 an hour. If you charge $1,000 for eight hours of surveillance, but you have to drive an hour both ways to get there, your ten hours are worth $100 an hour. For all the services you plan to perform, you need to create a weighted-average per hour charge.

In the Northeast, you can go from the low end of $35 an hour for Criminal Defense on court-approved indigent cases to $95-$200 an hour, depending on the specialties and expertise required. What the market will bear in other major metropolitan areas around the country can be very similar to what was just described for the Northeast.

The small towns far away from the metropolitan areas can have pricing from $45-$95 per hour. There's no hard and fast rule as to what is being charged or what the market will bear. What you'll charge per hour for your services should be figured out now before we calculate your critical number. Who is your customer, what is their need, and how much are they willing to pay for your services? How much expertise you bring to the table may allow you to charge premium rates.

When you look at what you will charge for flat rates, hourly, budgets and specials, you have to make an educated guess of how many of each you will sell to arrive at a weighted-average per hour charge.

Projections

$150 Billable Rate (high end)

- 6 hours billed per day generates $900 a day or $4,500 a week.
- Working 48 weeks per year yields $216,000 annual gross
- Less $6,000/month ($72,000/year) in business expenses = $144,000 net
- Multiply by .60 for taxes+SEP = $86,400 annually or $7,200 monthly

$125 Billable Rate (medium)

- 6 hours billed per day generates $750.00 or $3,750 a week.
- Working 48 weeks per year yields $180,000 annual gross
- Less $6,000/month ($72,000/year) in business expenses = $108,000 net
- Multiply by .60 for taxes+SEP = $64,800 annually or $5,400 monthly

$100 Billable Rate (low end)

- 6 hours billed per day generates $600.00 a day or $3,000 a week.
- Working 48 weeks per year yields $144,000
- Less $6,000/month ($72,000/year) in business expenses = $72,000
- Multiply by .65 for taxes+SEP = $48,600 annually or $3,900 monthly

SECTION FIVE: NEEDS ANALYSIS

Critical Number

Take your monthly personal expenses and add to them your monthly business expense, then divide that amount by 4.2 (the number of weeks in an average month). That subtotal is how much your weekly expenses are.

Tony's monthly expense is $7,407 / 4.2 = 1,763.57 weekly. If Tony charges $150 an hour for his services, he needs to bill 11.7 hours weekly. His accountant told him to set aside 1/3 of his revenue for taxes. **So, Tony multiplies his 11.7 hours by 1.33 and comes up with 15.63 hours a week to break even and pay taxes.**

Beth's monthly expenses are $9,459.50 /4.2 = $2,252.26 weekly in the more price-sensitive consumer/commodity pricing. She can only charge a weighted average of $95 per hour for all her services. She must work 23.7 hours to break even, and her accountant told her to set aside 1/4 of her revenue for taxes. **Beth multiplies her 23.7 by 1.25 and sees she needs to work 29.6 hours to break even and pay taxes.** You can see why she needs employees to absorb overhead.

John monthly expenses are $7939.50 / 4.2 = $1,890.46 weekly. John's weighted average for the insurance industry is $131 per hour. John must work 14.4 hours, and his accountant has him setting aside 1/3 of his revenue for taxes. **John multiplies his 14.4 hours by 1.33 for 19.1 hours a week to break even and pay taxes.** John needs employees to absorb overhead as well.

Before you get too giddy that you only have to bill X number of hours a week and you start dreaming about going fishing on three-day weekends, you have to account for administrative hours and non-billable hours that you can't charge the client for. There are marketing hours. There are travel hours that might be charged-off at a reduced rate. There are hours where you involved in managing your business or ownership hours such as doing bookkeeping. The hours spent in your business and working on your business add up quickly. What about the time you take going to conferences or watching webinars to stay sharp and self-improve? What about vacation time and that week you were knocked out with the flu?

> Tip: Add your billable hours up EVERY day and total them at the end of the work week, to know if you made your weekly goal. This is arguably your most critical number.

SECTION SIX: WHAT'S IN A NAME

NAMING YOUR BUSINESS

You're starting your business with a business name; however, you have to think of what that name means when you end your business if you plan to sell that business. You have to think about what that business name means to a potential buyer of your business.

Most importantly, you have to think about what that business name means to the possible customer of your *services*. Does your business name give them the confidence to begin the process of learning to know you, so that they can like and trust you?

Take a moment to visit private investigator companies online. Type in "private detective" or "private investigator" into Google just to give you an idea of what names come up. Would you be comfortable with some of those names on your business card? Is that really the way to present yourself and your business to the outside world? That is the prospect's first impression of your business.

Your website is second. Look at some of the websites. Would you hire that company?

Personally, I think some private detectives do themselves a disservice by playing into the stereotype of the 'Shameless Seamus' or that of the hard-boiled detective. Some detective websites carry the mysterious tough guy thing a little too far.

Take a professional approach to naming your business. Think about the needs of the customer first and your ego second. However, you're entitled to do what you want. Think about it as being synonymous with your name and reputation, though I wouldn't go so far as tattooing that business name or logo on any of your body parts.

There are times when you will name the business after yourself because you are the brand. Whatever you decide, calling your business is something that you need to address at this stage.

As you saw, my first company's name was Independent Special Investigations. It was named for the work that I did. I was an independent, and I did special investigations for the insurance industry. There was an immediate connection with that name. Later on, in another business I owned, I named it Squire Investigations, quite frankly, because I could not come up with a better name. I was transitioning away from the insurance investigations into general local practice and was trying to find the right market niche.

I understand what the naming of a business means now. I later tested a business concept with the name of an online company called Critical Locate Solutions. In our proof of concept, we wanted to provide a premium location service for high-end law firms and corporations. Unfortunately, our research showed the prospects were not dissatisfied enough with their present solutions to change to a higher cost solution, even if it was more effective. The pain of switching providers was more significant than the pain of not finding the party. My proof of concept was not expensive, and it saved me a lot of time, aggravation, and money.

I sell my DVD, *The Ultimate Guide to Taking Statements* from my website *The Department of What Happened*. Clear product name with a catchy website name.

Elm City Detectives was the name of another of my businesses. It clearly explained to the people who lived around the city of New Haven (nicknamed "Elm City") that I was pretty much a local general investigator in the greater New Haven area.

Browser Searches

Your branding and that what you name your company will affect the search algorithms on the various browser networks and a poorly chosen name could place your business on the second page, instead of the coveted first page. Why use a cutesy name that doesn't improve your search rankings?

There are ways to compete to be on the first page of your browser, and those can be very expensive. Rather than bid against companies spending a fortune for the first and second spot, select a good solid name for your business and carefully craft the first several words that are cached in the description of your link.

Domain Names

It's getting harder to find a business name with an available match but try to get a .com name and maybe the .net so that copycats have less of chance of stealing your branding.

Make the name short enough that people will bother to type it. Try to avoid using words such as hallellawfirm where the lack of spaces between the words confuses. Use Whois or GoDaddy.com to see if your domain name is available, and then I recommend going to GoDaddy to register and pay for your domain name.

For domain names, web hosting, and a robust web site builder, 1&1 is also a good choice. HostGator, DreamHost, and Wix.com are similar and have excellent pricing plans as well.

I tend to utilize GoDaddy for my domain names and BlueHost for my web hosting service. I like both GoDaddy and BlueHost because if I get jammed up on something that is keeping my website from loading or working, I can get a warm body on the phone relatively quickly. They are only two hours' time difference from me, and they speak American English. I'm not trying to be derisive by saying that, but there's something to be said about someone you can understand when they're trying to fix your website.

The next item to consider for your hosting is what is referred to, in the business, as Up Time. You want to make sure that your host's Up Time rate is as close to 100% as possible and that any recovery time is minimal. If they have to do any regular maintenance, make sure they promise it will be at night or on the weekends, when it doesn't cause a problem.

I recommend building your website on a WordPress platform with Thrive Theme Builder. WordPress content management software can be installed on most hosts, including Wix.com, Go Daddy, 1&1, Weebly, SquareSpace, and many others. Wordpress is a platform with a proven track record regarding Up Time that offers seamless integration of patches and fixes along with the ability to take on third-party plug-ins.

Website Builder is a program that allows you to create a website without the need to write or edit code. Website builders are web-based, meaning you don't need to download or install software, you need a browser such as Google Chrome, Mozilla Firefox or Safari, and an Internet connection to start building your website.

Tony's website is the least complicated because of the nature of his business, his branding, and his customer base. In a P2P company, search engine optimization is not as critical. He could pick a domain name from Go Daddy and build it rather quickly with Wix.com or Squarespace. He might need to have some help on WordPress to get started, but mainly those would be my three recommendations for Tony for a rather static site that does not have to have much fresh content.

John's website had to be more interactive. He decided to host a blog and a newsletter for email subscribers to get new information from his offerings. It was important that he had a robust front page which included video testimonials.

John used GoDaddy for the domain name, BlueHost for the host server, WordPress for the platform, and Thrive Architect for the website themes.

It was vital that he could change the content frequently. Refreshing content and good search engine optimization went hand in hand. We can talk about that later, as it is paramount.

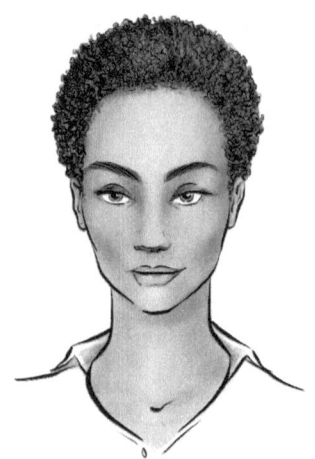

Beth is going B2C. She is competing for eyeballs on the first page of search indexes. She definitely has to be the first or second result on the first page, below the paid ads so people will be attracted immediately to her website where she can entice them into the sales funnel. To do this, she offers her new visitors a free monthly newsletter and ebooks.

She will ask satisfied customers to go on camera and create video testimonials for her. Those videos will feature in a prominent location on her website's home page. In a B2C world, it is probably the most active marketing material you could have.

Her website is the center of her business. Beth utilizes a Go Daddy registered domain, BlueHost for the hosting server, and WordPress with Thrive themes for her website structure. Her website also has to have a robust e-commerce plug-in where customers can enter into agreements, make assignments, and—most importantly—enter credit card or PayPal payments. She needs a very robust platform coming out of the gate.

Beth has little experience with website maintenance, so she hires a reliable IT person available to help her update content, fix bugs, remove dead links, and otherwise keep her website up and running.

The Biggest Mistake Private Investigators Make On Their Websites

Homepage

The biggest mistake that investigators make is that they talk about themselves on their homepage. You might think it's intuitive to tell the customer about yourself so that they will know, like, and trust you.

As much as you think you are selling yourself with your website, you need to be focused on the customer. It's important to understand what the customer's needs are and use your homepage to speak to their needs. That takes practice. Then you follow up with what their wants and desires are.

Your next pages talk about how you can meet their needs. As an example, with Hoda Investigations, one of the first things we listed before our refresh, was a newspaper article about the case involving a wrongful conviction exoneration. That link went to a compelling headline and video. This sends a clear signal to the criminal defense bar that Hoda Investigations works on the most serious criminal cases in the state of Connecticut. That content was immediately followed by four testimonials of well-regarded, highly respected, heavy-hitting lawyers in the state. The message is clear. The best lawyers use the best investigators. You should too. This is the social proof that prospects are looking for. This would be the type of website Tony would want to make as it supplies an immediate know, like, and trust through the first couple of minutes that a visitor spends there.

About Page

The about page is where you talk about your background, your successes, and your history, but again, scripted for the needs of your target market. This is not a place for your resumé. The content needs to reinforce further why the prospect will want to do business with you. Is there anything that is on this page that would turn them off? Please take a look at other websites of private investigators and look at their About pages. Judge them as though you were searching to hire someone with their skill set. We are talking about professionalism in the business here. We're trying to convince people to part with their hard-earned money. We're talking about the lawyers or other businesspersons that are involved in the most important thing on their desk at the time they are shopping for a Professional Private Investigator. Do you want to come across as the Shady Seamus or, worse, a rough and tumble kind of PI?

Whether it is a wife suspecting her husband of cheating on her, an attorney looking to find the facts to support the innocence of his client, or an SIU investigator needing a thorough investigation into a suspicious claim, you have to demonstrate you have repeatedly earned that trust in the past and will give them your best effort. Do you see that promise reflected in the websites of your competitors? It is rare at best.

Most PI websites talk blandly about being everything to everybody. There are other investigators in your geographic area that are a master of the skill that is specific to the needs of your Target Audience. So rather than putting out a watered-down website trying to cast a broader net, be very, very specific about the people you want to work with and speak to them about their needs on your **Services page**.

NAMING YOUR BUSINESS

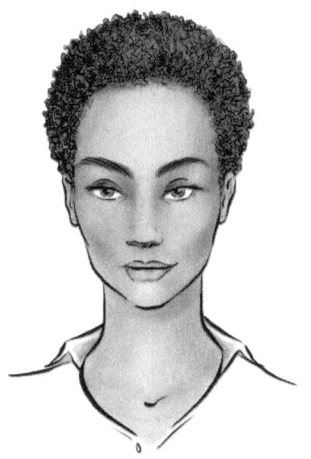

Beth will be very clear that she's working for the little guy. It bears repeating here that she's working for regular people in Family Law cases. Her goal is to provide fast, reliable, and quantifiable results for a fixed price, on a retainer that is price-sensitive for the individuals whom she's trying to attract.

Tony's services have to be very, very specific to all the lawyers, small business owners, and CPAs he wants to work with. He has to show results in the types of cases he wants to work on.

SECTION SIX: WHAT'S IN A NAME

John, in servicing the insurance industry, has to be very clear about special investigations and complex cases. His newsletter and testimonials have to be about achieving great results on those types of cases.

FAQ Page

Hint: If the prospect is on your FAQ page, they are interested.

Here, talk about lowering barriers to making the assignment and overcoming any perceived objections to using your services.

Be sure to provide information on:

- Payment methods accepted
- Reporting: media delivered in person, by email, text, cloud-based file sharing, or phone
- Territory
- Working office hours

Search Engine Optimization (SEO)

Search engine optimization is essential for Beth's B2C segmentation. As described earlier, she has to be first or second on the first page of Google below the paid ads.

As I type this, I am overlooking Lake Winnipesaukee in New Hampshire. I decided to perform a web search for 'New Hampshire private detectives' as if I was a local customer in need of PI services. The first result was a paid ad for an out-of-state company that most likely cannot do investigations in the state of New Hampshire. They did not disclose a person's name or contact. I don't see anything on their website that convinces me they can do work in the Granite State.

Google's keyword tools will help you determine the keywords being used by the websites that have paid ads and decide what words most resonate with what people are searching. You must understand it's not what you want to tell them, it's that you must answer what the prospect believes they are looking for. Those keywords typed in by your target audience have to be a natural part of the content of your website, not in a repetitive fashion, but in a way that makes it clear that you are concentrating on the prospect's needs and not on what you do best.

In checking for "New Hampshire investigators," a private investigative firm from out of the country comes up as the first paid ad. Really? Certainly they are not in a position to be able to assist the people in either Manchester or Concord, New Hampshire's larger cities, or anywhere else for that matter.

Sales Funnels

As the Internet matures, it is becoming clear to all marketers that, by creating a sales funnel from the time you generate an inbound lead, to qualifying the prospect, and then bringing them through the sales process, can all be done digitally within a properly structured website. This is done very expertly by all those businesses selling goods on the Internet. How many times have you gone through an online sale and ended up adding something to your cart that was steeply discounted?

The same technique applies to the businesses of both Beth and John. Their websites will allow for an up-sell opportunity for an additional investigation that is presented as a logical add-on to the investigation initially requested. This up-sell is a moneymaker and a valuable service provided to the customer that they did not initially think (or even consider they needed).

Autoresponders

Persons coming to your website which will give you their email in exchange for valuable content can be put into an email auto response sequence to walk them through getting additional content or more value in their engagement.

This helps the prospect move from learning about you to knowing, liking, and trusting you.

Digital reports, newsletters, and video webinars all move the lead to become a prospect and hopefully to a buyer.

Email Capture

Mailerlite, MailChimp, Convert Kit, and Infusionsoft are all services that allow you to capture emails and create email campaigns. Just starting out, I would recommend Mailerlite or MailChimp. Their free versions are easy to set up and hard to break.

The guides that AppSumo publishes on capturing emails, and how to craft your own emails, headlines, and content is worth spending time with.

The phrase **know, like, and trust** is very much embedded in the sales process before a person will decide that they want to do business with you.

In all cases, people are people. Whether they are a personal consumer, claims manager, business person, or an attorney, they need to have a sense of knowing whom they're dealing with and liking and trusting you before they'll take the next step.

SECTION SEVEN: MARKETING FOR THE INVESTIGATOR

DEVELOP A PLAN

There are many different names for the act of securing your customers leading them through the entire sales process. Sometimes the method is called the sales cycle or the sales funnel, but make no mistake about it; the marketing plan you develop must be based upon behaviors you can the scale and replicate. This is how your business will grow.

The process falls into a very simple straightforward beginning, middle, and end. It starts with the lead generation to either attract prospects with your message (called inbound marketing), or you reach out to them with some way of helping to meet their needs (outbound marketing). There are whole volumes written on both methods, but for some business models, one way may be more effective than the other.

Inbound marketing works for companies providing surveillance on cheating spouses, whereas with law firms, more success is met with outbound marketing that reaches out to prospective clients and makes them aware of your services and how you can meet their needs.

Once you **generate leads**, either through inbound or outbound marketing, or some combination of both, you will **qualify the prospect** to determine if you can meet their needs with the services you provide, at a price that would be acceptable to them.

During this phase, you want to provide **assurances** to the prospect that you can solve their problem, either by providing services for them or by connecting them with services provided by your affiliates or associates. We get into affiliate and associate discussions later on in the series, but they allow you to assure prospective clients that you can help get them closer to a solution for their specific problem.

Ask them **clarifying questions** about what their problem is after you offer them the above assurances. Too many salespeople across all types of businesses will launch into a sales pitch before understanding completely what their prospects needs are. This is a mistake. Every minute the prospect spends explaining the situation to you is one more minute they have invested in you being the solution to their problems.

Depending on the complexity of the situation, and after you have clarified their needs, tailor a **presentation** to them (which is probably the least amount of time spent in the conversation as opposed to the most).

Alternatively, you can offer them a ready-made solution, such as a flat rate. You know from work you've done in the past how to put together a budget for a flat rate. Based on the required skill sets and the time you know each will take to complete, and the related expenses, you can estimate that flat rate with some certainty. Plan for at least a 50% profit margin on that time and expense in order to make it viable.

You may receive **objections**. This is where you spend time going over the prospect's needs, explaining how your solutions meet those needs. They begin to understand the benefit they will receive from having the work done professionally and at a cost that can be agreed upon.

Tip: Sometimes the approach to overcoming objections is to understand the exact reason for not making a decision and help the prospect overcome that resistance. Too many times you may hear the objection is about money, but in reality, it could be having to live with the consequences of their decision. They are afraid of moving forward. Sometimes, you have to paint a picture of what the future looks like once they possess the information.

It would help if you made the decision simple for them and then you seamlessly flow into **getting the assignment**. You start the process of taking the information from the individuals, no differently than a car salesman would begin the application process for a car loan.

You now agree on pricing. It is here where it can be as simple as a handshake, getting a retainer signed, or filling out the contract.

However, wait, there's more. Once you've reached an agreement on the original assignment and the customer is relaxed and ready to move forward with the task, talk about other skills sets that you possess for the logical leads that would be tremendously beneficial to the customer to further their goals.

This is the **up-sell** I have mentioned a couple of times, and in the business of private investigations, it means taking an assignment and increasing the number of investigative steps, while providing more value to the customer.

Sometimes the up-sell includes a discount for an additional service or flat rate. Sometimes it involves expanding the initial scope of the investigation to be more comprehensive. This is an opportunity to increase the lifetime value of that new client after you agree on the initial assignment.

During your work for the client, there are times when the upsell will occur after the initial work is done to your client's satisfaction and because the investigation uncovers additional information or leads. Following up on those can increase the value of the case by providing the customer with additional services. Sometimes the upsell is done during the initial sales process. Sometimes the upsell comes after the work is done and has exceeded your client's expectations. While they're delighted with the work, further opportunities to expand the investigation are more accessible to digest, and they are open to engaging you for additional work. You might think this is not part of the sales cycle, but it is.

After you receive the assignment and agree on the price, talk with the client about their **preferred communication method. This is probably more important than the work itself.** Establishing communication expectations from the onset will increase the client's satisfaction with your services.

Ask whether they prefer email, text, or phone calls for status updates, and how often they want to receive updates. A question like that goes a long way towards improving the customer's satisfaction quotient.

Many Private Investigators think that receiving payment for completed work is the end of the sales cycle, but it isn't. Two additional aspects of the sales cycle are essential to the private investigator, especially one starting their business.

The first is asking for **testimonials**. Second is asking for **referrals**.

When the client is so happy with the work you've done as if they're willing to leave a testimonial, a well-formed testimonial spells out the specific benefit they received for a real need they had and how you were able to solve their problem uniquely. **When asking for a testimonial, give the client an example and let them adapt it to their case.**

Customers will often only be willing to include their first name and last initial in their testimonial. Other clients are less bashful and will grant you use of their full name and title, depending on the type of work you're performing and the type of client they are.

Getting a testimonial for a job well done is a crucial aspect of your marketing.

Hint: Upon receipt of payment, make a phone call to the client thanking them for the payment. Ask them how happy they were with the work you did and then, assuming they had no complaints, ask them for a testimonial or send them a customer satisfaction survey with an ask, "Can I quote you?"

Testimonials should not be left up to the client to decide how to word. You should send them a brief sample. Let them know you plan to use the testimonial on your website or in your marketing materials.

Too many investigators are bashful and do not ask for testimonials. They're happy they've been paid and are too busy working cases to ask. However, you must make testimonials part of your marketing strategy.

The more **social proof** you have that you meet the needs of your target audience, the easier it is for prospects to know, like, and trust you.

After you receive payment on a couple of cases from a happy client, there is nothing wrong with calling that client and asking for **referrals**.

This is, again, something investigators are loath to do and I don't understand it. Quite frankly, you've done an excellent job for this client, and your work shines. Their needs were met at a fair price. They're thrilled with the results, very happy with the effort that you expended in their investigation and, although they might have some difficult things to deal with; as a result, you got them the straight facts. In their minds, you are the person anyone should go to for that same issue.

SECTION SEVEN: MARKETING FOR THE INVESTIGATOR

Merely ask who else might they think of who would benefit from your services.

Just ask for permission to contact the other person, or have them introduce you to the other person.

By having them making contact with their friend or colleague, you get the benefit of both a testimonial and a referral. Better still, tell them their friend or colleague should mention their name to you for a **10% referral discount**. That is a double win for your client and their referral.

This has the benefit of that client becoming a true fan of your business. If all this sounds daunting, take it one step at a time. After all, how do you eat an elephant? One bite at a time.

In the next book in this series, we cover entirely marketing for private investigators, with techniques that will take less than five hours a week.

For now, plan to devote 10% of the time you will spend on your business marketing your business. If you prepare for a fifty-hour week, five hours of weekly marketing effort should be a rule of thumb.

Sadly, most investigators spend zero hours marketing after their website is built. Then they complain that they don't have any customers, that they're scraping for customers, that they have to accept any customer that walks in the door, or that they have to offer ridiculously discounted rates to keep the lights on.

This is a huge part of why 85% of private investigators fail to renew their license after their second year of being in business.

DEVELOP A PLAN

Here's the other axiom that is probably the most beneficial advice I've ever received.

The diet that you do is better than the diet you should do, but don't.

The exercise that you do is better than the exercise you should do, but don't.

The marketing that you do is better than the marketing you should do, but don't.

This is a time to think about the marketing method you feel most comfortable with, one that aligns your business with your target audience and puts your skill sets in direct line with their needs.

This is how you begin promoting your business. When I ask other investigators how much marketing they do, they say they do some marketing and explain what it is. I ask them to tell me how many hours a week they spend on that and they offer a guesstimate. In reality, they really don't know. I'm going to tell you now to track your marketing hours as you do your billable hours so that, week after week, you know whether or not you're following the most important numbers for your business.

I place billable hours first and my marketing hours second. If billable hours drop, it has an immediate effect on cash flow. If you cut the number of marketing hours, the income drop is not quick, but it does impact your ability to attract and retain customers to put more cases in your pipeline later on.

Tracking your marketing activity is extremely important, and though it is only mentioned here briefly, I go into more detail later in book two of this series, *How to Market Your Private Investigations Business*.

It would help if you utilized a customer relationship management software. There are several different products on the market, ranging from free, to relatively inexpensive, to very expensive. It can be as simple as a Google Sheets spreadsheet or another type of free customer relationship software with minimal features and benefits. If your needs are more complex, or specific, there are other paid CRM solutions such as ACT! for use with Windows operating systems. InSightly is a very robust CRM that I use to keep track of my leads, which works well in the Apple environment.

A higher end CRM called Hubspot has integrations with email and other platforms, reducing repetitive key stroking across platforms and how many screens you have to toggle between.

For more business-to-business severe ventures there is Salesforce.

The spectrum of your CRM options ranges from free to expensive. The option that will work best for you to track and grow your business will depend on what your needs are.

Full disclaimer: I still keep a simple spreadsheet of newly acquired customers and their email addresses. Each time I get a new customer, I put their name into one column, their email address in the second column and then use either **MailerLite** or **MailChimp** to send out any mailings I have. I send out newsletters, special announcements, or occasional specials that I run. I keep all my prospects in my **Insightly** database.

Several years ago, when I was forced to rethink my business model, I decided I would run my business almost exclusively from an iPad, and I left the Windows environment. I now run 90% of my business from my iPad. The other 10% is bookkeeping with my same accountant, who prefers I do my accounting on QuickBooks in Windows. I kept an old Dell PC for that reason, but otherwise, I run my entire business from an iPad.

Utilizing an app called iThoughts HD. I used the app's Genogram template to identify what my marketing streams were going to be and to see how effective those marketing streams were, in terms of both the number of prospects as well as conversions from leads, to prospects, to actual clients.

From my earliest clients, I received referrals to other prospects, who later became clients. The Genogram template kept a genealogy chart of an entire 'family' of clientele that entered my database as referrals by great, great, great, great, grandparent clients.

I decided that each marketing stream would be like the great, great, great, great granddaddy. I was able to track each marketing stream of leads, prospects, and customers. I continued to do that for several years. I was able to show what was working and what wasn't visually. The Genogram allowed me to go in daily to see what leads I needed to contact that day, and what I had said to those leads previously. It allowed me to grow my business and see where my company was coming from, all from a $12 app. You could simulate the organization in a spreadsheet by assigning an alpha designation for your marketing stream, like C for Chamber of Commerce or P for Public Defenders office. Then you could easily sort and filter your leads, prospects, and customers.

This CRM allowed me to track the numbers and my five hours a week of marketing my business. I did this marketing between 8:30 am and 9:30 am, Monday through Thursday, and then a recap of activity Friday and Saturday for the remaining hour. At 9:30 in the morning, I finished my marketing chores for the day and was able to go on to do the rest of my administrative and billable hours.

If I waited until too late in the afternoon to do my marketing, I might be too tired or, if I had an excellent billing day, I might think I really didn't need to do any marketing because my cases were going so well. By getting my marketing out of the way in the morning, which was the best time for me, I was able to then return phone calls during the course of the day and my marketing would fit seamlessly with my travel time.

SECTION SEVEN: MARKETING FOR THE INVESTIGATOR

Marketing Plan

At this point, I would keep your marketing plan on one page. In keeping with the advice I quoted above, making a one-page plan is better than the multi-page marketing plan that you should make, but don't.

An additional benefit is that a one-page marketing plan can be kept somewhere in front of or near you; somewhere where it can stare you in the face every day. This plan will serve as a constant reminder of your **Why, How, and What**. Keep them front and center in your workspace so you can focus on what you're trying to accomplish on a daily and weekly basis. This works better than a plan that looks beautiful after you spent hours crafting, only to bury it in your desk drawer where it is forgotten. An out of sight marketing plan doesn't do anything for you.

Use the **S.M.A.R.T.** technique to spell out what your marketing will look like. S.M.A.R.T. is an acronym for Specific, Measurable, Achievable, Results, and Time. Each heading gives you direction how to craft your marketing actions. Pick goals which are specific, measurable, actionable/achievable, results-oriented, and have a time frame for completion. If you make your one-page marketing plan S.M.A.R.T. compliant, you will be much closer to achieving your goals. Remember, the marketing you do is better than the marketing you should do, and don't.

Ten percent of your work time, spent marketing, could be the difference between success and failure. Take the time to understand what your marketing approach to your target market is, and continuously and methodically tweak it until you see the results you're looking for.

Not all new business people are marketing geniuses coming out of the starting gate, but getting your Private Investigation business to lift off the ground is a matter of marketing, and a case of seeing what works, disregarding the things that don't, or tweaking things to make them better.

Unfortunately, too many marketing gurus and business coaches want to convince you an investment in their marketing course can fix your problems. In reality, the fixing has to be based upon their advice, but you have to do the work to get the desired result.

Most times, marketing plans fail because you are not aligning your skill sets with your customer's needs and, then, you are not completing the sales cycle to convert leads to prospects to clients to referrals. Most marketing campaigns fail because they are poorly conceived and executed.

"Where do I find my customers?" is always asked, but rarely are the answers easy to tease out.

The time spent making your marketing plan is best spent on making one that is Achievable. This is probably the most important of the of the five letters in the S.M.A.R.T. acronym.

Failure to make a sustained marketing effort is probably one of the most significant causes for a private investigation business to fold.

After the initial push where a PI meets with some success, they get swallowed up in the administrative and billable activity associated with providing top-notch service. The investigator fails to keep up their marketing, thinking they do not need to go further with marketing and forget to ask for testimonials or referrals. In short order, the pipeline dries up, and the investigators are left scratching their heads, wondering how to get more customers. By that time, it may be too late. Cash flow has dropped to dangerous levels, and they have to abort the mission.

SECTION SEVEN: MARKETING FOR THE INVESTIGATOR

Sample Marketing Plan 20XX

- Daily calls for 60 minutes replaced by actual appointments.
- Email inspirational story to clients with a newsletter every quarter.
- Track in CRM and Genogram. Continue to use Martindale-Hubbell lists.
- Thank every client for their business and ask for more. Mention Flat rates.
- Go back and sell Flat Rate Statements and Locates as Introductory offer to all phoned prospects that did not buy last year.
- Create Asset check Email Blast in Mail Chimp for clients, then for prospects.
- Test Collateral in 20XX seminars. Track conversions.
- Make one daily referral request of my clients.
- After each 20XX success story, craft a testimonial letter for the client.
- Get the assignment. What do you need? What have you already done? When do you need it by? What's your Budget? Set a budget then talk up-sell.
- End of the year Holiday Greeting cards get lost in all the traffic. Get a jump on your competitors and send your hand-signed greetings at Thanksgiving.

The above is just a sample marketing plan, mostly geared to the P2P business Tony is involved in, to give you an idea of how to be **specific**, how to **measure** your successes, **achieve** your goals, the **results** you're looking for, and the **time** frame involved, following the S.M.A.R.T. process. It could be easily adapted for the B2B model John was contemplating in his 1997 launch as well.

Beth's marketing plan for the B2C category needs to be focused on inbound marketing. The clientele she wants is out browsing the Internet for investigative solutions for their personal needs. Additionally, she has to be very adept in the cultivation of testimonials and a referral network based upon happy customers. Much of her marketing time will be spent tweaking the search engine optimization, making sure she stays on the first page and that the keywords she utilizes match the keywords being used by prospects to search for the services she renders.

She has to continue to work on her website pages, walking the lead through the sales funnel to the place where they are willing to leave their information in a **Contact** form, click the **Chat Now** button, or make a phone call to discuss their case with Beth. She has to keep fresh content on her site with suitable free reports, e-books, and newsletters. Part of her testimonials should be a video of satisfied customers. This is crucial in a B2C market. She needs to show real people give compelling testimonials as to why the prospect should take the next step.

Part of Beth's marketing plan in the greater Austin area is to ingratiate herself with persons in the **Chamber of Commerce Leads Groups** or in the **BNI Business Network International** groups.

Beth needs to grow a list of affiliate marketers, people who would receive a commission for referring prospects that result in paying customers. Beth wants to concentrate on leads from upscale hair salons, gyms, wellness spas, and nail and beauty shops.

SECTION SEVEN: MARKETING FOR THE INVESTIGATOR

If you want to hunt wildebeest, you go where the wildebeest drink.

One PI I know joined co-ed softball leagues in up-scale towns and sponsored teams with his company's name on the team shirts. Right demographic for fidelity investigations, for sure. This would be an excellent tip for Beth. Are the professionals in your state-mandated to get continuing education credits at seminars? Sponsor a seminar or have a table. Do the businesses you want to do business with go to a trade association meeting? Do they have local chapters? Sponsor the happy hour. Guess what, you get happy prospects.

AIDA

This acronym spells out the sales process of moving a prospect through the process of becoming a customer.

Attention: Get the attention and keep the attention of the prospect

Interest: Create interest with how you can meet the prospect's needs

Desire: Make compelling arguments for the prospect to want your service to the exclusion of others.

Action: The Call to Action is most often ignored in most marketing content generated by Private Investigators. Stop the pain! Don't Delay! Act Now! Ask About Our (Season) Special.

Your marketing content language should fall into one of these four categories. Any discussion of marketing that fails to include the acronym AIDA would be lacking. It is the overlay on any of your marketing activities.

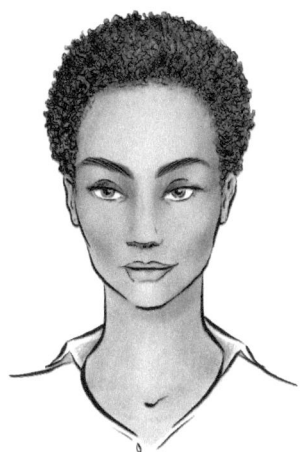

In Beth's case, her website captures attention immediately with a strong headline or sub-headline that details the benefits she provides, as well as stating the problem she can solve. To create interest in her services, she includes an informational video and testimonials. Before she was able to gather testimonial videos, she displayed thumbnail portraits of the persons next to written testimonials.

To create a desire for her services, Beth shows how much it may cost for another investigative firm to provide the same services and then shows how her prices are much more user-friendly and reliable. Beth argues the difference between an open-ended hourly rate which could drain the prospect's checkbook, versus a Flat Rate or Budget contract. Again, she includes more testimonials debunking objections while reinforcing the benefits of choosing her services.

Most importantly for Beth, is an attractive call to action. She includes a contact form with room for the prospect to spell out the assignment. It even consists of a boilerplate contract and an e-commerce button to secure a refundable deposit for a free consultation by credit card, PayPal, or bank draft.

Can you imagine the client going through the sales process, filling out the assignment information, then signing the terms of an agreement (boilerplate retainer), then providing a credit card for the fixed amount on the initial assignment? Beth wakes up the following morning, and she has in her inbox a completed task and a retainer, requiring only a confirmation by email, text, or phone, as the client has specified.

All of that to me seems to be a pretty good way of making money.

SECTION SEVEN: MARKETING FOR THE INVESTIGATOR

Tony wonders all about this marketing and selling stuff. He thought he could do it, but now he is having second thoughts. After a short stint working in the trades as a laborer after high school, he decided to join the police department. What he feels about selling was gleaned from roles played Al Pacino in Glengarry Glen Ross and Leonardo DiCaprio in the Wolf of Wall Street—not exactly right role models.

Selling has a bad connotation to him. Then there is the barrage of telemarketing calls on his phone and pop-ups when he does a google search for the Mets score.

Worse, as he starts asking professionals how they market, he gets a blizzard of answers and, as a trained investigator, realizes they are as clueless as he is.

How do they stay in business? he wonders.

Tony realizes this is a weakness and his own pre-conceptions are getting in the way. He knows he will make mistakes until he feels comfortable with listening to his clients' needs and learning how to meet them.

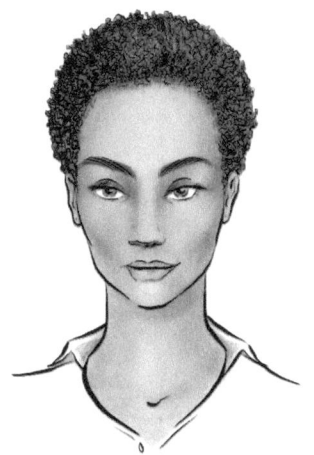

Beth is coming into this sales pipeline process with open eyes and says very clearly. "My branding, marketing, and sales materials are all about the consumer. My services will allay their fears and help them with the decisions that they need to make."

She is building her business around her Why, How, and What. She looks to other Service related e-Commerce sites and hones her process to capture eyeballs and convert leads to prospects. This is the new language she has to learn. Sitting in on prisoner of war debriefing sessions in Afghanistan taught her how to learn new languages, and now, as then, she has to learn the new language of selling.

SECTION EIGHT:
THE BUSINESS OF YOUR BUSINESS

WHAT IS YOUR BUSINESS ENTITY GOING TO BE?

Sole Proprietorship

You may want to consider the unincorporated option, sole proprietorship, if you don't have any employees and the business is just you. This is an ideal choice. Profit from your company goes to your personal tax returns, and all of your business expenses are deductible. The revenue and expenses are written upon an IRS form called a schedule C.

Since you will be filing a Schedule C at the end of the year, you'll need to keep track of every receipt and go through your expenses carefully with your accountant and bookkeeper.

My preferred paper method is to remove all the expenses and credit card statements from my monthly folders and then aggregate them by the type of expense. With an accounting program, you need to transfer the information from your program to the Schedule C. Many bookkeeping programs, like QuickBooks, have integration with tax prep apps like Turbo Tax.

Quarterly Estimates

You need to track all your income so that you can pay your estimated taxes quarterly. Some people suggest that 33% be set aside of each check your company receives. I'm in a high tax state of Connecticut, and 33% works well for me.

Partnerships

This is a straightforward discussion for me, because of the way that Tony, Beth, or John have set up their businesses. None involve a partnership.

A partnership is a business formation you can aspire to after you've already launched and established a running private investigations business. Consider adding a partner or two when doing so will give your business a synergetic boost when the sum is greater than the parts. Most partnerships, however, are a dilution of assets and capital and run the risk of imploding because no agreement was hammered out in the beginning. Most marriages end in divorce and most partnerships, where even more effort is made to spell out responsibilities and expectations, also tend to fall that way.

It is difficult to imagine how your business can grow in its earliest stages when it is dependent on a partner whom you have no control over.

Limited Liability Companies

An LLC, or limited liability company, is a popular option with small business owners because it has even more significant advantages than an S Corp., especially if you want to offer employees a part of the business. This is now the most popular legal entity type as it is the best of both a C or an S corporation without the restrictions. A single member limited liability company is not allowed in some states, however, so you should check with your accountant to determine whether or not you can form a single member LLC.

Forming an LLC puts you at arm's length, away from any liability action that can be taken against you or, as you grow your business, taken against your company because of the actions of your employees.

S or C Corporations

A corporation confers limited liability to the corporation and not the members. The individual assets are protected in the absence of exceptional circumstances like a fraud. C Corporations are relatively easy and inexpensive to form but may be subject to **double taxation**. This means that the corporation pays tax on the profit and then the shareholders pay tax on the money they take home from the profit. You can avoid the double taxation issue with an S corporation. With an S corp, you maintain the protection from personal liability, and you avoid the double taxation issue that often arises with a C Corporation. The S Corporation operates like any corporation with the establishments of officers, directors, and shareholders. You do need to file a great deal of paperwork like a C corporation. It is more expensive than the unincorporated options because you need to hire a lawyer and an accountant to file the paperwork for you, but for small businesses, it is an option. Listing "Inc., P.C." after your company name in the B2B world confers some additional legitimacy as the prospect can verify your corporate status.

Some restrictions apply, and you should review the details with the professional who files your taxes for you. I'm not a lawyer nor an accountant, nor do I play either on TV.

My feeling is that an LLC or limited liability company is the preferred route should you plan on growing your business to include employees or subcontractors that could all bring liability to your company with their actions. However, if you plan to be a solo operator, then a Sole Proprietorship gives you the ease of the only business formation you'll need, but understand the risk.

This writer chose to create an LLC which allows for business growth with employees.

Employee Identification Number (EIN)

This is a requirement by most of the states to tax your revenue and is required by the IRS. Your bank would also need an EIN if you're planning to open a checking account in the business's name.

The Internal Revenue Service does require an EIN number for your sole proprietorship when classified as a limited liability company, Partnership, C Corporation, or S Corporation.

It makes sense for you to secure this number after you have named your business so that you're able to do your banking and secure credit cards under that name.

Banking

It is strongly urged that you create a separate checking account for your business operating account and separate all your business deposits and expenses from your personal income and expenses.

For the same reason, it makes sense to have a separate business credit card.

Your choice of credit cards depends on whether or not you want cash back or airplane miles. Depending on what your lifestyle goals are, there are some excellent airline mileage cards with no travel restrictions such as Capital One, and some great cashback cards such as a Discover or Amazon Prime card which gives you cashback and discounts while making purchases from preferred stores. (I do not have any affiliation with any of these financial institutions; I am just offering these as suggestions.)

Additionally, it makes sense to have a second business account that you keep solely for retainers that you receive and for money set aside for your quarterly federal and state tax estimates. The more you keep these monies segregated from your operating accounts, the less you will be tempted to use this money to meet cash flow.

Part of the reason to keep retainers out of your operating account is if you have to return the retainer, as per the terms of your agreement. That you have the money on hand when the retainer is fully earned out, you're able to transfer that money into your operating account then. Law firms are required by the state laws to have trust accounts for their clients, and they work off their retainers by moving the funds from their trust account into their operating account. This is a good practice to get into from the beginning to keep yourself out of problematic situations.

Debit Card

Your bank will offer you a credit card that has a debit card capability, and it makes sense to have it so you can withdraw funds out of an ATM for Cash or miscellaneous expenses, without incurring fees for cash advances against your credit card. My recommendation is to choose a bank that has many branch offices in your area of operation as well as at least one that is close to your residence.

Even though more and more banking is done electronically as mobile apps replace the need for a personal visit to a bank branch, it is good to have a relationship with your local bank manager and that relationship could do wonders for you later on. Case in point: I was traveling out of the country and received a call from my bank manager and told the bank had made a mistake and deposited funds into the wrong checking account. I received a contact from the payroll company saying the payroll checks would bounce. There was nothing I could do from Florence, Italy at the time this happened! However, because of my good relationship with the bank manager, the bank made sure the funds were put into the proper account and paid my expense to have the payroll company issue the checks on a special run.

By establishing a relationship with your bank manager, you're in a position to take advantage of offerings at the bank, such as a credit line and home equity loan should there be an opportunity for you to grow your business. That is not to say I'm recommending you take out a credit line or home-equity line for your business. Rule of thumb would be not to engage in a home equity loan or a line of credit if your business is in trouble. This is not the way to address the issues while your company is hemorrhaging money. First, look at a viable plan to downsize before you take on additional debt. What happens, unfortunately, in most cases, is that a home equity loan or a line of credit is extended and that extra money doesn't fix the problem, and now you have additional debt.

Hiring An Accountant

Your relationship with your bank manager is only second to your relationship with your accountant. When interviewing an accountant, make sure that they are a certified public accountant (CPA). Confirm that they offer services related to small businesses and have them give you the names of other sole proprietorship's or small companies they deal with. Request permission to contact them and see if they are satisfied with the services of their accountant.

Be sure you know how often your accountant wants to meet with you, and whether or not you're using an accountant in combination with a bookkeeper. There are times when an accountant will offer a bookkeeper at a reduced rate as part of your relationship. You'll also want to know how many times you need to meet with the bookkeeper and/or accountant to do the bookkeeping.

You want to know exactly who is going to be working on your books and if the accountant you meet is going to be the exact person that will be filing your tax returns.

Also of importance is what bookkeeping system they plan to use. My accountant is an expert in QuickBooks and, although QuickBooks is one of the more expensive options for me, I am happier that my accountant is satisfied with his preferred software as he can save time fixing problems I create with my record-keeping or bookkeeping.

Most importantly, you need to know that they can go toe-to-toe with the IRS when faced with paying interest and penalties. Also, you want to make sure your accountant can explain to the IRS any honest mistakes that were made and be able to amend the tax return at the lowest possible additional cost to yourself. We are not talking about evading taxes here, but avoiding paying more taxes than required by law.

Is your accountant available for phone calls or emails? There have been times when I've been able to get a text reply from my accountant on a Saturday within a few minutes of making the request. This is the kind of relationship you will like to establish, as well.

I would say that after about 18 or 19 years with the same accountant, his services are pricey. However, I will also say the services he provides me are priceless, in that I know where I stand at the half-year mark, I know where I stand just before the holidays when he gives me an idea of where I'm going to be on tax day. I know he also helps me understand my tax liabilities for the upcoming year. There are no surprises on tax day.

I think of both my bank manager and my accountant as professionals that I can use as sounding boards with my business, even after 22 years of being in business.

Licensing, Bonding, And Insurance

When you apply for your license, it is a good idea to have the name of your company in mind, as they will ask for it. It also makes sense to know the type of business you're going to be, as different states have different dues for licensing based upon the type of business organization your private investigation business will be.

It also makes sense to have the type of business in your business name, such as Arrow Investigations, Inc. Willis & Associates, LLC for your EIN and on your business bank account.

Have the name ready when you go for professional liability insurance as required by your state licensing board (you should also think about it, even if it's not needed).

Think about the insurance as being precisely what it is: an insurance policy for your professional conduct. You're about to enter into a business that, if you're a sole proprietor, may expose your equity in your home and your other assets to a frivolous civil suit.

I carry a $1 million in an Errors and Omissions policy, with a $2 million aggregate, so that, should multiple people make claims against my business for a particular incident, there will be enough coverage there to handle that event.

Many states require bonding. I would suggest you make contact with your local private investigator association or the state Private Investigator association and talk with the leaders of that association. Please introduce yourself and ask questions about whom they prefer for their errors and omissions coverage, professional liability coverage, and their bonding. Some state associations have secured discounts with preferred vendors, and you might try joining your state organization. The discount from the insurance coverage may make up for the cost of your membership with that organization.

Reporting

I do 99% of my reports on my iPad and have a template that creates an invoice once a report is finished. Both the invoice and report are sent either by mail or by email to the client. The invoice is then manually entered into QuickBooks under the customer account. However, other investigators invoice directly through their QuickBooks or other accounting software. Many of these software allow for electronic payment, yet the float time on having access to the funds can be longer.

For longer reports, you may consider a transcriptionist or use a software titled Dragon Dictate. I dictated this book into a portable recorder and transcribed it through Dragon Dictate. It saves time and effort versus typing voluminous reports by hand.

The other thing about dictation is that, if you're working on multiple cases during the day and are running and gunning, as they say, you may not have time to sit after each event and chronicle it, but it might be easier to pick up a $40 digital recorder and record that case into a digital folder named for that case. Then, at the end of all your dictation on that case, put it through a transcription software like Dragon.

Dragon Dictate is designed for the Windows platform. This writer uses an older version for Apple and finds he is still delighted with the accuracy of the transcription.

What follows is more an investigative tip than a procedural tip with reporting, but the reality is the longer you wait to compile your reports after the actual work is done, the more a report may look like a synopsis, and many of the essential facts you gathered may be lost in the truncated reporting weeks later. Additionally, the information you possess that day may get lost if it's not recorded correctly.

In the early years of my investigative career, I had a separate dictation tape for every single file I worked on. The transcriptionist would receive a tape after the case and transcribe it from beginning to end. I was able to reuse the analog tapes.

From a billing standpoint, being able to dictate your reports while you were traveling on your cases reduces the administrative time spent on your cases. At the end of the day, if you use some of your travel time to dictate your reports, you will allow for more billable time and more marketing time, rather than being tethered behind your laptop, typing out what you did that night or the previous day.

Customer Relationship Management Software (CRM)

Long gone are the days of a Rolodex, where you kept your stack of business cards. That ship has sailed. If you wish to minimize your time administrating to marketing chores then using a customer relationship management software is imperative.

By keeping track of your leads, your prospects, and your customers, you're able to know when to follow up with them, to move them further down the sales funnel, or to ask them for testimonials or referrals. You can use CRM's email compilation features to provide your prospects and customers with newsletters, announcements, or seasonal sales.

At the time of writing, I am offering a special 10% discount for new customers on our flat rates between now and Labor Day. It is our summer special.

An email blast went out to 279 prospects. It took 45 minutes to create the sales copy in a **MailChimp** campaign, and it has already netted several thousand dollars and a half dozen new clients. If I did not retain the name of the prospects and their email addresses, I would not have had that opportunity for any of that return. By keeping this data in a simple spreadsheet where I can filter between leads, prospects, and customers, it's not difficult to filter or sort in a way that allows me to easily cut-and-paste email addresses into the proper marketing campaign.

I use a combination of Excel spreadsheets for customers and **Insightly** CRM for leads and prospects. It's not difficult to set up a spreadsheet or to all learn the basics of a CRM software package such as Insightly or **ACT**.

The time you spend key-stroking the prospects' information into your CRM is recouped by the long-term value of all the prospects you received by following them up with regular marketing.

I have followed up with some prospects as long as three years after first meeting them and have received a significant income because the time was right for them, even though it was not right for them at the time of the initial engagement. Over the years, they became disenchanted with their previous provider, or their previous provider moved away from Connecticut, got sick, died, or retired, and by having regular and ongoing contact with me, they accepted the latest invitation to engage.

Assignment log- keeping track of your assignments and their report due dates is imperative to make sure you don't lose your assignments and that you're on top of your work. You are providing regular and ongoing status reports to your clients until the cases are completed. **This is the number one reason why professionals will give up on their present provider. They are dissatisfied with the lack of regular reporting and communication.**

Another purpose for keeping an assignment log is to see where your work is coming from geographically, by type of work, and by customers. How many cases your different customers are giving you is a significant detail in the B2B world as well as in the P2P world, though not so much in the B2C business to consumer sphere, as many times this is a one-off engagement. However, keeping a record of when you receive these cases, how often you receive them, the type of assignments that you receive, the money that you make on the cases, and successful up-sells are all important metrics to follow to make sure you know how your business is performing.

If you're doing 15% better than you had budgeted for the year or, conversely if you are doing 15% less than you planned for the year, what is the reason for this? Can you point to the reason not only from your accounting software but also from your assignment log? With both your assignment log and your customer invoicing, you can gauge the effectiveness of your marketing.

At the time of this writing, I compared the first two quarters of this year to our budget projections, and then to the same quarter of the previous year. I was able to immediately pinpoint our growth and where I have been falling behind.

The loss of income during that period was not made up by the marketing efforts in my other marketing streams, so it was decided a new marketing stream would be would be added to my business model to see if I could the pump up the numbers for the second half of the year. However, without having an assignment log, you are left scratching your head wondering why things are happening as they are.

Your assignment log not only points out what is not going right—which is very, very important—but it also helps to understand what's going well and what you could do to make what's going well even better. Here's a chance for you to leverage your business from satisfactory to above average by applying more effort and more monies towards the things that are working.

If you don't know what's working and why then you don't know how to allocate resources accordingly.

Simple column headings such as date opened, date closed, which investigator is handling the case, which the client is, the name of the case, where is the case located, the type of the case, what marketing stream it comes from, whether the case is a flat rate or an hourly, and possibly a short narrative field for recording essential notes about that particular case (important if that case is an outlier). That's just nine pieces of data to input into a simple spreadsheet.

Time Management

Obtain a small pocket calendar that breaks each day down in quarter hour increments. If you don't have a planner or a little pocket calendar, Day-timer is a great start. Just mark off blocks of time that are more than .25 as either B for billable, N for non-billable, A for administrative, O for ownership, M for marketing, or T for travel. Block off M for breakfast, lunch and dinner and G for goof-off time. Be honest with yourself. If you goof-off during working hours Monday through Friday, ask yourself why are you in business.

Keeping this record day in and day out over the first year that you're in business is well worth it. You capture your billable time and your marketing time and get to analyze how you are actually spending your time. Keep in mind you have to have X number of billable hours attributed to a particular week for you to stay in business.

With this method you can see:

- How much administrative time or non-billable time is you are engaged in to support the billable time?
- Are you doing your marketing? When are you attending to your ownership duties?
- Did you meet your goals? Did you exceed your goals? What is the total number of hours for the week related to your business?
- Is something getting in the way of you being able to do all the hours necessary to perform in your business? List those in your planner.

SECTION EIGHT: THE BUSINESS OF YOUR BUSINESS

Peter Drucker said it best when he said, "that which gets measured, gets done." By managing your time, you'll find out that you get more things done.

Finding excuses for why you can't get things done will become glaringly evident in your time management log, and it's also going to be part of the answer as to why your bottom line isn't doing so well. Keep searching for ways to reduce your administrative and non-billable time during prime time. You will be able to expand the number of billable hours.

If you can grow these new time management habits, it will benefit you as you move forward. When you start working closely with associates or employees, the amount of your supervision and management time will go up and should be measured too.

For the time being, tackling your time management is the most critical day-to-day task that you can do. Attempt to make sure you are giving yourself enough time in the areas that are important such as billable time and marketing.

Budget

You should create a budget for the year you start so that you can compare your actuals against your business plan. How else will you know how well you're doing?

Making sure you have a budget set up for the following year, in either a paper fashion or in the accounting software, is a worthwhile exercise. How else do you keep score? How do you know how well you're doing? Of course, the final score is that you have money in your business checkbook week after week, month after month and that you don't have to dip into credit cards or a line of credit or a home equity loan. You're able to not only fund your living and business expenses, but you're also able to think in terms of growth because you don't have to take on additional debt to expand.

WHAT IS YOUR BUSINESS ENTITY GOING TO BE

SECTION NINE: COUNTDOWN SUMMARY

BUILDING BLOCKS

Each section is to be worked in order. Once you have gone through all the exercises and checklists, you may be wondering, "How do I put this all together in my countdown from Day 90 to Day 0 and lift off?"

I recommend visiting the **Red Light / Green Light** checklist as you get a clearer picture of your business. If you are not having a "Hell, Yeah!" reaction to creating your business by this section, you should rethink your decision to spend time, effort, and money for your lift off.

If it's "Hell, Yeah!" then let's go.

Knowing your numbers is essential. It would be best if you nailed down your living expenses, business expenses (projected budget), and revenue projections. Know your weighted-average hourly rate so you can calculate your critical number. If these are foreign concepts at this stage of the book, I haven't done my job of explaining them to you.

Numbers first, because you are entering the **business** of Private Investigations. Otherwise, you will drift into thinking about this endeavor as a "paying hobby." There is nothing wrong with paying hobbies, but very rarely will they keep the lights on. When I was a solo working on Squire Investigations, I put in extra hours Monday through Thursday and Saturday morning, so that I could play with Hoda Genealogy all day Friday and Saturday afternoons. That time eventually morphed into Part-time, then Most-time, then Full-time as the money I was making with Hoda Genealogy surpassed my revenue from Squire Investigations. After one prominent case, I was able to fund the start-up of International Missing Heir Finders, LLC.

But I digress.

After you nail down the numbers needed to feed yourself, your family, and to pay Uncle Sam, we shift the focus to where it belongs: **The Customer.**

Why do you want to go into business and why is this important to you? My Why was to create a team of highly trained experts in insurance fraud investigation. My How was applying all my supervisory and managerial skills to my expertise in insurance fraud investigations. My What was investigations for the property and casualty insurance companies.

Most Private Investigators are the hammers always in search of a nail. The shift in thinking required is this: How does your Why align with customer needs? How does your How meet their needs with What services or products that you will provide? Are you open to learning new skill sets to meet more of your target audience's needs?

John planned to launch Independent Special Investigations from his Rolodex of contacts. These people already knew, liked, and trusted John from their previous experiences with him.

John had hired private investigators throughout the geographic area in which he wanted to compete. He knew who was where, and how much they charged.

As a start-up, John decided to price his offerings slightly below the market average to lure his contacts away from their present investigative solutions.

It worked. In less than four years, John had nine investigators working for him in New York, Massachusetts, Rhode Island, and Connecticut, with plans to move into New Jersey and Northern New England.

Tony's plan is to align his Why—the desire to work on his own out on the street again with no bureaucracy looking over his shoulder—directly to Professionals closer to his home by offering his What—high-end investigative skills and 27 years of contacts—with his How—scripted phone calls to set up face to face meetings with Attorneys, CPAs, Property Managers, and Financial Planners. His marketing and business plan looks very much like the example provided earlier in the marketing section.

SECTION NINE: COUNTDOWN SUMMARY

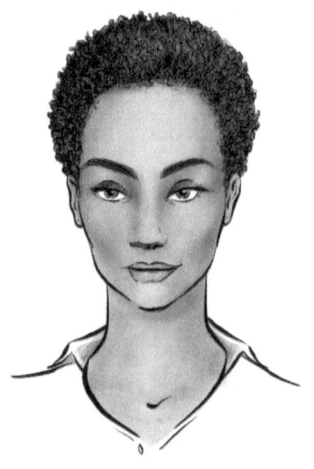

Beth's plan is more ambitious. Her personal expenses are low but having to replace all her life, and disability benefits in her business will be more expensive than for Tony, who has pension benefits, or John, whose wife's career provides all the benefits for the family.

Beth's business expenses are higher due to the IT costs of maintaining a website with e-commerce capability and a robust sales funnel.

Her Why is much like Tony in that, between the Army and working in the Armed Guard industry, she has chafed under the layers of management and is looking to be her own boss. Like John, she wants to train apprentices or newbies in her methods.

Beth's How is to attract inbound leads with an SEO-rich first page listing in the browser search results and to lead the customer through the sales funnel using e-Books, Free Reports, and Video Testimonials to get them to fill out the contact form. Beth consults with them via live chat, to qualify them, converts the sale by getting the assignment, getting them to fill out the retainer, and make payments through the website with a credit card or PayPal.

She, like Tony, will attend a Chamber of Commerce leads group, join Business Networks International (BNI). She will institute a referral program with high-end hair, beauty, nail and wellness salons. Her business cards will be displayed in independent coffee shops and area gyms.

She engages customers with her What, fairly-priced flat rates or budgets. She prices her surveillances in four-hour and eight-hour blocks.

Have you decided what your WHY, HOW and WHAT are?

Are you ready to Countdown? Say **Hell, Yeah!**

Day 90

- Decide on a Business Name and Type of Business. Secure Domain name.
- Secure your EIN number.

Day 89

- File for your LLC, S or C Corp., if you are not going to be a Sole Proprietorship.

Day 88

- Apply for your PI license *find out if your State has an exam requirement.
- Memorize the gun carry laws related to Private Investigators.

Day 87

- Open business bank account.
- Secure a business Credit Card.

Day 86

- Interview Accountants.
- Decide on your Accounting Software.
- Determine if you need to upgrade your computer and smartphone.

Day 85

- Immerse yourself in bookkeeping and accounting tutorials with your accounting software. (Rainy Saturdays are good for this exercise.)

SECTION NINE: COUNTDOWN SUMMARY

Day 84

- Move your expense and revenue numbers into a monthly budget in your accounting software. Create an annual Profit & Loss.

Day 83-82

- Begin planning your website build. Decide on DIY or get help. Be sure that your guru can't lock you out so you can refresh content.
- Engage a professional designer for your company logo. (List your job on Fiverr or Upwork.)

Day 82-81

- Decide on a web host server and website software

Day 80-79

- Rough out the website look and wiring (e.g., select your Wordpress theme)

Day 78-77

- Rough draft of Home Page and Services page content

Day 76-75

- Rough draft of About page, Contact Page, and FAQ content

Day 74-73

- Set up your e-Commerce plug-in and customize those templates.

Day 72-71

- Reach out for testimonials.

Day 70-69

- Create Grand Opening Newsletter

Day 68-60

- Create a FREE REPORT or e-Book for Target Audience.

Day 59-58

- Identify search terms with Google Keyword analytics.

Day 57-56

- Go over the content rough draft, adding in keywords without diluting the message.

Day 55

- Decide on Contact Page and Email Capture software.

Day 54-53

- Begin loading content on your website.

Day 52-51

- Add Auto Responders

Day 50

- Build Assignment Log

Day 49

- Test Accounting software for sending out invoices or from your Word Processing software email feature. Can your Software talk with your bank? Can you reconcile checking online?

Day 48

- Decide on a CRM method.

Day 47

- Play around with CRM tutorials. Create some fictitious customers.

SECTION NINE: COUNTDOWN SUMMARY

Day 46

- How are you going to track your time? Now is an excellent time to start.

Day 45-44

- Hire a designer to create business cards with your brand spanking new logo.

Day 43-40

- Hire a designer to create brochures, flyers, and sale promotions using your Logo.

Day 39

- Attend Chamber of Commerce leads groups and ask for advice on your design mock-ups. Point them to your website for additional suggestions.

Professionals are glad to offer advice over coffee but don't abuse or monopolize their time.

Day 38

- Introduce yourself to BNI. Float your Why, How, and What in your "Elevator Speech." A Private Investigator is always the coolest kid at the lunch table. Be professional and don't play to stereotype.

Getting to know business people before your launch date allows them to get to know, like, and begin trusting you, without the pressure of a sale.

Day 37

- Find out where your wildebeest (target audience) drinks. Don't be bashful. Go and observe.

Day 36-35

- Tweak your marketing copy on your website and in your collateral.

Day 34

- Check on business filings and licensing. Once your license has been granted, apply for the databases you need for your investigations.

Day 33

- Talk with your State Association about joining, the meetings schedule, and their preferred vendors for your Errors & Omission Coverage and your Surety Bond

Day 32

- Apply for your E&O and Surety Bond.

Day 31

- Meet with your final choice of accountants. Place upcoming milestones on your calendars. Run your budget by them. Does anything jump off the page at them? Come up with a realistic bail-out date, in case your revenues do not start to meet expenses and you hemorrhage cash at a dangerous rate.

Day 30

- Do you need letterhead and office supplies? Look for my stapler story at the end of this section. Plan your exit strategy from your present situation. How much notice do they require? If your banked personal days and vacation time is "Use it or Lose it," make sure not to leave any time on the table.

Day 29

- Decide on phone and fax capability. I have an old-fashion fax machine, and a dedicated line left over from the early days. Call me old-fashioned.

SECTION NINE: COUNTDOWN SUMMARY

Day 28

- Offer complimentary assignments to key influencers in exchange for testimonials and to test your processes.

Day 27

- Start marketing for a soft launch. Begin populating your CRM with soft targets. Practice listening to clarify their needs.

Day 26

- Begin daily practice on your outbound phone call scripts with soft targets. Put these activities in your schedule now and build your habit, before it matters.

Day 25-21

- Meet with prospects following the AIDA process.

Day 20

- Sit with your supporters and go over what you have done and what still needs to be done.

Day 19

- Find conferences or seminars to attend that will provide an opportunity to sharpen your investigative and marketing skills. Make sure those expenses are in your budget.

Day 18-10

- Prioritize all remaining tasks. What's not done needs to get cleaned up here. If you are on target, continue to market, but now for paying clients.

Day 9-8

- Return to Chamber of Commerce leads groups or BNI meetings. Renew contacts and make new friends. Showing up is half the battle.

Day 7- 1

- You are a short-timer at work now. Let as many people know at work or in your work sphere that next week, you will be in business for yourself. Do not tread on non-competes. Respect everybody and don't burn bridges. On nights and weekends, market and work on any soft launch assignments.

Day Zero

- Liftoff!

Congratulations! Look at what you have done to prepare yourself for this day. It all started when you said, **"Hell, Yeah!"**

SECTION NINE: COUNTDOWN SUMMARY

My Stapler Story

Back in 1997, I was getting ready to leave a significant corporation and go out on my own. We were just at the dawn of the Internet and Email was still something new (with an AOL account). I was in my company's supply closet, drooling at all the supplies in there. Everything I needed for my desk at my new office at home was in arm's reach. I made my list of what I needed instead and went to Staples.

Back then, we stapled our invoices to paper reports and folded them to fit in a printed envelope. Yes, I even licked the stamp and walked the finished product out to the mailbox. Email is so much easier and faster.

At Staples, I bought a **Swingline Stapler** that I still have on my desk today, twenty-plus years later and a box of 5,000 staples. They weren't expensive at all, but I paused for a minute and thought about it before I put it into my basket. If I went through that whole box of staples, I would be stapling tons of invoices to tons of reports. Hell, if I went through that entire box, I was darn sure I'd be still in business.

Sometime in December of 2008, my accountant was going over my books and reached for the trusty Swingline. It was empty. I went to the supply drawer, and that box of 5,000 staples was empty. I told my accountant the story. We laughed. It was a good day.

He then used a paper clip.

Tony has come a long way from wondering what it would feel like to retire from the only real job he ever had. As much as he cursed the suffocating stratification of the NYPD, it was comforting to know a paycheck arrived magically in his checking account every month. Those benefits he took for granted have a real price tag on them now. He is learning how to budget his personal expenses. He learned how to build a business budget in the software his accountant recommended. Every once in a while, he visits his website to see his company's name, logo, and his photo. When he mentions that he will pull the pin, people begin asking him for his business card. Even better, he starts gathering contact information in his simple CRM.

Little steps taken in order, one step at a time, work for him. He gets a handle on his numbers and figures out who his target audience is, and he focuses his message in a way that doesn't sound salesy or scammy. He can look the professional sitting across his desk in the eye and not blink when the subject of price comes up. Some cop skills are transferable!

Each step in his journey is the next logical step on his path. He is excited to leave the comfort of the lagoon and start swimming in the ocean surf.

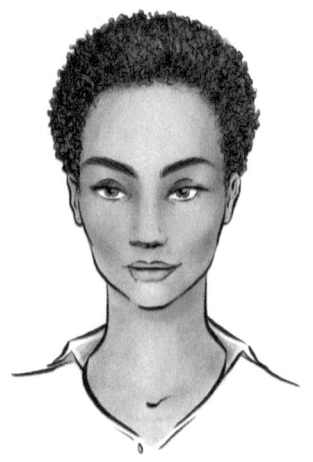

Beth is working extra hours on her job while she bootstraps her company. She cherry-picks an employee from the guard service to train. They work together during the soft launch and are a good fit. The website works; all the buttons and links do what they are supposed to do. The Free Reports attract email sign-ups, and a six-email autoresponder sequence moves the prospect further into the sales funnel. The live chat function gives her immediate access to leads, and she qualifies them on the spot. She learns to separate the tire-kickers from the motivated buyers very quickly. She directs them to the contact page, the terms of agreement button, and the shopping cart.

Yes, Beth Clark has a shopping cart for her business and almost all the buyers want her Open Source Intelligence (OSINT) special. What they learn about the subject of the investigation is well worth the up-sell to them, and it was painless to add, as Beth found out after the first couple of nervous asks.

People are buying what she has to offer. She receives interest in her referral program, and she does a few freebies for hair stylists who thought their lovers might be stepping out on them while they were cutting and coloring.

She and her employee provide excellent service. Testimonials are abundant, and Beth has already added compelling videos to the website. All of this while she is part-time. Of course, she's working long hours, six or seven days a week, but it's time invested in the goal, and the light is there at the end of the tunnel. She is her own boss and loving it. Looking at the numbers, she thinks both she and her employee can go full time sooner rather than later.

SECTION TEN: BONUS STORY

AN ANECDOTE

I will never forget the time or date. There I was on a rainy Friday afternoon, September 21, 2012, approximately 2:31 PM. It was the last day of summer, and I had just received an attachment in an email on a significant case. It came in while I was talking with my senior Certified Genealogist, Claire.

Sure enough, the information contained in that attachment blindsided us. The story behind it is for another day; however, suffice it to say the news was disastrous.

I had started International Missing Heir Finders, the missing heir research and forensic genealogy firm, seven years earlier.

Primarily how the business worked was this: I would find estates in Probate where people died without a will and where, in a small handful of those cases, not all heirs were accounted for. I would use Forensic Genealogy to find who they were and my Private Investigation skills to locate them. I made a simple pitch. I told them they were heirs to an estate. For a percentage of their inheritance, I would tell them where it was and would hire an attorney to get their money for them. The heirs would not have to front me a dime or pay expenses. I would get paid when they got paid. If they got nothing, they would owe me nothing and would not have to pay any expenses. High Stakes. High risk, and high reward.

Earlier that year, I had elected to close down the business slowly. This case, along with a handful of others, was meant to carry me through 2013 and into 2014.

I had been sitting in a co-working space and stumbled out to my wife's car. She asked me what was wrong. I explained the situation to her. This sad news just drove home the point to her that I'd been engaged in a high-stakes, high-risk, high-reward business and here she was, again, hearing what appeared to be seriously bad news.

I had trouble sleeping that night, and at about three o'clock in the morning I trudged downstairs to my home office desk and started going over the research again. I realized the information I had received in that email was severe, but not fatal to the overall case. On Monday morning, we would embark on the way to salvage the case, which we eventually did, two years later but, after paying off our extensive legal bills, only received about a tenth of what we should have.

Through that summer in 2012, I had undertaken a couple of proofs of concepts to see if there was viability to ideas I had on a couple of online B2B specialty niches. Within six weeks of each proof, I realized performing the proofs of concept saved me from expending a lot of capital and time in determining whether or not there would be customers for those business models.

Unfortunately, the bad news late that Friday afternoon meant the money I was to receive from that case, which was earmarked for paying down the business credit line, funding my salary for 2013, and paying for my daughter's advanced degree had evaporated into the rainy mist.

Now, over the first sun-splashed fall weekend of 2012, the decision had to be made—quickly—on how to return to profitability.

I had kept a handful of private investigative clients over the years from 2005 through 2012 and looked to them as the rebirth of my private investigation business. However, first, I had to get a handle on my expenses. The missing heir research business had been very profitable for me, and it allowed me to place more emphasis on revenue. Somehow, a fat checkbook took the pressure off of me to keep a sharp eye on all my expenses.

For the next three weeks, I slowly reviewed my credit card statements for the past three years, along with my personal and business checkbook registers.

I was shocked by what I found. The amount of fat in my expenses was eye-popping. I saw that the I was paying for monthly charges for internet radio on cars we no longer owned. We had gym memberships to gyms we no longer attended. There were duplicate bills or other expenses for which there were no explanations. I saw how much money I was spending at Dunkin' Donuts and Starbucks every month. I saw how much I was paying for lunches and how much we were spending going out to eat. Needless to say, during those seven years, we took more vacations and spent more money on those vacations as a percentage of our total expenses. Vacation costs had crept up on us over the years.

It was the first time we sat down and analyzed our personal budget since I first started my business in September 1997. My review of bank statements and credit card statements had eroded as the company grew and became more profitable.

SECTION TEN: BONUS STORY

It was a real eye-opener to see how much money we were spending.

Before launching a new business on January 1 of 2013, the first matter of business was to get a handle on our personal expenses—similar to what you have been asked to do in this book.

Next, I determined what the business expenses were, and what business expenses would remain or change for 2013. A careful review of the budget and actual expenses for several years gave a clear indication, again, where I had taken on extra costs that were no longer needed. I was still paying a monthly subscription fee for databases we no longer used. I ended those quickly.

From a revenue standpoint, I had a look at every one of the remaining missing heir research cases and determined high, medium, and low payout probabilities. I placed them on a spreadsheet to gauge the earliest and latest times these cases might pay out. Having had several years of tracking these numbers allowed me to estimate a reasonable schedule of how much the handful of cases would pay out and when.

This bought me some time. I also realized I did not have to hit the ground on January first earning a full replacement income. The monies I would gradually earn during 2013 could be supplemented by the occasional missing heir research case payment.

When I saw my actual living expenses and business expenses, I understood the urgency to create a new business. I looked to build a scaled-down, solo PI business and mapped out the timeframe by which I had to reach sustainability.

Years earlier, a good friend and former employee, Jon Sitek, had shared the idea of naming a company Elm City Detectives. In Connecticut, many towns have nicknames. Bridgeport is Park City, Danbury is Hat City, Waterbury is Brass City, and Hartford is Insurance City. New Haven was known as Elm City. I thought about how I wanted to go about this business, and what this business meant with the end in mind. What was I going to do with this business? Where was I going to go for customers? How was I going to attract these customers?

I had concerns about returning to high-level private investigations again, as I had to invest most of my time and energy from 2005 to 2012 into forensic genealogy and the investigative skills associated with it.

I'd worked up a few criminal defense cases in the intervening years, and handled some cases where the locating people were of the utmost importance to my still existing clientele. Since my expertise in location services was part of my missing heir research work, it was easy to extend those skill sets to all lawyers who had to locate parties to their cases before going to trial.

However, it was validation from a group of private investigators I'd known for years, through my time as a Regional Director for the National Association of Legal Investigators, that finally prompted me to jump back into the game. They had no problem telling me I could blow the rust off my old skill sets and very quickly get back on my feet. That validation was important to me because I was concerned that if I were to return to this business again, I would not be able to work at the same high level as I had done previously. This would be a source of high stress for me.

So from early October through Christmas of 2012, things began to fall into place rather quickly. Starting with the end in mind, I decided I would start up Elm City Detectives as a sole proprietorship until my retirement date, which had now been pushed back because of the evaporation of that significant case, as well as losing the opportunity to sell International Missing Heir Finders to my employees.

Elm City Detectives would stay in business until my retirement date. At that time, I would give my clients sixty days' notice and

SECTION TEN: BONUS STORY

then would work off the remaining cases in that period. I would turn off the proverbial lights and lock the door behind me.

This was to be a lifestyle business. I would work directly for attorneys in the greater New Haven area, mostly in criminal defense investigation and personal injury investigation. I still had one or two clients from the insurance defense days, and the transferable skill sets were still there. I remained interested in working to obtain proof of reasonable doubt for criminal defense attorneys, as well as working personal injury cases for attorneys with clients who needed to find the evidence that the other party was indeed at fault.

I dissolved the LLC for International Missing Heir Finders and created a sole proprietorship for Elm City Detectives. I created two new business checking and savings accounts at the bank under Elm City Detectives, as well as a new credit card. Elm City Detectives would officially start January 1st and monies coming in from the Missing Heir Research cases would flow into that checkbook. A new QuickBooks account was set up, and a new budget was created for 2013.

With the Fall colors on display over the New Haven Town Green in mid-October, I sat down in the Chamber of Commerce offices overlooking the Green, as I had done in previous years, and worked on my marketing plan. I had a clear understanding of my target audience, who they were, and how I was going to market to them. I used the iThoughts HD app for my marketing genogram and created a Google spreadsheet for my assignment log. I would keep a separate list of prospects and customers in an Excel spreadsheet.

I planned to send out a quarterly newsletter to both prospects and clientele with special announcements, news releases, and seasonal specials.

I registered the domain name for Elm City Detectives and built a WordPress website. The Home page, About page, Services page, and FAQ page were created in rapid succession. I gathered testimonials while also trying to expand my customer reach by contacting customers I had before 2005, and ones that I retained over the eight years.

On November 12, 2012, I was contacted by a criminal defense attorney working on an appellate case for a young man who had been in jail for six years on a murder he didn't commit. I had worked on the co-defendant's, and in May 2008, the codefendant was acquitted.

Just before that trial, this young man's attorney at the time pled him guilty to 38 years in jail for the homicide he didn't commit. Since I understood the underlying case, I was the logical choice to work on this young man's appellate case.

In December 2012, I was anxious about the launch of Elm City Detectives and how it would be received. I attended a Christmas party hosted by a law firm that I had stayed friendly with. That evening, one of their attorneys threw his arm around my shoulder and told many of his friends to utilize my services. He went out of his way to extol some of the more creative ways I uncovered the facts for him. He told them about some of the cases I'd worked on and what the results meant to his bottom line.

That evening I picked up a dozen business cards and, the next morning, titled the header of one of my genogram marketing streams with the name of his law firm + Holiday party. I entered those twelve lawyers' names as having received glowing testimonials and referrals underneath that law firm's family tree.

Several months later, during a business lunch, that same attorney turned me on two additional law firms doing work in New Haven, and one of those law firms became one of my largest customers.

In the beginning, my marketing plan included contacting lawyers in the Greater New Haven area. These were my target audience. I scheduled appointments to meet with them and talk about how I could upgrade their investigative solutions.

With a leaner personal budget and a leaner business budget for 2013, the push to my critical number could be gradual. Within a short period, I reached the required number of weekly billable hours to break even, and make a profit that year using the steps outlined in this book.

I made five calls a day, Monday through Thursday, for an hour. I received callbacks on four of those five phone calls, and during that callback, I followed my scripts which allowed me to qualify the prospect.

Two of those four callbacks agreed to meet me for a 15-minute appointment before morning court.

Of those two law firms that I met with and made a presentation to, one would proceed to hire me and provide assignments within 60 days. The other one, although they were happy with their present PI and did not to hire me immediately, with persistent follow-up over the years, eventually came into the fold.

Gradually, I moved many prospects onto my customer spreadsheet. I sent out press releases on our headline cases from the New Haven Register and the Connecticut Post, the Bridgeport paper.

I tracked everything.

At some point, I retired my Massachusetts and New York State private investigators licenses and concentrated only on the clientele in Connecticut.

I realized that lawyers outside of the Greater New Haven radius were reticent to utilize my services, thinking that I only handled assignments in the Greater New Haven area. Reasonable, given that Elm City Detectives is nicknamed after New Haven, so I went through a rebranding exercise and changed the name of the company to Hoda investigations, LLC. I gave the limited liability company the tagline Serving Connecticut Trial Attorneys Since 1997. This clearly expressed that I worked all over Connecticut for trial attorneys, whether they be personal injury, criminal defense, insurance defense, or divorce attorneys.

I instituted flat rates. I noticed that over the course of several years, I received repetitive assignments from many of my customers, requiring the same skill sets. By logically completing those tasks and utilizing best practices, I was able to determine how much time and expense they would take. I crafted my flat rates to be profitable for me while assuring the client there would be no additional cost and no "stair stepping" of their expenses.

I also instituted what I called the CashFlow Snapshot, which allowed me to see the status of the company with a glance on the 15th and the 30th of every month.

I started with my operating account checkbook balance and subtract out my outstanding checks, that tells me how much money is available in there. I look at my budget for the month and see what one-time-only expenses are coming up, and the average costs that I will incur. I subtract them from my net checkbook balance. Sales tax and monthly tax withholdings are next, and they are moved to the tax account.

How much I could take as an owner's draw was dependent on how low I could bring the checkbook, what my monthly draw was, and how much in receivables I had coming in. I manually count the invoices in the closed and unpaid cases to see how much is coming in. If receivables were low, then I kept more in checking as a cushion. Remember the adage "Cash is King."

I can tell you there was no magic in this build out. It was incremental, based upon executing a marketing plan, keeping track of the numbers, and watching my metrics to make sure I was doing what I said I was going to do. Over half of my work now

SECTION TEN: BONUS STORY

comes from attorneys outside of the Greater New Haven area, and I made inroads into other practice areas where my skill sets matched up very nicely with their practices.

I can tell you "90 days to lift off" is possible. I did a massive pivot from early October of 2012 to New Years of 2013.

When you decide you want to go out on your own as a private investigator follow the steps outlined herein. Don't skip any of the exercises. Take the time to make sure of your numbers. Check them twice.

You really should get buy-in from your loved ones, close family members and friends. They should be there to support you during this time.

Get your financial house in order. Make sure you understand what your expenses are.

Determine how much revenue you have to make to replace the loss of income from your job and to cover your taxes.

What is your Critical Number?

Does your one-page business plan and one-page marketing plan make sense?

Make sure you have the plans in place before you offer your two weeks' notice or change careers.

Go back to the Introduction and ask yourself the **Red Light/Green Light** questions one more time. Give yourself the time to get your business running, but have a bail-out date on the calendar at which point you will call it a day if you are hemorrhaging cash.

As an old homicide detective once said, "There ain't nothing to it, but to do it."

I believe this book offers you the opportunity to use your energy and enthusiasm to overcome all obstacles, to find out what your true North is and to follow your roadmap to success.

I thank you for staying with me to the end.

I hope I've earned your time and your trust.

Now go out and do it.

BOOK TWO

HOW TO

MARKET
YOUR
PRIVATE INVESTIGATION
BUSINESS

LESS THAN 5 HOURS A WEEK, REALLY!

OVERVIEW OF THIS BOOK

WHAT TO EXPECT

Section One: The HoneyMoon Is Over (Page 183)
- Six Months To Two Years After Launch
- Examples From Our Characters
- Reasons Why Sales Go Flat
- Marketing Plan Revisited
- Checklist
- Why
- How
- What
- Target Audience
- Pricing
- Services
- SMART Goals
- Competition

Section Two: Keeping Score (Page 203)
- Paragraph
- Time Management
- Critical Items First Thing In The Morning.
- Crm For B2C, B2C, P2P
- Saturday Morning Projects
- Old-Fashioned Flip Chart

Section Three: Branding (Page 219)
- What Does Your Website Really Say?
- What Does Your Collateral Really Say?

Section Four: Targeting The Right Audience (Page 239)
- General V Specific
- User Versus Buyer
- Go Wide Or Go Deep
- Examples Of Targeted Audiences
- Summary
- Checklist

Section Five: Guess What? You Are Always Closing. (Page 257)
- Basics Of Selling AIDA
- Selling Steps
- Example
- Resources

Section Six: When You Are A Hammer, You Are Always In Search Of Nails (Page 281)

- What I Learned From The Parachute
- Examples Of Transferrable Skill Sets.
- "I Don't Do That."
- Refer It Or Learn It
- Beware Bright Shiny Objects
- Beth's Side Hustle
- Summary

Section Seven: You Can Market Less Than 5 Hours A Week. Really! (Page 299)

- Why Less Than 5 Hours A Week?
- Examples Of 5 Hour Marketing Habits
- Your Plan

Section Eight: Flying Fortress (Page 313)

- Conclusion

OVERVIEW OF THIS BOOK

SECTION ONE:
THE HONEYMOON IS OVER

DON'T GET SWALLOWED UP IN YOUR SUCCESS

After you launch your business, regardless of whether it is a soft or a hard launch, you can get swallowed up in minutiae of your own success. You might take on a weekend case for a new customer, or offer a discount to someone that could give you more work or a great testimonial or both. You might be swamped with the fulfillment part of the business (services), all the while thinking, *this is great!*

You don't realize how much time it takes to log a case in, set it up, work it, report on it and bill it, enter it into your accounting software, receive payment, make the deposit, and close the file. You might be taking on new work that requires slightly different skill sets that has a steep learning curve.

Back in the day when you were mining someone else's gold, you might not have returned to a faraway location until the next time you were out there in the hinterlands. Now, you make special trips just to impress your new customers.

It's fun, it's new, and it's exciting. You are building up the checkbook. You are paying your bills. Your family and friends are impressed. You pinch yourself. *Is this real?*

SECTION ONE: THE HONEYMOON IS OVER

Then reality sets in. You bust your butt to get that impossible video shot of Mr. Smith and Mrs. Jones who have a thing going on. You send in the video with your bill, and the client complains that the video is jiggly. You patiently explain the difficulty of obtaining the shot, but you can't get them to understand that this is not Hollywood. The client wants to negotiate your bill—*the nerve.*

Your virus software didn't catch the latest attack from those zany guys in Eastern Europe and you are staring at tons of work to be input, and at least 2 days of having to re-enter data because you thought you were backing up to the cloud, only to find out, unfortunately, that you never tested your back-up plan.

The associate who was scheduled to work with you tomorrow calls you at the last minute, while you are staring at the blue screen of death, and says they can't work with you. You hang up the phone muttering and cursing that ten-year-old nephew of your associate who had to have a birthday party on the same day as your big case.

You have more unplanned work. You have to cancel the big case or throw another warm body at it and to add insult to injury, you notice that you haven't received a new case in a while. You were so mired in fulfillment and the business of your business, you failed to notice that by the end of next week, you will hear crickets when the work dries up. It's then when you slam the new desk drawer closed (and it breaks) you realize the honeymoon is over.

I am about to tell you how Private Investigation marketing is really done. Raise your hand if this applies to you:

- You market when you run out of work.
- You take all comers.
- You discount pricing to keep people on the payroll.
- You wait until after you do everything else, including taking out the trash, before you lift up a phone and dial a prospect.

- Alternatively, follow-up with that prospect from the other day, oops it was last week, ugh no, it was two weeks ago. *Fat chance for that one, bunky!*
- It's been a long day, and you're tired. The launch adrenaline has worn off. The long nights and days have caught up with you.
- *I'll do it tomorrow,* you say. But you don't.
- You don't have a plan.
- You haven't done any marketing in a while, and it feels awkward trying to ask for business again.
- You had gotten so busy you turned off the Live Chat button on your website.
- You haven't put up the new video testimonial that is just sitting there waiting to be uploaded.

Let's check in with Tony, Beth, and John

Russo & Associates has gotten off to a good start. He is hitting his numbers from day one thanks to a soft launch where he used his unused vacation time and comp time to work on cases and go to Chamber of Commerce Leads Groups and BNI meetings. A former District Attorney that he knows invites him to a bar association meeting and introduces him around. All of this leads to coffee or lunches with prospects. At first, he is nervous talking to people about his business, but he learns to shift the conversation to their needs, and how their needs are not being met or not being met satisfactorily. Tony is six months into his new gig.

SECTION ONE: THE HONEYMOON IS OVER

He and his wife are still adjusting to his working at home. Yes, he could put the clothes in the dryer after his marketing calls, no he wasn't vacuuming the stairs on a workday. He likes taking a case in and working it quickly to the happy surprise of his clients who have never received such royal treatment. His bills are fair, and when the first payment checks arrive at his post office box, he feels like a kid a Christmas. He photocopies the first one and frames it, placing it on the same wall as his commendations and awards.

He takes the time to learn how to do his bookkeeping, and his accountant is pleased with his effort. Tony sets aside enough money for taxes and tightens his belt on personal expenses for a while. He can start paying down credit card balances faster than expected. This lifestyle business of P2P resonates with him. The hours are not killer, but he has been warned there will be some adjustments to being the chef, cook, and bottle-washer.

The marketing is still hard to accept. The lure of doing the work is higher than the diligence of marketing, even if only for a little while each day. He tricks himself into thinking that if he gets up early and goes out on his cases, it will create more billable investigative hours.

However, by watching the numbers, he sees his numbers are actually flattening out. He looks at the stack of business cards on his desk. These were people he met, but he got too busy and hadn't bothered to put them into his CRM and follow-up. *Was it too late to call them? Did he fail to strike while the iron was hot? He looked at his watch. 4:30 pm: no, it is too late in the day. He'll call in the morning.* His friend, the former DA, has a case that he wants to talk to Tony about. He will call first thing.

Note: Tony will find out that, in some businesses, calling after the receptionist has gone home means he can leave a message directly on the prospect's voicemail. This generates more return calls than if he had gotten the receptionist in the first place. Provided it is the right message, of course.

Truth Be Told Investigations, Inc. is celebrating its first year in business. Beth Clark and her senior (and only) investigator Mary Chambers are at their favorite taco joint in Austin, Texas. Billy White, their wunderkind IT guy, working on his third beer, is enjoying the music and the cool evening breeze at a picnic table with his two favorite private investigators.

It was this exact spot where Beth had originally drawn up the idea of her business. *Her business!* It was here she was fortunate to have met some of the good folks at App Sumo who recommended Billy to help build out her website. App Sumo understands e-commerce for small business, and there was a chance for Beth to apply their know-how to Private Investigations. So naturally, it is at this taco stand they celebrate. Beth and Mary flip a coin to see who will drive Billy to his apartment—his car will stay there tonight, at the rate he is going.

The numbers are amazing. Working nights and weekends on her armored guard job and the opposite of Mary, cherry-picked from the same company, they can quickly roll out their B2C fidelity and personal private investigations to Austin's upscale community. Her website is SEO optimized. She keeps the leads clicking through the site with video testimonials and a free checklist. Capturing their email with free reports, she converts those leads to prospects.

As important is the website's Live Chat function. Beth and Mary take shifts fielding those calls. Billy made it so easy for them to convert the prospects into customers with the terms of an agreement (contract) baked into the credit card or Paypal payment options on the shopping cart page.

SECTION ONE: THE HONEYMOON IS OVER

Beth attacks the market with reasonably-priced 4-hour or 8-hour flat rates, but what is really eye-popping is the up-sell to use her intelligence skills and OSINT (Open Source Intelligence) to throw more ammo at the target. She raises the price of that up-sell to nearly triple its introductory rate and buyers do not even blink an eye.

These are giddy times, but she knows that her business has to grow substantially if she is to move out of fulfillment and marketing. She doesn't mind that the number of assignments is slowing down. Both she and Mary are getting stricter in taking on new clients from their Live Chats. They do not fully listen to the opportunities people come to them with. If the cases don't fit into the easy to digest flat rates, they pass on them. *They are passing on potentially more significant and long-time hourly assignments they could work and fit into their schedule.* This is nagging Beth but doesn't bother Mary whatsoever. Mary didn't have an equity stake in the business and wants to work the 4-hour cases because they are easier. Tonight, however, they will celebrate.

DON'T GET SWALLOWED UP IN YOUR SUCCESS

John was turning green from the Cuban cigar he was smoking outside of the Toronto hotel where the International Association of Special Investigation Units was holding its annual conference in 1998. It was almost a year to the day that he started Independent Special Investigations, LLC. His employees, Jon and Chris, were there with his soon-to-be surveillance manager Frank. They were all wearing identical white polos with the ISI logo embroidery. They were the only private investigators attending the conference.

Yes, they had business cards and brochures, but no booth. The conversations with the other attendees were amiable and not focused. Qualify prospects? What's that you say? His company provided Insurance Fraud Investigations to this exact group. Everyone in attendance was a prospect. He tended to saddle up to the bar with other investigators and didn't ask for an introduction to their supervisors in attendance. He talked about being in southern New England but didn't emphasize being able to work in New York City at all. Attendees didn't know what John's Unique Selling Proposition (USP) was. John picked up a few business cards and didn't follow up on any of them.

They were there for the training, or so he thought. He went to a Toronto Blue Jays baseball game with some of the directors of the association and didn't introduce himself, same for a tour of the Space Needle. He had more work than he could handle and would be adding two more investigators in the next six months and a surveillance group under Frank's guidance. What did he have to market for?

SECTION ONE: THE HONEYMOON IS OVER

What a missed opportunity!

John, in the months leading up to his launch, used his contacts from his days as an SIU Quality Control Manager for a major insurance company to land three major Property & Casualty insurance companies as clients. They made up exactly 3/4th of his work. The other 1/4th was comprised of a smattering of smaller Self-Insureds and (TPA) Third Party Administrators and local claims attorneys.

John was flying high and didn't know about the danger on the other side of the white puffy clouds he was about to enter.

REASONS WHY SALES GO FLAT

Service

This is the number one reason why customers switch providers. The customers have deadlines by which they need to make decisions. They have to make repeated contacts with the PI to chase down the reports. When they finally get ahold of the PI, the litany of excuses solidifies their decision to look elsewhere. They feel like they are talking to a kitchen remodeler!

If you cannot complete the majority of the assignment in the agreed upon time frame, let the client know as soon as possible what the problem is and how you are going to fix it. Keeping the client in the dark is the worst practice possible.

Process

You don't have one! Okay, I am not asking you to make McDonald's burgers and fries, but you must have a procedure for taking cases in, acknowledging assignments, and agreeing on the price and due dates. If you need to have a checklist in your assignment log to reinforce this, then do so, until you have committed these practices to memory. Do you jacket a paper file? Where do you keep the "stuff" that you have to forward to the client, such as police reports, DVDs, or sketches/drawings? This leads to the next category.

Product

An excellent report with average results will resonate better with the client than a poor report with great results. Before I produced reports for paying clients, I was the paying client. Some providers sent me the prettiest three-hole punch tabbed reports on professional letterhead, along with the hefty bill. As I sifted through the meticulously-formatted and perfectly-spelled words, with photos inserted by the latest word processing software, I had trouble finding the facts I needed to support a claim's payment or denial decision. As they say in Texas about talkers, not doers, such reports were "All Hat, No Cattle."

I had other providers that did an excellent investigation, but couldn't put two coherent sentences on paper. Getting them to send me a report **and a bill to pay** was like pulling teeth.

Today it is so much simpler. Build the templates for the reports that you regularly do and change out the information as needed. I tend to include my summary first then follow with the chronology of events and supporting documentation. I cover sheet the report with an invoice on letterhead.

Pricing

In my experience, flat rates work better than an acknowledged budget and much better than itemized bills.

Ask your client how often they prefer to be billed. A whopping bill at the end of a long-term assignment may get some pushback. If you charge by the hour and for mileage, the report should justify the time spent and where you went.

The client might pay you for your first case with them but will never call you again if they felt that you charged too much for the results they received. More often than not, this is because you didn't prepare them for the bill by **not** keeping them updated about the time and expense it took you to do your investigation. You failed to sell them on why the bill you sent them is appropriate. They were shocked when they received it.

Surprisingly, most private investigators **underprice** their services. I address that in more detail in the next book in this series. *How To Boost Your Private Investigations Business into Orbit.* The issue is not market-related. It is how you communicate your pricing on the front end and during the life of the case, so they don't have a heart attack when they get your bill.

So, if you have strengthened your **service, process, product**, and **pricing** then why are sales flat?

What is your brand? Are you attracting the right customers?

If you are the logical choice for your services, why isn't your inbox full of assignments or your phone ringing constantly from potential customers?

It boils down to lead generation, qualifying prospects, getting the assignment (converting), agreeing on price, fulfillment, testimonials, and referrals.

The checklist below will help you flesh out your one-page Marketing plan. That's the one on the wall in your workspace you look at every day, not the pretty one tucked away in your broken desk drawer you now have to fix over the weekend.

SECTION ONE: THE HONEYMOON IS OVER

CHECKLIST

Take 18 minutes to watch Simon Sinek's 18-minute TEDx talk on YouTube if you haven't already. He replaces Mission, Vision, and Value Statements with a Golden Circle of Why, How, and What. It is a much better way to align your passion with your customer's needs.

Why
What is your Why? What gets you up and working on a rainy Saturday?

How
How do you plan to go about getting to your Why?

What
What do you do for your customers to meet your Why?

Target Audience

Take the time to visualize who that person is or who that group is. The more detailed you make them, the better you will come to understand them, where to find them, and how to engage them.

Pricing

Can you make money turning a repetitive task like surveillance into an attractive flat rate? When you talk with the client, can you steer the conversation to a budget for spelled-out work to be performed by X date? If you must discuss an hourly rate, it only comes after you have thoroughly understood the client's needs. You then charge either a premium (and spell out why) or a discount from your premium rate (which is your standard rate), for which the customer is grateful.

Services

Don't try to be everything to everybody, unless you are the only game in town. The quicker and more efficient you are providing the services you can nail, the better. I will talk about nails in more detail later. For now, do what you do best. Your customers will begin telling you their other needs. There will be time to learn new skill sets, but for now, "stick to the knitting," as they say.

S.M.A.R.T. GOALS

Specific

I will do A, B and C.

For example, I will market the list of Trust, Probate, and Estate attorneys in my county and the adjacent county where I want to seek clients. I will do this on an ongoing basis. On Friday afternoons, I will contact each client where we had successful outcomes upon receipt of payment and ask for referrals.

Measurable

Following my call scripts, I will make 5 calls a day starting at 8:30 am Monday through Thursday, and I will enter my leads into the CRM.

Achievable

I will work with the Chair of the TP&E Bar association section to develop a lunch seminar on investigative topics relevant to their practices for presentation in May-June.

I will create a quarterly newsletter for my clients and prospect lists, highlighting successful cases that showcase my skill sets.

Relevant-Results

From my calls, I am looking to have callbacks from 65% of the leads. From those callbacks, I am looking to qualify and secure meetings with half of them. Half of the prospects will convert with assignments in the first six months.

Timely

I will hand-write and hand-deliver, where feasible, Thanksgiving cards to my best clients for this year.

Competition

Don't compete on price. It is a race to the bottom. Figure out what they do and offer something different or better, or something differently better. Learn from their mistakes. We will learn more about what they should be doing but aren't. Lucky you.

I don't spend much time thinking about competition these days. They are in the same boat as I am. You should be looking at the horizon for the storm clouds of well-funded start-ups that can disrupt your industry.

"What gets measured, gets done."

—Peter Drucker Management Guru

SECTION TWO: KEEPING SCORE

WHAT GETS MEASURED, GETS DONE

You track the hours you bill for each case, but do you track the hours you bill each day? Each month?

You receive inquiries (inbound marketing), but do you track them? What percentage convert to customers?

When you make calls to lists or pick up leads at seminars, lead groups or chamber of commerce sessions (outbound marketing), do you count them and segregate them into categories. Do you analyze what works and what doesn't?

Drucker said it best. "What gets measured, gets done." It's almost magical.

You will pay attention to the numbers you track. If you don't do any marketing that day, that week, that month, the ZEROES will stare back at you with an indignant look.

Conversely, when you see the number of calls you make (dialing for dollars) and the number of connections you make which result in appointments granted and assignments generated, you feel a sense of accomplishment. You see yourself putting a plan into action and how well it's working.

It becomes very plain to see you are engaged in a plan. Can you improve your message? Do you need to change your scripts? Are you talking too much during the presentations? Are you teasing out the client's real objections? Do your solutions meet their needs?

The investigator—oops, I meant to say the seller of investigative solutions—leaves a presentation meeting wondering why they didn't close the sale and thinks about what they need to change or improve. How much different is that from doing a cold call interview on a rainy night in a lousy neighborhood? Did you come at the right time for the witness? In the first fifteen seconds, while they sized you up, did you frame the issue and establish rapport? Did you have visuals to thrust in the door before they closed it on you? Did you have your rescue question ready to revive a stalled conversation?

Why do I juxtapose a street interview with a reduced sales call?

You weren't a great interviewer when you started, but you saw other investigative mentors, and you learned. It is the same with a sales call. You have to learn something new, and maybe a little foreign to your nature, and it's difficult. You are doing it without a mentor in most cases. I can say from experience, plan the work and work the plan. You might get tongue-tied the first couple of dials/callbacks or meetings/discussions, but with time, you'll relax, and it becomes fun. Yes, fun!

Time Management

I cannot stress this enough. Track your time. Are you nimble with your smartphone? Enter the time spent on tasks in your favorite app. When the ice age ended, and I came out of my cave, I used a pocket Day-timer. I tracked time by the quarter hour every day for years. It was automatic. It served as my record for billable time on cases, but I also tracked non-billable, travel, administrative, managerial, and supervisory time. Owner duties and bookkeeping were added when I went out on my own. Day in and day out, rain or shine, whether I felt like it or not. 52 to 56 hours a week were commonly tracked. Sometimes it jumped up to 60 and 70 hours, but only when I was cranking out more work or planning a new campaign.

It must have been around 1990 or 1991, years before my 1997 launch of Independent Special Investigations, that I learned the name of what the nuns called my lack of "self-control" or "obedience," those behavior labels on the left side of my report card. My scatter-brained hectic lifestyle was given the label ADD, Attention Deficit Disorder. Finally, I got an answer to why I was the way I was.

Saying good-bye to the good Sisters of Mercy, after thirteen years of Catholic schooling, I was ill-prepared for the rigors and freedom of college. With bad grades and a low draft number, I learned if I didn't get my act together, my next stop would be the University of South Vietnam, Mekong Delta campus, School of Warfare. I came back my sophomore year with a determination to succeed and to graduate. I was able to schedule afternoon classes, as I slept all morning because I started studying after 10 pm when the dorms quieted down. Nicotine, caffeine, and noise-canceling headphones quelled the distractions. I read and highlighted the text books and wrote notes furiously in class. I re-read the highlights and notes on Friday nights. I found study buddies for the classes that were Greek to me.

At home on Thanksgiving break, my mom was stunned to find out I was actually studying at the local community college library when she brought me a lunch one day. The amount of effort didn't immediately transfer into higher grades, but I didn't have to worry about exchanging my Criminology textbooks for an M-16.

Junior year, I made the dean's list, and in my senior year, I received back-to-back 4.0s.

I am not bragging here, just talking about turning a weakness into a strength. It was hard. There were no short cuts. I had to fall a lot before I could walk but, with time, it got easier.

Managing your time and working your plan is the key to marketing. Setting aside time for the to-do list where you are clear on your goals is paramount, but mostly measure your progress.

Drucker was not a dummy.

Critical Items First Thing In The Morning

Get your desk ready for marketing. The reports to bill out, non-sales emails to return, and the bookkeeping can wait. Other than confirming your appointments for the day, focus on your marketing.

I will tell you this secret: the sirens of email and Facebook will call you; ignore them. Putting the finishing touches on the report to bill out is very tempting, but it can be done later when your energy is lower. You have some easy stuff on your to-do list to check off. Wait, there will be time later. Fight the distractions and get to work on the life's blood of your business, sales, and marketing.

For those folks who rely on their website to generate inbound leads, it is like going out to the garden in the morning while the dew is still on the vine. Listen to the calls that came into the dedicated answer line. Return them right away. Emails to the contact form? Give a personalized reply and ask them to engage you by phone, if they can, for a free consultation. Qualify and convert. Sell and up-sell, if their situation warrants it. Start filling the pipeline. Each day that passes, the prospect may go to a lower-cost provider who will pick up the phone on the first ring. Each day that passes, their interest may wane.

For outbound marketing, called that because you are reaching **out**, there is a process to follow in identifying your leads, calling or emailing leads, calling leads or emailing again to leave a slightly different message, and talking to the leads with the singular goal of qualifying the prospect and getting the appointment. Can you meet in person? Great. If not, can you give them a link to an app where they can see you and your presentation materials? I suggest Skype or Screenflow, Google Drive Presentation with Keynote, or PowerPoint.

Resist the urge to send them your stuff by email or snail mail. You can't possibly know how to meet their needs without knowing what their pain or fear is.

People will buy from you when they know, like, and trust you. Separate yourself from the herd by providing a listening platform for your prospect's needs. More listening and less talking allow you to seize the opportunity to ask for the 15 minutes you need to move them from not interested in interested in meeting you.

On the days you have a marketing appointment, work your investigative assignments around that marketing call.

What about prospects that you cannot drive to? Is it cost-effective to fly to meet a customer? I would say yes if you can make up the cost of the airport parking, flight, hotel, meals, and time away from billing with the case, or in the first 5-6 cases with the potential of more. Pre-qualifying these leads are paramount.

Do this heavy-lifting first thing in the morning. Plan your first investigative appointments to allow you to market and drive to your first stop.

> You will find if you get in the habit of doing your marketing first thing, it gets done.

CRM For B2C, B2C, P2P

Part of keeping score is how you retain your marketing leads.

- ACT in the Windows platform
- Insightly CRM in Apple
- Hubspot
- Zapier if you are looking to integrate your CRM with other applications
- Salesforce is the big daddy of them all

They all give you features and benefits that range in cost from a couple of hundred dollars a year to a couple thousand. Smaller platforms might mean you may have to keystroke the same data into your assignment log, accounting software, and email lists. Zapier might ease that pain, as it helps integrate popular applications.

The most important feature is the follow-up feature. You meet a prospect at a gathering, or you make a call and leave a message. In your CRM you note whom you talked with, the date, and a note, then **schedule a date and time for the follow-up.** Some mornings, I sit down at my desk and have an hour's worth of follow-up calls to make. They are all queued up.

What if you were able to import hundreds or thousands of qualified leads into your CRM? What if you were able to send them then a six-email autoresponder sequence with links to your website and your sales funnel?

What would a four percent conversion rate on a thousand leads with a profit margin of 50% on an average sale of $800.00 for a Flat Rate look like in your bank account? Hint: $16,000.

Would you pay $1.00 a lead or $1,000 for that list? With a 16:1 rate of return, you would do that every time.

However, wait, there's more. With a better marketing message, could you increase your conversions to say 6%? Maybe add an upsell at the end of the sale to increase the profit margin to 60% on a higher $999 sale for your flat rate and premium background check (you could go with $1,000 for the sake of round numbers, but there's a bit of marketing psychology to that $999).

Now that original $1.00 per lead cost brings in $36,000 just on 2% more in conversions with 10% more on margin on $200 more on the average sale. Get the picture?

This works exceptionally well in the B2C world where the customer is a one-time buyer, but what if you could cross-sell the B2C customer with another service, or have an affiliate link with other professionals that could service that customer with follow-up services? Divorce attorneys or CPAs come to mind.

None of this, so far, includes the referral commission program your customers could enter. With a profit margin on your higher end offerings of 60%, you could easily give your customers 10% for each referral that results in a case, plus a 10% discount given to the referred customer.

Keep an email list of your customers. You might be surprised how sending them a follow-up email 60-90 days after the one-time service, thanking them for the assignment and mentioning the referral program in a non-salesy or spammy way, could result in follow-up work for them on top of what you have already done. Gee, all you did was thank them.

Add in testimonials, and you get the picture.

All this talk of CRM and email lists might make your head swim but look at it this way: today's prospect may become next year's customer. If you rely on them to dig your business card out of their desk drawer or go searching for your email, you have less chance of connecting with them than if you sent them an occasional news release, free report, newsletter or sales promotion.

For instance, at the time of this writing, I am running a "Summer Special" offering 10% off all my flat rates for first-time customers. That sale has an "act now" feel as I end it on Labor Day. With 10 days to go, I have landed 9 new customers and $5,400 from an email blast to 239 prospects that took me 45 minutes to compose in MailChimp's Constant Contact.

Personally, I use Insightly CRM in conjunction with MailChimp and two Numbers (Excel) spreadsheets, for prospects and customers respectively. I use customer billing templates in Pages for my reports and invoices and have my QuickBooks preloaded with the customer data. I also keystroke out a seven-field assignment log.

For a B2C focus, your website buildout should have, at a bare minimum, a contact form and email solution to capture leads. You may have to move them manually into a CRM if you don't use an integration app like Zapier.

With B2B, it is imperative to capture and enter Prospect data into a CRM where you track a prospect's progress through your sales funnel.

We will talk about P2P with Tony's sample below.

Saturday Morning Marketing Projects

Plan them and execute them. It is so easy to slough off any of your repetitive tasks to Saturday morning or Sunday, depending on your weekend commitments, but if you carve out time to work on the occasional project, say from 8 am to 10 am, you can boost your marketing exponentially without giving up half your weekend.

Some ideas of Saturday morning marketing projects are:

- Work on creating or updating your Free Report
- Compose a mail campaign for your Newsletter

- Work on creating or updating your Free Checklist
- The Testimonial Ask
- Promotions
- Sales Special
- News Release
- Tweak the website with new content
- Add new video or written testimonials
- Develop or update your brochures or sales sheets (AKA leave-behinds or collateral)

Put these projects on the calendar as the opportunities arise. As a content provider, you want to offer value to your prospects and clients. Make it easier for the former to know, like, and trust you and give the latter more reason to stay with you and not succumb to the temptations of your competitors, who are knocking on their doors constantly.

I did use the words 'content provider' on purpose. You self-identify as an investigator first, and it is not always intuitive to think about yourself as a content provider. Think of it this way, before someone will part with their own or their company's money, they would like to know more about the investigator who might be able to meet their needs. The more your content creates a likable bond with the lead, the more they will see themselves prospectively trusting you with the most serious problem they are facing or have to get off their desk. If your content identifies their fears and provides a reasonable solution to their problem, the less resistance they will have to select you for their private investigation needs.

Old-Fashioned Flip Chart

A simple flip chart sits behind me in my office. The top sheet, right now, is all about the Third Quarter. Across the top are nine categories that I measure. Along the side is the week, ending on Saturday.

Thirteen weeks a quarter, four quarters a year. The first two quarters are taped on the wall above my side table. With a glance, I can see how I am doing. Last year's numbers are kept handy. I can pull out the Third Quarter from last year for easy side-by-side comparison and see that I'm doing better this quarter than the same time last year.

This is what I measure:

- Weekly Billing goal: example $4,270
- Weekly "Actuals": example $4,690
- Delta Example: "$420" or "-$420"
- Color-coded by specialty area:
- Stick count of Flat rates
- Stick count of Budget cases
- Stick count of Hourly cases
- Stick count of leads called
- Stick count of callbacks
- Stick count of appointments made

The numbers don't lie. Am I making goal? Are my marketing efforts generating the cases I want to work? Am I doing the marketing I said I would do? Am I getting appointments?

Okay, it's summertime, but that doesn't mean I don't market. Yes, my clients take vacations in the summer, but they don't take the whole summer off. No excuses.

That flip chart keeps me honest and shows me the most important numbers for my business. Mr. Drucker would be proud of me and my very simple tracking device.

How many leads became how many prospects, turned into how

many appointments, resulted in how many cases? What kind of cases paid me how much money? If I keep putting the numbers on the flip chart and keep it where I can't hide from it, I am motivated to maintain my numbers in the black column and to keep the numbers out of the red column.

The best marketing plan, with the best tools and the most compelling message aligned with your target audience's needs, won't be worth a hill of beans if you don't prioritize the time actually to do the marketing.

I turned time management and organization challenges from a weakness into a strength, and I want to share my learnings at the School of Hard Knocks with you.

I guess you can blame it on my ADD.

You are welcome.

> *"Your Brand is what other people say about you."*
>
> —Jeff Bezos, CEO founder Amazon

SECTION THREE: BRANDING

WHAT DOES YOUR WEBSITE REALLY SAY?

I am in Western New York as I type this. I type "Private Investigator" into the search bar in my browser. The first four searches are paid ads for Online PI firms that specialize in Fidelity Investigations. Most of those firms will take your money and send out to a local PI for cents on the dollar. You will deal with a firm that is pandering to the masses.

I click on one of the first PIs who comes up after the paid ads, in the organic search results. Their Home page loads showing royalty-free stock photos of busy streets and skylines. Pretty generic stuff. Nothing compelling. The contact form pop-up loads before the rest of the Home Page and you have to dismiss it to read the Home Page content when it finally loads. I repeat, I had to X out of the contact form and close it to read the home page. Will I bother to search out the contact form after I closed it?

The portrait of the owner shows up in a thumbnail. A thumbnail! I've seen better mugshots, quite frankly. It is not a professionally taken photograph—if it was, the PI should get their money back. A run-on block of text goes on and on about the lineage of the company and how they come from a family of former Law

SECTION THREE: BRANDING

Enforcement. I tell you there is **nothing** on that first page that addresses the customer or their wants, needs, or fears. Nada. To me, the home page screams, "We are more important than you are!"

Next, you scroll down to a mis-mash of services. B2B, B2C, Security Guard Service, Very Specialized Debugging.

When everybody is your target audience, you are connecting with nobody.

The site offers no testimonials and no pictures of satisfied persons or companies.

So, I move on to the next site in my search results. I see one tag line about the customer's needs, then a confusing Nav bar of services and directions. This PI is a Surveillance hammer in search of Surveillance nails.

Are they B2B or B2C? Today it is a case about a cheating spouse. Tomorrow it is a case about a disabled man out on Workers Comp helping a buddy move. Who is the target audience? They don't say.

Then there is a video. It is a disjointed, re-purposed video that talks about the PI coming from the long line of cops, the gratuitous shot of guns and very little about the client's needs. I didn't watch it all the way through.

Remember, a video of satisfied customer talks to the customer. This site's video talked to the ego of the PI, in my humble opinion. Next.

The next website is slick. It has a slider of stock photos of CIA types flashing across the top third. They are generalists pretending to be specialists. We do everything for everybody, but we do it well. They have a chatbot. I didn't bother. I scanned the site to see if they had any testimonials or copy that speaks to the needs, wants or fears of at least one type of client. They can't provide that because they are trying to be everything to everybody.

However, because they have a slick website, they can charge a premium. Is there anything there that marries a benefit or feature to a need or a want? Nope. Nada. Nyet.

I have to stop. You get the picture. Now go and type in "Private Investigator" and your bustling burg's name into your browser search bar and see what turns up for you.

Do the websites have cutesy names or do they say what they do individually? Bonus points for a website with a specific customer need baked in. The first website I built was www.siuonline.com. My company name in the B2B sphere was Independent Special Investigations, LLC. My target audience was SIU managers and Claims adjusters. I couldn't make it any clearer.

Do the names of the firms have a name that plays to the Gunslinging Gumshoe or Shameless Seamus stereotype? Deduct points for pictures of owners depicting people for whom, if they were standing on her front porch, you would tell your mother not to open the door.

Are the sites customer-focused? Do they spend more time on their own needs and wants to move money from a yet-to-be-described customer, than the needs and wants of the customer?

Do they throw up on you in their About Page? Is there any connection between their background and the specific needs of their target audience?

Do they offer a press release, newsletter, checklist, free report, eBook, or video testimonial?

Your brand is what your customer says about you. What do their customers say about them? Is the target market identified? How are objections and resistance dealt with right on the home page?

SECTION THREE: BRANDING

Is there any Gun-slinging Gumshoe or Shameless Seamus stuff there?

Let's say you are a Personal Injury or Family Law attorney looking to replace your present investigative solution and you have one of these firms referred to you from another lawyer that you trust. You compare this website with the paid ads or other top of the page search returns in Connecticut and tell me, what would you do?

In the P2P market, your target market already has a solution. I learned I have to keep my face out there for that time when that other PI moves to Florida, becomes too old, tired, or sick to work, or for those PIs who decide to quit without telling their customers. After a couple of unreturned phone messages, the client gets the picture.

The professional in need of an investigator will reach out to their friends in the business, whom they **know, like, and trust** to ask for a referral to a PI that their friend, you guessed it, knows, likes, and trusts.

Now, let's talk about your website:

Can you, or someone you can talk to 24/7, add, subtract, or modify content easily?

Does your website take forever to load?

Is it Search Engine Optimized for keywords your customers will use in their searches?

Access your website from your smartphone or tablet. More people search from their phones these days. What does your website look like on the phone?

Does your company name and logo (including colors and fonts) speak to your target audience?

Does your content address the wants and needs of your target audience?

Do you have a target audience?

Who is your ideal customer?

What do they eat for breakfast? Okay, that's going a little too far, but remember if "everybody" your target audience then you are talking to nobody. Get serious about exactly who you want to talk to and understand their habits.

Do your benefits and features give you a unique edge over the competition?

How can you phrase it to express that you are better, faster, and less expensive than the herd? (Getting the job done right the first time is less expensive, charging a flat rate where you have a healthy profit margin is less expensive than the unknown in the client's mind.)

Being the cheapest has you in first place in the race to the bottom. You provide a professional service, not a commodity. More on that later.

Do your images express what you are trying to say to your target audience? Do they detract from your message? If you have no photos or graphics, why not?

Can the client read a News Release? Can they click on a Newspaper headline, or see a video of a TV report? This is social proof of how good you are.

Do you give the target audience a checklist, free report, eBook, or other value that keeps them thinking about you and what you can do for them?

What about your testimonials? It doesn't matter if you are B2C, B2B, P2P, or hybrid. Testimonials pre-qualify your prospect. If the viewer can stand in the shoes of the person giving a testimonial, they are on the road to knowing, liking, and trusting you.

What is your CTA? That is your Call To Action. "Act Now!" "Don't Delay!" "Call or text me at (123) 456-7890 to discuss your needs. I will pick up my phone or call you right back when I get out of the shower."

Does each page have a CTA at the bottom with your phone or email? In today's connected world, "operators are standing by," because the prospect's connection to you is from their smartphone to yours. Live Chat in the B2C world is a CTA. In the business or professional world, the prospect is more apt to call or email you directly.

WHAT DOES YOUR COLLATERAL REALLY SAY?

What is collateral? Answer: business cards, brochures, flyers, leave-behinds, and promotional sheets. Digitally speaking, it could be your newsletters and free reports, or price schedules (although, people smarter than me say not to have your hourly rate on your website—flat rates or promotional rates are different).

Jimmie Mesis, the former owner of PI Magazine, has an answer for that question about rates. He always responds with, "It depends." He recommends you ask questions about the assignment to qualify the prospect, learn what has already been done, the urgency, and what they have budgeted for the work. I will tell you more about Jimmie and how you and he can make money together in *How to Boost your PI Business into Orbit*.

Dr. Jeffrey Lant, in his seminal work *Cash Copy* back in 1989, wrote that most marketing copy:

Doesn't target people who need you

Doesn't speak directly to these people

Doesn't tell these people precisely what you can do for them

Doesn't work to allay their anxieties about taking immediate action

Doesn't use past buyer testimonials indicating specific results attuned to get prospects to buy

Doesn't hammer home a consistent believable, client-centered message.

He advises, "The best marketing copy is an exciting dialogue between two people—you, the seller, and the single prospect/buyer who is reading what you have to say about them, their problem, and how you will solve it."

John says:

Identify their needs and how they will benefit from your service. Lead with needs, follow with benefits.

What are their fears, how can your services address their fears?

Create your target customer and talk to them.

Every marketing piece has to have a Call To Action.

Can you offer a time-sensitive discount, free consultation, or free report (in exchange for their email)?

Separate your company from the herd. My company competes with a lot of retired coppers. In face-to-face meetings, I say that I am **not** retired. I am not tired, and the best is yet to come.

Tease out your Unique Selling Proposition (USP).

Back in 1997-1998, I wrote this about my first company:

INDEPENDENT SPECIAL INVESTIGATIONS

Was formed to bridge the widening gap between Independent Adjusters and Private Investigators.

Independent adjusters know policy coverage and claims-handling procedures and specialize in the adjustment of the claim.

Private investigators know how to investigate but lack the claims knowledge to service the Property and Casualty Insurance Industry amongst a diverse clientele.

No one combines claims experience with ins. fraud investigation expertise until now

SECTION THREE: BRANDING

TESTIMONIALS

Here is a sample email to your satisfied client who just paid you and sent a thank you note with their check.

Hi Ed or Edna:

Thank you so much for your kind words. I am glad the case turned out well for you. Could I ask you to please give me a testimonial?

I have made it easy for you to provide me with one—it should only take a moment. As I recall, you told me you had a trial date looming and needed to contact a witness who you just learned about. All your attempts to locate that witness had failed. I answered the phone on the second ring, and we talked about your needs. By talking about your case, I teased out that other persons whom the witness worked with were identified. In quick order, I located one of the workers and they told me the witness's ex-wife's name. I was able to find her, and she told me that her ex was on probation in the adjoining county. I made contact with the witness at his next probation appointment and served him with a subpoena to appear. If you agree, I can write something up for you.

SECTION THREE: BRANDING

Just to be sure, may I use your last name and title in the testimonial?

I will send it to you for your review and approval.

Thanks again

Jack or Jackie, Owner

Brass City Investigations

A day later......

Hi Ed or Edna

Here is the testimonial. I hope you like it:

I had a trial date in 12 days and just learned about a witness whom I could not find. I got hold of Jack or Jackie at Brass City Investigations right away, and they combined their computer and people skills to not only find the guy living in Springfield but also to serve him in time. His testimony made all the difference at trial, and my client was ecstatic. The work was professional, performed quickly and the bill was exactly what they quoted.

-Ed or Edna Jablocknicki, Attorney at Law

If you agree, I will use this in my brochures and on my website.

Thanks

Jack or Jackie, Owner

Brass City Investigations

If for some arcane reason you are put off by supplying the client with a well-crafted testimonial that they agree to, you may instead give them a template.

Hi Ed or Edna:

Thank you for your kind words. I am glad the case worked out well for you. Could I impose on you for a minute to provide me with a testimonial that I can use on my website and in the brochure I am working on?

Could you describe the problem you had and how easy it was for us to talk? My clients have that problem often.

Can you add how easy it was for us to brainstorm the solution? This will help the reader want to trust me with their problem too.

In your own words, could you then describe what we did for you and how that helped your situation become very clear?

How did that make you or your client feel?

A quick ending on how fast we did the work and our pricing with your full business signature would be perfect.

Whaddya think? Can you help us find more great clients like you?

Sincerely Jack or Jackie, Owner

Brass City Investigations

SUMMARY

All of this leads to permitting you to rebrand and to refresh your website and your collateral. I can feel your "sunk-cost bias" pressing down on you. I can hear you say, "I spent X number of dollars or number of hours just building my site. Am I just going to throw out those beautiful brochures I just had printed up?"

Just remember the words of Jeff Bezos. **Branding is what other people say you are.** His little company Amazon is trading today for a share price where I wish a had a few hundred shares —just saying

SUMMARY

*"When you hunt wildebeest,
you go to their watering hole."*

—John A. Hoda, CLI, CFE

SECTION FOUR: TARGETING THE RIGHT AUDIENCE

WHERE DOES YOUR TARGET AUDIENCE DRINK?

Stay with me on this. There is a good story coming.

One PI firm I know sponsors a co-ed softball team in an affluent town. Twenty-Somethings and Thirty-Somethings are playing softball after work. Each team plays the PI's team at least twice a summer. The PI's players are wearing their company name and logo on their IBM blue jerseys. Most of these players are the PI's young employees, and the PI pays their tab to go to the local watering hole where the teams congregate.

A couple of hundred age-appropriate people (infidelity investigation prospects) meet the PI's people in a relaxed setting. Alcohol and pub grub make for relaxed conversations. Those couple of hundred people have thousands of relatives. Is it possible that maybe more than a handful may not be in good relationships? Those softball players usually play for the company they work for. How many co-workers do they have? Those players have hair stylists, gym buddies, play date parents, dog park attendees. You get the picture.

Do the professionals you market have annual, quarterly, or monthly meetings? Can you be a speaker? Can you put together a

"Seven Deadly Sins" PowerPoint that places your services directly in the path of their needs? Can you sponsor the cocktail hour?

How about a vendor table with a table skirt embroidered with your company name and logo on it? You could easily carry in a couple stand-up displays with content matching your services to that wildebeest's need.

Tip: Keep your audience in mind. Don't bring your signage and leave-behinds for lions and tigers to the wildebeest watering hole.

Everybody loves to hear war stories from Private Investigators. Can you offer to speak at the Chamber of Commerce, the Kiwanis, or The Rotary Club? The same multiplier is in effect as the softball league, except you are trading the jerseys and ball caps for nicely-tailored power suits.

Holiday cheer and holiday parties. Golf outings. Association Year-end parties or mid-summer picnics. Go to where your prospects gather.

Can you drop off reports in person to your client and ask them for referrals within the building or nearby?

It works like this:

"Hi Chris, I was just dropping off a report of a (briefly describe the successful investigation) with Pat (client on the eighth floor, and Pat told me to come by and introduce myself. Pat told me you have a similar practice. I'm curious. How do you meet your investigative needs?"

Out of politeness to their colleague, Pat, they will spend a minute with you, and you can qualify this prospect.

If they are a good fit, say to them, "I know you're busy now, but can I come back next Thursday before court and explore your needs for 15 minutes. How does that sound?"

Hint: Next Thursday before court usually works and if it doesn't, you have them giving you an alternate time and date. It's incredible to see how simple this is.

"Smokestacking" refers to an old-fashion route salesperson coming into a new town. They would look for the smokestacks and make a cold call, or they would walk the length of Main Street and stop in each store, say hello, leave a card and ask the shopkeeper if they could tell the salesperson whom they should talk to.

In today's world, when you are working a case on the street, and you literally have to walk by a prospect's office to get to your car. Do you make a quick detour?

Do you keep business cards, press releases, brochures, and price sheets in your folio?

Which brings me to the question of how you attire yourself when you are on the street. I always dress for the most important person I have to establish rapport with that day. I dress differently for cold call door knocks in a not-so-nice neighborhood than I do for an appointment with a prospect. I would instead tell my prospect the story of why I am wearing a polo and khakis than explain to a witness why the older man that I am is wearing a business suit and knocking on their door. I think the former would be more understanding than the latter. What do you think?

For years, my favorite attorney has invited me to his holiday party. It is The Event to go to every year. This large law firm invites their own families and tons of other attorneys-spouses as well. They rent a five-star hotel ballroom and have a locally renowned jazz band play.

Attendees eat their way around the room with the best hand-carved meats, hand-rolled sushi, and hand-made desserts. I'll stop there. You get the picture, and it's making me hungry.

Anyway, most of those previous years, my favorite attorney sat on a local town board, and they met on the same weeknight as the party, but in 2012, the dates didn't match up, and he attended his own company's holiday party.

I arrived early and was chatting him up about a case I had just done for him.

It was mid-December, and I had taken a sandwich board to a busy intersection on the same day of the week, at the same time during morning rush hour as the accident. The sandwich board read, "Did you see the motorcycle and bicycle accident in October? Call John Hoda at (123)-456-7890"

A polar vortex had our little town in an Arctic grip of sub-zero weather that day. It was freezing cold, just after dawn, and my attorney was very appreciative.

What made this case special and worth re-telling is the motorcycle was being operated by a police officer who had just finished working the midnight shift and was gunning it to beat the light. The boy on the bicycle was entering the far side of the intersection on a green light before the collision. When the motorcycle hit him, he flew high in the air. His left leg required multiple surgeries, and the possibility of walking was still up in the air.

Can you imagine what the police report said? Were there any witnesses noted? What do you think? This is why I had to find a creative solution. More importantly, what do you think the witnesses I was searching for would say?

It was this story of the sandwich board that my favorite attorney told his friends as they walked into the party. These were other high-powered attorneys who respected him and trusted him. I would go fetch drinks and appetizers for my favorite attorney between times he regaled his steady stream friends with this story of my creativity.

I haven't missed any of their parties since that night.

General versus Specific

Does your website call to the whole jungle or one or two related species?

Are you hunting with a sawed-off shotgun or with a hunting rifle?

Can you meet the needs of the general public with several services? Absolutely.

Looking at the reverse, should you be offering those services to the general consumer B2C and B2B simultaneously? I argue not. If you are hunting B2C and a B2B wanders in, you can take your shot, but don't start watering down your marketing message. Be specific in your message to exactly who you want to talk to. Talking to everybody means you are addressing nobody. Be specific.

User versus Buyer

This is an easier decision in most cases. You talk to the person with fears, needs, and a desire for change with their issue. Once you have the investigative objective and can determine the cost, you make a presentation to the buyer with high, medium, and low pricing (unless the assignment can be done quickly with a flat rate, then you pitch that). A two-step sales pitch is required with the user and the ultimate buyer. Never forget who writes the check. That can become a nasty surprise.

What about in B2B where you want to become a service provider for many users of the business you are targeting such as a Claims Department, Corporations, Governmental agencies, Chain Retailers, or Franchisors. Do you create a suite of services to meet the needs of an entire industry? Whom do you pitch and what is your pitch? How is your pitch to a Claims VP different than to an SIU manager? I will address that question in Section Eight-Flying Fortress.

Going Wide versus Going Deep

There are arguments on both sides for this. The deeper you go, the more specialized your services are and the more you can charge. In a lifestyle business, having a specialty for a loyal group of high-paying clients is ideal. On the other hand, market forces out of your control may cause that business to dry up. Having a broader customer base smooths out the sales cycles. In both cases, all your marketing materials and your message should be consistent with the audience.

Tony's detectives in Mid-town Manhattan handle many financial crimes and work with the Feds on joint cases regardless of who was the primary case investigator. Tony is well-positioned to approach the professionals in Queens about his services. Their needs become more evident to him as they talk about their civil remedies. Finding witnesses and interviewing them becomes his most-requested service, followed by asset checks of the targets. Tony learns to suggest the asset check immediately after he gets evidence on the target, so the client will know if it is worth going after the target with more costly litigation.

CPAs in his home borough work with hundreds of small businesses who are getting ripped off by employees, vendors, sub-contractors, and dead-beat customers. They turn to Tony to find the evidence and help them bring the cases to small business attorneys to prosecute the thefts and frauds civilly. Those attorneys begin using him on their other cases with larger clients. The Russo & Associates brand is starting to form with the triangle of CPAs, Small Business Attorneys, and mid-size corporations in Queens.

However, it is his friend, the former DA, that tells Tony he has an innocent client sitting out in Nassau County jail. Tony reviews the discovery into the murder case and goes about his investigation. He locates witnesses that completely discredit the sole eyewitness while bolstering the alibi witnesses the locals had ignored. The Nassau County DA has to drop the case. Tony is there when his attorney's client is released from jail. The front-page headline and photo of the trio accompany the article in which the attorney credits Tony for gathering the evidence of his client's innocence. Tony uploads the video of the TV reports and the Newspaper Headlines to his website.

Tony catches some gas from his former squad, but in the end, they know Tony is a straight-shooter and that he never let them get away with cutting corners or taking short-cuts like what happened in this case. Tony had never considered working Criminal Defense, but in the days following that headliner, he receives overtures from other Nassau County Criminal Defense Attorneys. He doesn't want to go against NYPD, his former employer of nearly three decades, but has no problem with taking on the boys and girls in blue in the adjoining county. This work energizes him. He had never considered it as a possibility, and now he looks forward to the cases he reviews for those Defense lawyers.

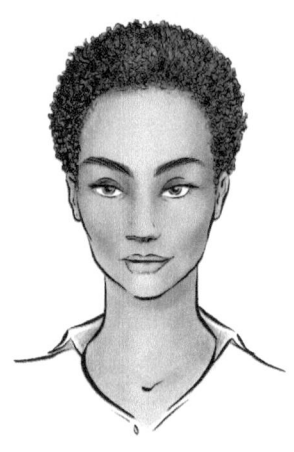

Truth Be Told Investigations, Inc. captures leads when prospects give their email to Beth to obtain a Free Report. She takes turns with her employee answering the Chat Live calls and can convert the calls into paying customers by walking them through the shopping cart. Her outbound marketing to the high-end hair salons, wellness centers nail salons, beauty shops, and gyms is focused on upscale women in Austin's booming economy. After six months of modest pricing, she increases her hourly and flat rates twice without any clients blinking an eye. The split is also showing her the upscale clients are coming from the outbound marketing almost exclusively. She and Mary can say bye-bye to the Armored Guard jobs when the cash flow forecasts show they are way ahead of schedule. Beth's professionalism and processes are appreciated by her customers which increases her word of mouth referrals. Her numbers are evenly split between inbound from her website and outbound from her marketing to upscale women where they congregate. However, outbound marketing is providing more than twice the income per assignment. She needs to double in size and knows her processes have to absorb the added administrative time. Her brand is slowly moving from taking all comers to meeting the needs of higher-paying longer-tail cases. The work is also bringing her in contact with Austin's high-end law firms, who are contacting her to conduct more detailed Open-source Intelligence (OSINT) investigations, which pay very well.

Independent Special Investigations grew on schedule and expanded into insurance surveillance. John's marketing stalled as he did everything except the bookkeeping. His training was hands-on, and his new employees accompanied him as he handled cases. Later, he accompanied them until they were comfortable with the work and managed their own caseload. The work took them from Connecticut into Long Island and NYC, as well as Boston and Providence. They drove longer distances, and the clients balked at paying for extensive travel time and mileage. John created billing points for the clients, but still paid his employees' drive time and mileage, portal to portal. The billing points cut into profit margins, and his next hires had to be in NYC and Massachusetts. Revenues were growing, but so were expenses. The second year of ISI showed mixed results. Still, John and his top employee created in-house training seminars for his customers and the annual IASIU in Dallas, Texas. He attended local state association lunch meetings in Connecticut, Massachusetts, and Rhode Island. He created a quarterly newsletter for his customers, and his sub-contracted secretary mailed them out for him.

John was one busy hombre. He brought his expertise to his target audience where they worked and where they congregated.

SECTION FOUR: TARGETING THE RIGHT AUDIENCE

SUMMARY

As you begin to learn who your best customers are, keep looking at your message and make sure you are talking to the people you want to reach. Marketing is not a spectator sport for Private Investigation businesses. You can see the prospects meet for work, then eat and drink for play. You have to manage your time to go to these events. Some may require late evenings while others may require you to travel to conferences. Your marketing is the lifeblood of your business, and you have to sacrifice billing time to invest.

SECTION FOUR: TARGETING THE RIGHT AUDIENCE

CHECKLIST

- Chamber of Commerce Leads groups
- BNI (Business Network International) groups
- Rotary, Kiwanis, Library nights
- Association meetings
- Conferences
- Bar association gatherings
- CPA association gatherings
- Golf outings
- Bowling or Softball leagues. (Sponsor a team if you're not a kegler or baller)
- Create a power point (i.e., Seven Deadly Sins) for your target audience Continuing Ed Requirements, or create their in-house training where their needs intersect with your services.
- Take the claim adjusters, paralegals, or CPAs' bookkeepers to lunch day.
- "Smokestack"—Do you keep marketing materials in your folio?

- Deliver brochures to other prospects in your client's building.

"Makes sense to me, what do you think?"

—Stephan Schiffman from *Closing Techniques that Really Work*

SECTION FIVE: GUESS WHAT? YOU ARE ALWAYS CLOSING.

BASICS OF SELLING

From *How To Launch Your Private Investigation Business: 90 Days To Lift Off*

John came to Independent Special Investigations with no sales skills and no marketing plan, per se. He had an old-fashioned Rolodex and long-standing relationships with many SIU managers who knew liked, and trusted him. He launched his company at a time when SIU units had hired as many investigators as the Claims Department budgets allowed, and the SIU managers needed to outsource investigations due to higher volume or geographic considerations. John exceeded their expectations and did so with reasonable pricing. He made believers with his work product and training presentations. He counted Insurance Companies Claims Departments and SIU units as his target audience and marketed at the local and regional level.

SECTION FIVE: GUESS WHAT? YOU ARE ALWAYS CLOSING

Tony is wondering all about this marketing and selling stuff. He thought he could do it, but now he is having second thoughts. After a short stint working in the trades as a laborer after high school, he decided to join the police department. What he feels about selling was gleaned from roles played Al Pacino in Glengarry Glen Ross and Leonardo DiCaprio in the Wolf of Wall Street. Not precisely good role models.

Selling has a bad connotation to him.

Then there is the barrage of telemarketing calls on his phone and pop-ups when he does a google search for the Mets score.

Worse, as he starts asking professionals how they market, he gets a blizzard of answers, and as a trained investigator, he realizes that they are as clueless as he is.

How do they stay in business? he wonders.

Tony realizes that this is a weakness and that his own pre-conceptions are getting in the way as well. He knows that he will make mistakes until he feels comfortable with listening to his clients' needs and learning how to meet them.

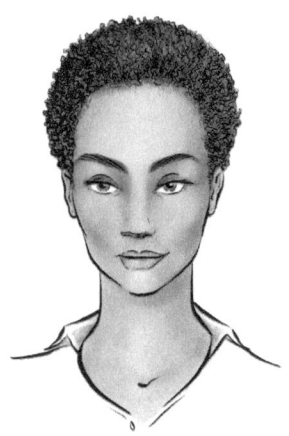

Beth is coming into this sales pipeline process with open eyes. She says very clearly, "My branding, marketing, and sales materials are all about the consumer. My services will allay their fears and help them with the decisions that they need to make."

She is building her business around her Why, How and What. She looks to other Service related e-Commerce sites and is honing her process to capture eye-balls and convert leads to prospects. This is the new language that she has to learn. Sitting in on prisoner of war debriefing sessions in Afghanistan taught her how to learn new languages and she has to learn the language of selling.

SECTION FIVE: GUESS WHAT? YOU ARE ALWAYS CLOSING

> Where you came from before deciding to market your Private Investigation business is as important as where will you go from here.

The mantra, "the marketing you do is better than the marketing you should do, but don't," combined with having a plan to market just 5 hours a week is a bridge to where you want to be.

This comes from a guy who openly said he would instead take out the trash than pick up the phone and market. What changed? Well, for one, the business climate. I will cover that in Section Eight: Flying Fortress.

Secondly, I learned one technique at a time and measured my progress. I studied what worked and more importantly, what didn't and why.

Slowly over time, I began to realize if I wanted to succeed as a Private Investigator in Business, I had to learn about business, and central to that premise was learning how to market and sell investigative services.

I had to make some hard decisions and decide what conferences and training seminars I would attend. Do I spend time and money on investigative classes or marketing classes?

I spoke about wanting to continually upgrade my investigative skills as my motivation.

Why do you resist sales and marketing activity? Does it leave a funny taste in your mouth? Are you disdainful of the process? Do you feel like a snake-oil salesperson?

I understand your feelings. Most professionals feel cheap when they have to hawk their wares, **the work should speak for itself, or so the thinking goes.**

Can you reframe those feelings?

Can you see that you offer a valuable service and people need it? Can you make more people aware that you can help them solve their problems?

I traveled the path from not knowing what I didn't know, to knowing what I didn't know.

Stated differently, I went from being unconsciously incompetent to becoming consciously incompetent. It was a difficult process, but I was determined to learn. Slowly, I began to know what steps to follow in what order.

With that came the confidence to grow my sales persona to where I could pitch a prospect on a return phone call, even as I was getting out of my car for a long walk to do a door knock. That didn't happen overnight. I had to take baby steps at first, and as my confidence grew, I began seeking out more courses on marketing.

A few years ago, I went to SumoCon in Austin, Texas, where I met Noah Kagan and the good folks at App Sumo. They are the Sumo wrestlers in the internet e-commerce arena. That's why I wanted Beth Clark to work there in the B2C world and have them chatting over tacos with her.

If your business model is B2C, you owe it to yourself to leverage your website with inbound marketing. Inbound means the prospects are looking for a solution to their problem and if you can give them value during their search phase and drip content to them with email autoresponders they can begin to know, like, and trust your business.

The following year, I traveled to Alexandria, Virginia, from Connecticut to immerse myself in the Ben Glass Law "Great Legal Marketing" course.

"Whoa, what's that?" you ask.

Why would I spend four days of time and all that money for tolls, two tanks of gas, three nights hotel, and food to learn marketing geared to lawyers?

My reasons were two-fold. Where else could I have a large group of my sample target audience under one roof for four days? They were under no sales pressure from me, and I was able to ask them what they valued in a Private Investigator and what would motivate them to switch service providers? The trip was worth the consensus of answers I received.

As a bonus, I watched how Family Law, Personal Injury, and Disability practitioners overcame their fears and prejudices and learned to begin employing strategies in their businesses. Just the "before and after" recordings of how some law firms answered their phones was the best comedic attention grabber of the conference.

Then there was the montage of TV spots where the lawyers looked tough, acted tough, and talked about themselves. Later, the client-focused TV spots were aired. A handful of converts allowed Ben to play their own TV spots before and after applying what they learned through the GLM course.

Combined with other client-focused strategies, graphs on the ballroom screens showed growth in the number of cases taken, per case average settlement/verdict growth, and eye-popping, chart-topping revenues. Ben also emphasized taking the stress out of their business by empowering others and honing processes so they could concentrate on what they did best.

Great lawyers were learning how to become good marketers.

I will tell you a secret. Lawyers are a risk-averse bunch and are loathe to change. However, these attendees had reached a pain point—they had been spinning their wheels or revving in low gear, not realizing the full potential of their practices for a long time.

Something had to change. They were ready to address their pain.

Let me save you some pain, time, and money. Just bring an open mind and plan to incorporate one or two ideas you learn here for five hours a week to start.

SECTION FIVE: GUESS WHAT? YOU ARE ALWAYS CLOSING

A.I.D.A.

Attention

The prospect is looking to address a pain point. They are going on the Internet to find a solution. Professionals tend to reach out to other professionals and ask for a referral. Separate yourself from the herd by talking directly to them in your marketing copy. Again, from Dr. Jeffrey Lant's 1989 *Cash Copy*, in two words, you care.

- Care to understand what your prospects are trying to accomplish.
- Care to let them know you can help.
- Care to tell them (sometimes with the most utmost candor) how your service can help them realize their objectives.
- Care to inform them what will happen to them if they don't take action to solve their problem.
- Care to understand their worries and anxieties both about what you are selling and about you.
- Care to make sure that you address these worries and anxieties-and not treat them as inconsequential.

- Care to be flexible in how you do business and when you do business so that your client understands that you are genuinely interested in their comfort and ease.

- In short, empathize. **Put yourself in your client's shoes and run your marketing- and write your cash copy- from their perspective, not from yours."**

This last point turns everything upside down in some investigator's minds. You have a need, a burning need, to tell the prospect how great you or your company is. You have a need, a burning need, to impress them; how your firm and only your firm can meet their needs.

It takes practice, but you can change the direction of your marketing copy and in your conversations, become a good listener first before you steer the discussion with probing questions. Only then can you begin to address their problems with your solutions.

Interest

Okay, you have the prospect's attention. However, Interest is a double-edged sword. On one side, they want to move forward; on the other hand, they have objections.

How do you make it easy for them to move forward?

- Make it easy to contact you with website forms and a google voice number. (Bonus: Every time you see your Google number on your phone display, you know it's a prospect.)

- Answer your calls with, "Hi, This is (Your full name). How can I help you?" "Is this Blazing Arrow Investigations?" "Yes it is, and whom am I speaking with?" * I call investigators all over the country to give them high-paying and interesting work. I can't tell you how many times I get the phone company's generic default answer, 'Leave a message,' a terse response, "Adamchilski, who's this?" or worse.

- Ease of discussion via a free consultation. Active listening sometimes calls for empathy and restating the problem in a way that makes sense for you and gives them a chance to agree or clarify the problem.
- Give them room to describe their problem to you by making sure your contact form has a text field that allows for a paragraph or two.
- FAQ - This is to pre-empt objections. Your FAQ, either on your website or woven into your discussion, is meant to overcome objections before they are raised and solidified in the prospect's mind.

It bears repeating, become a problem solver. Once you identify the problem, you can offer a specific solution for the pain point. By doing so, you are building:

Desire

That's right. Desire for a Private Investigator to address the problem and give the promise of a better future.

You are the expert; you have handled cases like this before. Hopefully, you can point to the testimonials on your website or collateral to show this. Because you are an expert, you have seen many variations of this problem and have a track record of being adaptable to each specific case.

Restate the prospect's painful situation, how your solution will apply, and how they will feel when the case is completed.

But first they must take:

SECTION FIVE: GUESS WHAT? YOU ARE ALWAYS CLOSING

Action

The prospect wants to move towards acting. Why? Why will they part with money for your solution? How will they do that?

What follows is an example argument you might make in favor of your services.

"Mrs. Gabbagottio, You need to know what is really going on. You can't live a life filled with his lies and deceit. You can't change the past, but with the information gleaned from our investigation, you can move forward with confidence. You won't be guessing anymore. Yes, it will be painful knowing the truth, if it is what you suspect it is, but at least you will know, and then you can decide how and when to act based on the information we will supply."

"I just pulled up his DMV record and see that he drives a BMW 7 series, black in color, is that correct? Which of the social media pictures here is the most recent? You said you suspect the activity will take place when you go to your sister's house out of state this coming weekend. I want to suggest coverage from the last time you see Mr. Gabbagottio until a few hours before your return, or we will begin tracking him after work if that makes more sense? We will stay with him until we know what he is doing and can address your concerns. Our price range on the refundable retainer, with some conditions for this work, is between $x and $z. We need you to fill out the retainer agreement here, and here, and initial here on the conditions."

"Once I confirm the payment from you, we will be all set."

"Will that be by credit card or PayPal?"

(Or whichever digital transfer methods you accept)

"Yes, we do take cash. I can give you a receipt. Let's set this up now."

Pushy? This is a condensed version of what may take place over several conversations.

Direct? Yes. Problem, solution, contract, and payment follow a straight-line progression.

Professional? You are not a therapist, but you can be sympathetic. Is your solution the best alternative of several discussed? The action steps should be the logical and **ethical** response to the issue the client is facing.

In a B2C interaction, you are the professional, and they are the sometimes-emotional amateur. Your professionalism includes the ethical obligation to do right by your client; not to inflame their passions so that you can empty their checkbook.

In a B2B sale, you are continually circling back to make sure you have agreement on solutions, and by the time the ACTION step arrives, the client is ready to move forward. The money part is just the housekeeping both sides know has to be done between you and the ultimate purchaser of your services.

In a P2P sale, you are looking to confirm that you and the client have brainstormed the issues and cobbled together the best approach. Your quote comes after you can see the complete picture of your investigative objective. You might have to offer a discount for a first-time client, but you must be firm it is only a one-time offer so they can see how well your firm performs.

Note: I learned early to offer a volume discount only after the volume is established, not before. Action is a natural by-product once the desire to move on the issue with your collective solution is hammered out.

SECTION FIVE: GUESS WHAT? YOU ARE ALWAYS CLOSING

SELLING STEPS

What we are about to talk about is **your** activity during the sales process.

Opening, Qualify

Do you have their **attention?** Is your firm a good fit? Remember, you can refer them to another colleague if appropriate. You can also use the consultation time to help them understand they should skip GO, save the $200 or $2,000, and go right to an attorney or another solution provider. The opening is not about taking all comers. You need to understand their wants, needs, or fears.

Part of qualifying the prospect is establishing rapport. Here you have a leg up on most salespeople. You know how to establish rapport and make people feel at ease when they talk with you. If you can ethically convince someone to make a statement against their own interest, you can certainly speak to somebody about their needs and wants. What you have learned from your street work applies here. Frame the issue and get on their wavelength. Salespeople tend to rush this step and fly headlong into their sales pitch.

Get the prospect talking and relaxing into what they want to talk about. This is not the time to tell them how wonderful your firm is and how you can meet their needs. You are a sympathetic listener.

Interviewing/Information Gathering

This step is often brushed over in a hurry to get the sale. Undoubtedly try to understand the investigative objective. This should keep the prospect's **interest**.

If you see them fading, you may have to touch upon their wants, needs, or fears. Their ideas of what a PI can do may be informed by Hollywood, far from the legal or ethical rules we are bound by.

You need to adjust expectations to rebuild their **interest**. This is where you spend the most time in this four-step process. As a trained investigator, you are trying to understand their motives for wanting to utilize a PI's services, as well as establish the parameters of the case.

Imagine the most under-utilized step by salespeople is the most crucial step and as an investigator, **you** have the skill sets to do it well.

Presentation

By this stage, you have gathered enough information from the prospect from conversations, emails, or texts and can put together a presentation.

If you are not creating a **desire** during your presentation for the expert solution you have crafted for them, you have to go back and restate why they are qualified, summarize the information you gathered, and present your solution with the hoped-for outcome clearly defined.

You may have to overcome objections with a restatement of how the answer will bring about the desired result.

Close

You want the prospect to take **Action**. You qualified them after you got their **attention**, and you kept their **interest** up while you gather information about their wants, needs, or fears.

This is different from picking the Who, What, How, When, Where, and Why of the case.

You made your presentation and see that they **desire** the outcome your services will provide. Here is how you close. Wrap everything up with:

"Makes sense to me. What do you think?"

That's a winning close that I must credit to Stephan Schiffman! I will recommend his books at the end of the chapter. I recommend you read his tips to help take the fear and loathing out of the sales cycle.

John's Example

In early June, a few years back, John was standing at his exhibit booth long after all the other vendors had packed up and headed out for happy hour. This was his first booth exhibition at this particular day-long Bar Association meeting, and he was determined to get his money's worth. John was waiting for the last class to end. The lawyers were getting their CLE credit certificates handed to them at the end of the class, so they all had to stay until the end.

Since John was the last man standing when the doors opened from the class, he decided to hand each attendee his brochure personally, price sheet and business card all nicely paper clipped together. One lawyer lagged behind and read the materials while John finished giving a package to each attorney. John's messaging was consistent. The lawyer didn't say what the case was about, but that he would reach out to John when the time was right.

Six months later, the right time was the Monday, three days before Christmas. John received a call from the attorney who explained that the VP of a Financing company had an urgent case for him. John called the VP, and they met on Christmas Eve at 10 AM.

The financing company had a problem. A big problem. Their inventory practices were somewhat lax and preliminary indications were that much of the heavy equipment they had financed for a safety company providing services and equipment to the Oil & Gas Fracking industry had gone missing when the price of oil dropped to the point where further exploration was no longer cost-effective. Some of the equipment had been abandoned on the job sites as the market collapsed.

The partners of that safety firm were hemorrhaging cash and pointing fingers at each other, and at the General Manager who was not cooperating.

The VP wanted a solution in place before he started his year-end vacation.

The missing equipment had last been seen at job sites in West Virginia, Kentucky, and Ohio.

This is what John knew before he walked into the high class, well-appointed offices of the VP. Framed photos of the veep and his bride in Aruba became the ice-breaker. John and his wife wanted to vacation there, and he asked about it. The VP asked John how he took his coffee as he served him from a fresh pot on the credenza. He then thanked John for coming in on short notice and Christmas Eve, no less. Their offices would be closing at noon. John realized neither the VP nor his attorney had envisioned the scope of the problem. Criminal prosecution, Civil Fraud, and Restitution were all in play, but they had not yet gotten an accurate inventory from all the players. They were stymied. The previous year's inventory, supposedly done by a third-party vendor, was questionable.

John had a blank slate to work with, but not a blank check. The more probing John did, the more interested the VP became in brainstorming a solution. Long after his staff wished the VP happy holidays and the outer offices darkened, John and VP hammered out a two-step approach to investigative steps. Talk to the players first, then go out into the field and see what the locals and ex-employees had to say.

Every 40 hours of billable work, John would hand-deliver his reports and pick up a new retainer. During the presentation phase, John walked the VP through AIDA with his opening, qualifying, information gathering, and negotiation. A three-hour meeting closed with the VP pulling out the checkbook and handing John a five-figure retainer check.

After, John enjoyed a pleasant sleigh ride home, humming along to Burl Ives singing his signature Christmas song.

Resources

Three books I recommend for this section are readable, actionable, and will give you clear direction in your five weekly sales and marketing hours, of how to call and meet prospects by appointment. They are all written by Stephan Schiffman and can be found on Amazon:

Cold Calling Techniques (That Really Work!)

Closing Techniques (That Really Work!)

Upselling Techniques (That Really Work!)

For an investigator who would rather have taken the trash out than pick up the phone and market, these books saved my business. Really!

Does it seem redundant to overlay these four steps on top of AIDA? You might say yes, but here is the crucial difference. AIDA is all about the prospect's reactions, questions, behaviors and their movement in making a decision. AIDA is all about the **prospect** while Selling is all about **your** workflow.

SECTION SIX:
WHEN YOU ARE A HAMMER, YOU ARE ALWAYS IN SEARCH OF NAILS

IN SEARCH OF NAILS

The best example of this is Truth Be Told Investigations, Inc.

Beth Clark provides surveillance solutions to consumers, mostly for Infidelity Investigations. Now she is getting inquiries from the law firms who represent her upscale clients.

Those very happy lawyers tell their partners that represent insurance companies, governmental entities, and major corporations about Beth's outstanding results.

Those attorneys now want Beth to hammer on their cases. They pay a little more per case, and the lure is, where the consumer may approach her once or twice and make the occasional referral, insurance companies are steady clients.

At any given time, a litigation supervisor will have hundreds of cases on their desk where surveillance may be a useful tool in determining if a person is as hurt as they say they are.

Beth has to jump through hoops to get paid as the users (the attorneys) are not the buyers (claims adjusters), and the buyers are buried in paperwork and make payments when they get around to them.

SECTION SIX: WHEN YOU ARE A HAMMER, YOU ARE ALWAYS IN SEARCH OF NAILS

It is hurting cash flow, and she has to spend time chasing receivables. Hate to say it, but insurance companies view surveillance services as a commodity, and no one vendor is irreplaceable. They dictate pricing and decide if they will pay for travel time, mileage, and pre-surveillance database work-ups.

With the consumers, she gets paid up front. The consumer is usually the buyer and user of the information whereas attorneys are the users, but claims adjustors are the buyers.

The consumer cases are mostly night and weekends while the insurance companies like to see what the claimant is doing on the weekend as well. Beth and Mary are torn between two masters.

It's a no-brainer to prioritize the clients who give them tons of cases, but the people in Beth's B2C market suffer.

By working for the insurance companies, her responsiveness and quality suffer with her target audience.

Then a wealthy school district calls her. They seem to have many students matriculating who may not live within the school district. They want Beth to find out where the kids really live.

Not long after, the lawyer for a neighboring town contacts Beth to follow employees whom they suspect of working on side businesses while clocked in on the town's time.

In both cases, a bidding process must be completed, and purchase orders filled out. The reporting requirements are far different from what she supplies the consumer client or insurance client. They have restrictions on report and travel time, and they want to cap mileage. In both cases, she gets into a bidding war with a retired cop who had once been the preferred vendor. She has to bow out.

> Instead, what if Beth resisted the sirens' call of the repeat customer, with all their issues, and concentrated on offering more services to her target audience?
>
> Instead of going so wide outside of her nets, what if she goes deeper?

Already, she is receiving requests from the soon-to-be-divorced clients to find assets the errant spouse was hiding.

Then there are the pre-marital background checks. The wealthy parents are sure that Mister or Miss Right is wrong for their misguided and love-struck child.

Sam or Sally ask Beth to find their long-lost black-sheep sibling to attempt to make amends.

The skill sets necessary for Beth to meet her own high standards are similar to those she picked up doing Intelligence in the Army. Beth services the same target audience better with premium products and services. The testimonials and referrals are coming from consumers, not school superintendents or town supervisors.

What I Learned From The Parachute

What Color is my Parachute, updated annually by Richard Bolles, is a book geared to job hunters and career changers. The author has both a growing and recurring market. I often recommend this book to people who get blindsided in a lay-off or an unjust firing. He helps them dust themselves off and provides the tools to make their new job **getting** a job.

One of the things that attracted me to his writing, and to refer his book to you, is the information regarding transferable skill sets.

Think of a person like Tony Russo, who was a cop and a detective for most of his career. When you look at him, you see a person with an unusual occupation.

He might look at going out on his own through a more narrow lens. *What do I know about sales, marketing, and accounting?*

Yet his squad worked on enough economic crime cases to understand how thefts or frauds were perpetrated and find the evidence of the wrongdoing to make an arrest that stuck.

If he could understand the intricacies of economic crimes, he can follow the basic tenets of accounting.

If he could interview witnesses, persons of interest, and suspects, he could certainly learn about AIDA and the four steps of selling.

Many people who worked in the same job, doing the same type of work every day, might share that same narrow view about their skills.

Bolles uses checklists and questionnaires to tease out complimentary skills and widen their scope to see that they can do more than they initially thought.

Another resource is AARP's *Life Reimagined* tabs on their website. AARP realizes many retirees are healthy and still have much gas left in their tank. AARP sees these people need to do something different in their "second career."

AARP created a series of checklist and questionnaires to help retirees decide what they want to do while they are still healthy enough to do it.

If you have behaved, so far, like a hammer always looking for nails, transferrable skills are the other tools in your toolbox. Don't try to hammer everything. Explore what other tools (skill sets) you can use to serve your target audience.

The most transferrable skill for Tony to aid his expanding Target Audience is Criminal Defense Investigation. However, even here, Tony understands he has to sharpen his tools.

In quick order, he purchased Brandon Perron's *Uncovering Reasonable Doubt: The Component Method*.

He found the National Association of Public Defenders (NAPD) webinars compiled expertly by Jeff Sherr.

On the advice of his attorney friend, he became a member of the National Association of Criminal Defense Lawyers (NACDL).

To work civil financial cases, he joined the Association of Certified Fraud Examiners (ACFE) and planned to become a Certified Fraud Examiner.

He joined the New York PI Association, ALDONYS.

SECTION SIX: WHEN YOU ARE A HAMMER, YOU ARE ALWAYS IN SEARCH OF NAILS

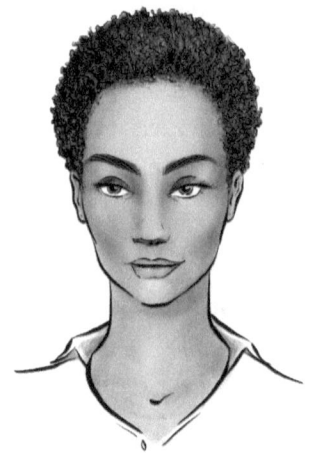

Open Source Intelligence (OSINT) investigation has captured Beth's passion. Right now, surveillance is paying the bills, but more and more consumers and Austin's high-end law firms are requesting her OSINT services.

She can charge a premium and has made it a "paying hobby" within her business.

Even as a start-up, Beth has a paying hobby now that the Armored Guard days are behind her. She attends the OSMOSIS conference, put on by Cynthia Hetherington in Las Vegas in the fall, and will be attending TALI's annual conference as well.

His target audience was Property and Casualty Insurance Companies.

Surveillance was not even on the radar when John started Independent Special's Investigations but slowly became a money-maker. Claims adjusters that requested insurance fraud investigations also required surveillance. It was a complementary offering and so specialized that he hired surveillance operatives whom he cross-trained to become investigators.

His margins were lower for surveillance, but it allowed him to keep his growing staff employed full-time.

The Casualty Adjusters also requested that John find witnesses and take their statements. He charged his investigative rates as opposed to the lower prices charged by Independent Adjustors.

He created attractive flat rates for Accident Scene Photography and Measurements. He performed other complex investigations for his target audience and met their needs with his specialized insurance knowledge.

As long as they were willing to pay his rates, he was willing to do the work. Teaching his people how to do casualty investigations was more straightforward for John than teaching fraud principles.

These high times were about to come to an end, but he didn't yet see what was on the other side of the clouds.

SECTION SIX: WHEN YOU ARE A HAMMER, YOU ARE ALWAYS IN SEARCH OF NAILS

I Don't Do That!

> How many times does a customer in your target market have to ask for a service you decline to perform before you will sit up and listen?

As long as it is not unethical, illegal, or immoral, you better have some clear reasons why not.

If it's not in your proverbial wheelhouse, and you feel uncomfortable saying yes to a task that you may fail at, you must receive the umpteenth request with a more open mind.

You can always refuse a prospect that asks for bargain-basement pricing; you can refuse to go to farthest edge of your geographic reach on short notice; and you can refuse to handle a case on a holiday weekend (but you can also refer them to them to other investigators and take a 20% commission off the top line for the trouble).

However, multiple reasonable requests for a skill you don't yet have should be a signal that it's time to expand your skill set.

You get a call from one of your best clients. It is the Wednesday before the four-day Labor Day Weekend. They want you to do around-the-clock surveillance in East Bumrush?

"I'll check on my availability and get back to you," you say.

You contact your buddy in West Bumrush and sell it to them at your rates, minus your 20%. They are happy to do it, and you get paid when they get paid. You call the client back and tell them the bad news first. You can't do it, but your good friend and business associate from West Bumrush is standing by to take on the assignment, and you would be more than happy to make the introduction. Best of all, since the client is a great client, you won't charge a rush premium. The client is doubly grateful.

If you have been turning down work from your target audience because you lack the skill set, what if you learn the skill so you can charge your regular rates for it, or even a premium?

If the work doesn't bore the living bejesus out of you, what is holding you back?

The services performed will help your target market—the exact people you are sending your message to. They might be using you regularly, but if you don't add this service to your offering, you are telling them to look elsewhere for a solution. Better you look elsewhere for them, vet a provider, and present your client with the answer.

Why do you really turn down work?

Richard Dawson's Family Feud Survey says:

- "I don't do that type of work."
- "Fear of failure." (But you never say that you make up some other BS excuse.)
- "It will take too long, and it will take too long to get paid."
- "I can't do it on such short notice."

Maybe you could turn those reasons around and see the opportunity for what it really is, a chance to learn something new and to try something new. Maybe, just maybe, you might like doing something different for a change, instead of the same old, same old.

Maybe you can learn something about this case you can apply to all your clientele. But...

SECTION SIX: WHEN YOU ARE A HAMMER, YOU ARE ALWAYS IN SEARCH OF NAILS

Beware BSO - Bright Shiny Objects (AKA Magic Bullets)

Maybe I am more entrepreneurial than some. I have tested a dozen proof of concepts over the years to see if they could sustain a business or a side business. I am not bashful about talking about any of them and the education that came from those experiences.

I once spent a summer's worth of Wednesdays and Fridays, and $46,000, with a team of really smart techies to unlock the secrets of connecting people to billions of dollars sitting in unclaimed matured savings bonds collecting dust in the US Treasury. Talk about a BSO.

In the end, we could not make it replicable or scalable. I worked long hours the other days of the week, and Saturday, to keep my company afloat while I tested this concept.

Do I have any regrets? Heck no. I learned more about data-mining in that summer than I would have in a college program, and every Friday we all went to a different Ice Cream store at the end of the day. I am still friends with the team.

What does that have to do with a Private Investigation Business, you ask. I joined a team asked to locate and talk to family members of a dead person whose Savings Bonds were not even collecting interest any longer. Getting good phone numbers for them was the most significant challenge as landlines were going dead every day, and mobile numbers were not yet showing up in the databases. We then had to establish rapport with the family members, interview them, and determine if they were the closest family of the decedent. It forced us to find different ways to locate people. From that summer, I was able to create a flat rate for Locates that I still sell every day.

Beware the single case that effectively shuts down your business for over thirty days and places your customers in second place. The customers will go elsewhere.

Beware the new customer that starts giving you plenty of cases but hasn't paid you for the first one yet. If they have that kind of volume, they were using somebody before you. Is this client a "burner" or will they grind you to give them a discount after the work is performed?

Beware servicing a customer outside your target audience at a lower profit margin. Would you be better off using that time to market your higher-priced offerings to your target audience?

Beware sub-contracting for less than 75% of your regular rate. I restrict my marketing costs to procure a new customer at 20% of my billable hour, so subbing at 80% of regular rates is okay. Anything less would eat into the profit margin.

Beware the case that jeopardizes your license, livelihood, or life. You must walk away when you realize what's going on.

SECTION SIX: WHEN YOU ARE A HAMMER, YOU ARE ALWAYS IN SEARCH OF NAILS

Beth's Side Hustle

Beth loved doing intelligence gathering and analysis in the sandbox of Afghanistan. She did two tours but had enough of the spartan army life.

After her launch of Truth Be Told Investigations, Inc., she is surprised to find so many different customer segments clamoring for her to gather intelligence. Whether it's on an errant spouse, a prospective spouse, or players in a big merger and acquisition deal, she loves the work.

When she doesn't have the eyeball on two-car surveillance with Mary, she whips out her laptop with a stable internet connection and gets lost in the data.

Somebody else might have pulled out a book or binge-watched YouTube videos, but not Beth. The importance of these OSINT cases dictates her fees.

Her upscale clients asked her to gather intelligence and told their friends Beth is a magician.

Almost from the beginning of her business, she tracks the time and money she is making on this side hustle. She spends half the time and charges twice or three times as much as she does for flat rates and budgeted cases. Beth uses it as an effective upsell after a successful outcome on her core business.

She devotes a page to her website just for OSINT, and the testimonials are rolling in. Her marketing of OSINT is purely organic.

What if she applies a mixture of inbound and outbound techniques to OSINT as she does for Truth Be Told?

SECTION SIX: WHEN YOU ARE A HAMMER, YOU ARE ALWAYS IN SEARCH OF NAILS

SUMMARY

Focus on all of your target market's needs, not just what you are best at. There are things you can learn and should learn, so you don't leave money on the table or worse.

Don't let your hard-earned clients go to another provider, who may have weaker skill sets than you but who isn't as rigid.

Avoid spreading your services outside your target market and instead drill deeper into your market with higher-margin offerings. If you specialize in Insurance Surveillance, it sounds counter-intuitive not to work an Infidelity case or vice versa but in the long run, working outside your target market dissipates your energy or focus. Of course, that is the object if you are working on your marketing. If you are not working on your marketing, and are taking all comers when the work dries up you have no pipeline. All you have is a scattered customer base that direct marketing cannot effectively engage.

Beware Bright Shiny Objects. They will derail you from your well thought out business and marketing plans. If you do engage in them, treat them like a paying hobby and do not let them detract from your business focus.

SECTION SEVEN: YOU CAN MARKET LESS THAN 5 HOURS A WEEK. REALLY!

WHY LESS THAN 5 HOURS A WEEK?

Because it is more than zero hours a week and implements a steady approach. You own your Private Investigation Business and marketing is part of your job now. Spending less than 5 hours a week marketing doesn't feel like Sisyphus pushing the boulder up the hill every day of eternity.

Five hours is 16% of a 40-hour week (and that is a short week for small-business owners).

5 out of 50 is 10%, 5 out of 55 is 9%.

Can you spend between 9 and 16% of your work week feeding your PI business?

Most PIs say yes, but the rub is not the time commitment, it is **how** to market.

How do you get started? Where do you start? How do you get your butt in the chair and do the work?

You have heard the saying many times: "Plan the work and work the plan."

The PI that markets:

- Has a SMART marketing plan— something they can pick up on Monday morning and get back to it.
- Has a CRM with leads in the pipeline that make it easy to start the week off.
- Knows marketing hours includes cold calls, appointments, fixing broken links on the website, warm-calling clients for referrals and introductions, gathering testimonials, and emailing prospects that downloaded your free checklist, free report, or e-Book.
- Walks a prospect through their sales funnel. By now, they know the acronym AIDA and how it works with the sales process of Introduction/Qualifying/Information Gathering/Presentation/Closing. Bonus: selling counts as marketing time.
- Attends Seminars, Conferences, monthly, quarterly, and yearly association meetings where they are the vendor or attendee with a marketing agenda.

The above are necessary marketing hours. SEO optimization and attracting leads to your website are a little more advanced, but can be learned and implemented, and will especially help if you are in the B2C world. I would tend to categorize time with your IT people or working on the website for B2C as admin time. Harvesting the leads your website gathers and nurturing them would count towards marketing time.

Tony's Five

Tony visits a leads groups meeting at the Chamber of Commerce every other Wednesday for an hour and a half, and a BNI every Thursday for two hours. These are face-to-face meetings with professionals he wants to connect with.

He also tries to schedule early morning hour-long appointments with qualified prospects for Thursdays and Fridays. He uses his association lists to call CPAs and business lawyers for an hour each day on Mondays and Tuesdays. He is getting better at getting call-backs as he tweaks his call scripts. He fields call-backs and enters all the data into the CRM on his laptop as it occurs.

Tony attends monthly Bar Association after-hour events and meets his clients there. He has them introduce him to other attorneys they are talking to. It usually results in a warm introduction and testimonial.

Boy, those Wildebeests like to drink.

Since the big murder case in Nassau County, he fields calls from Criminal Defense attorneys with cases there. He counts his free consultation with them as part of the marketing and sales time involved in qualifying the prospect's case.

Tony's marketing time sometimes creeps up to 10 hours a week, but he has a plan that has him marketing at least 4.75 hours a week.

Beth's Five

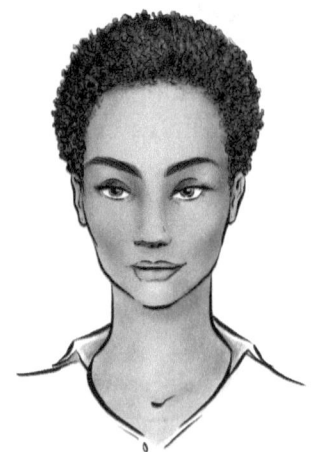

The live chat function on her website has her and Mary Chambers, her employee, fielding inquiries and qualifying prospects at least seven total hours a week. She hires and trains a new Administrative Assistant, Pat, to cover calls from 5 pm to 9 pm, when most of the calls come in. Beth finds that Pat converts a higher number of cases to hourly cases which pay better than the flat rates. Beth trains two new operatives to work the hourly and 8-hour flat rate surveillance cases. Pat becomes adept at scheduling the field assignments. Mary fields the daytime callers while working 4-hour flat rate jobs and the more natural background checks. Beth qualifies the prospects that make email inquiries.

Inbound marketing is clearly exceeding 5 hours a week

Beth, Mary, and Pat are working on their sales scripts to increase conversions, but quickly realize their niche has a lot of tire-kickers and persons who would instead not find out what is really going on when their loved one goes out for milk and comes back two hours with bread.

Beth's inbound marketing is automated, and the team is engaged in sales.

Beth continues outbound marketing with leads groups and visits where her upscale wildebeests figuratively drink.

She visits upscale hair salons, beauty and nail salons, wellness studios, and gyms in a twenty-five-mile radius of downtown Austin, Texas. She offers the workers a deep discount on flat rates, and they send referrals to Beth from their client base. The owners of those facilities and their workers split a commission that Beth pays. Everybody is happy.

Beth stops by these providers on her way out to her working cases and makes her marketing pitch. She does this less than five hours a week.

The results she gets for her upscale clients attract the attention of her clients' high-end lawyers. She drives some of the video and reports into the law firms and meets other lawyers in the firm. They ask if she can do different kinds of background checks, including due diligence. She takes on Bodily Injury and Workers compensation cases for these lawyers as well but finds the insurance company vendor requirements and commodity pricing off-putting.

Even though the lawyer is doing the hiring, they are passing Beth's bills to out of state claims departments. She experiences heartburn from trying to collect on past due bills. She is reminded that her user is not her buyer.

What is most surprising to Beth is the variety of uses for her OSINT (Open Source Intelligence). The law firms are her most prominent clients, followed by her upscale clients. This is all organic marketing, and when she sees the per-case profit-margins, she wonders why they are grinding out tons of B2C surveillance hours every day.

John's Five

Each newsletter took about 4 hours to create before he gave it to his secretary for mailing. The training classes were usually 4 to 6 hours, depending on whether John brought in Pizza and Salads for a working lunch. Many of the clients were out of state, so he made a marketing swing: AIG in Albany, Utica National in Utica, Peerless and National Grange in Syracuse, and Merchants Mutual in Buffalo before making the long trek home.

Training was a quarterly event. When he was in office, he filled out the mornings phoning new claims adjusters to chat, then followed up by sending them his brochures and price sheets.

In the two-plus years of servicing a loyal clientele, he found out claims adjusters move between jobs all the time and were his best evangelists with their new employers.

John leveraged this movement by meeting the new company's Claims supervisors, SIU, and Claims Managers. Free introductory cases and price-matching worked to dislodge their present contract investigators who had fallen asleep at the switch.

He used ACT to keep a record of his leads, prospects, customers, and clients. With B2B, he had lower margins on the surveillance work and his flat rates—which didn't allow him to charge for travel expense and time—weren't making up the difference.

Revenues were up, but so were expenses. His profit margin fell from 47% in year one to 31% in year three. Some of that had to do with 10% increases in salaries every year (the nationwide average is 5-6%). He implemented a bonus plan based on revenue and quality control goals.

He established contacts with Insurance Defense Law Firms but couldn't charge a premium on their most critical high-dollar cases. He did not market the law firms for their other types of cases and stayed focused on working for the insurance companies that hire the lawyers. He turned down Infidelity investigations and the occasional Personal Injury cases handled by those dyed-in-the-wool Defense firms.

He increased his pricing every year, but could not charge premiums for any of his services. Things were good, and he stuck to the knitting, as the saying goes.

John expanded his fraud investigation work with large and small insurance carriers, as well as third-party administrators. He sought licenses in New Jersey, New Hampshire, and Maine as part of his "Bangor to Baltimore" coverage.

Your Five

How you craft your five hours per week depends on your SMART marketing plan which is built upon your:

- Business Segmentation–B2C, B2C, P2P, Hybrid Specialist, Hybrid by Geography
- Target Audience–Claims Departments, Attorneys, Professionals, Corporate-Government-NGO, CPAs, Small Businesses, Landlords/Property Managers, Individuals, Other Private Investigators
- Brand–Range of Services
- Marketing Copy or Marketing Message
- Inbound/Outbound methods
- CRM and Email Capture
- Attendance at gatherings, meetings, and conferences
- Email, Phone, and Presentation scripts (Schiffman books are recommended)

Go into your marketing time knowing that you will have periods of discomfort. No baby started walking without falling down a bunch of times.

Tip: Set a timer for a 55-minute marketing session and don't get distracted until the timer goes off.

You may encounter reasonable situations that prevent you from marketing at your scheduled time. Immediately schedule a make-up time for the same day.

There will be times when a whole week goes by while you have done zero marketing. If you are keeping score and can see those zeros staring at you, you will be motivated to get up off the ground and try putting one foot in front of the other again.

If the pattern of avoidance persists after you have made an effort to create a viable marketing plan, you have no one to blame for the empty pipeline other than the person staring at you in the mirror. That sounds harsh, but rather than skip blindly along in the dark, think about why you are resistant to marketing. Is it the methods that you have chosen?

Were there some marketing activities you enjoyed more than others? Can you double up on them?

Do you have trouble getting the phone call or emailing engine started? Try calling a good customer you haven't talked to in a while. Then call another and then another. Count those calls as marketing calls and after you warm up with friendly voices, plunge into the cold calling.

Pull your calendar out and block off the first hour and a half of your business day every Monday-Thursday (except for the days where you have bonafide marketing appointments). Example: 8:30-9:30 am, Monday-Thursday.

What activity is the best use of your marketing time for that period? Is it cold-calling, warm-calling, or asking for testimonials and referrals? Is it creating free content for the website? Training for your target audience? Is it returning calls or emails to qualify prospects?

Set the timer and go for it.

Are you adding leads, prospects, and new customers into your CRM? Are you tracking how the leads come in?

How are you tracking conversions?

- Converting leads to prospects
- Converting prospects to customers
- Up-selling the right service at the right time for the right client.
- Converting customers into referral-generators or testimonial-givers.

SECTION SEVEN: YOU CAN MARKET LESS THAN 5 HOURS A WEEK. REALLY

Work your marketing plan. There are no shortcuts. It does get easier. With repetition, you will become more relaxed as see how your plan works.

SECTION EIGHT: FLYING FORTRESS

CONSIDER THE B-17

I understand why you might be resistant to change. I was there myself in the face of some pretty steep adversity.

Consider the B-17 Flying Fortress, an American heavy bomber deployed in WWII. It flew missions in both theaters of conflict. Most of this bomber's acclaim came from dangerous daylight bombing missions over Germany and Occupied France, without the benefit of fighter escort.

The bomber groups were alone in the sky, facing radar-assisted anti-aircraft guns, and defending themselves against swarms of enemy fighter aircraft.

TV shows such as *12 O'Clock High* and the Movie Memphis Belle added to the bomber's legacy as a warbird that could take incredible punishment and still bring its 10-men crews back to safety in England. If forced, it could fly on only two of its four engines.

In February of 2001, my figurative B-17, the high-flying Independent Special Investigations, LLC, was crippled by two blows.

Two national Private Investigation companies disrupted the Property and Casualty Insurance Industry with a well-funded

SECTION EIGHT: FLYING FORTRESS

marketing plan. "Disruption" is the proper word. Here is how they did it.

Where I marketed to local offices, they went to the Home Offices with two promises. They could take assignments anywhere in the country through one single 800 number, and then the assigning claims adjusters could watch the progress of their cases in a simple dashboard.

800 numbers were common at the time, but nationwide service coupled with the online dashboards was not. This was cutting edge. Think of how 1-800-Flowers disrupted FTD's stranglehold on ordering flowers.

Local branches of the XYZ and ABC insurance companies made up over 55% of my business. Then these competitors asked the Home Offices for—and received—one- or two-year contracts with the **entire** claims department of the XYZ insurance company and the ABC company, among other insurance companies. None of the local PI's were working with contracts.

Within 60 days, the time it would take to work out my present backlog on their files, I would be flying a heavy bomber with only two working engines. It was a long way back to the white cliffs of Dover.

What added insult to injury, those two companies tried to hire my crew and me for about 30% of our billable hour rate to service our own customers, who were forced by their home office to use the national competitor.

My customers were not happy and apologized to me but their hands, or more appropriately their purse strings, were tied. I quickly learned the difference between the user and the ultimate buyer. The Claims VP held the purse strings and wrestled back autonomy over the SIU units. Sadly, those national competitors were now eating my lunch and were charging more per hour than I was in my own backyard.

A month into this debacle, I went to a meeting in Phoenix and met with other similarly-affected PIs. Their shell-shocked faces told the same story. We realized we had all been watching the white fluffy clouds without any contingency plans for the trouble brewing on the horizon.

Most, if not all, of our incomes, came from one source, and that was local claim departments. This was a disruption, not just a faster, better and cheaper competitor. McDonald's was not moving next to Burger King. This was like what Uber and Lyft are doing to the taxi business.

One PI at the meeting was immune from this disruption. I met him a few times before and knew he had a successful company in the Windy City, Chicago. He was the go-to guy in Chicago for just about everything. It was his primary business to service the legal community. He had expanded to take on the newly created SIU work, but he wasn't entirely dependent on it. He supervised a group of highly skilled investigators and invested in office staff and a contract internet librarian.

I considered myself an expert in Insurance Fraud and not a generalist. In our earlier encounters, I wished him well.

Now, he was like a guru to the half of the group that wanted to survive (the other half went to the bar to drown their sorrows). My people were not going to drown in the English Channel, and I was going to bring my airship home.

First, I had to get over my attitude towards other Private Investigators. I had been with an SIU, and now I was Independent Special Investigations. That costly PI license didn't mean much other than allowing me to do privately what I had once done as a salaried employee, but I still resisted making the mindset changes.

I had to learn how to market. In all honesty, to that point, all I had done was copy my company employee mindset methods for gaining and retaining internal customers. The newsletter and training worked well for adjusters, but what if that spigot got shut off? Still, I resisted looking for other types of business such as lawyers or private individuals.

I was losing altitude and could run out of money, and still, I didn't change my target audience, even though it was forever changed by a technology that was out of my reach at the time.

The Nationals were investing in programmers at the earliest time in the Internet. I was having a hard time hiring an administrative assistant. I could not compete, because I couldn't afford it. Family loans had bankrolled one. I didn't have an extra hundred thousand dollars laying around.

I doubled down on what I did best. Marketing time increased dramatically. I began reaching out to other smaller insurance carriers, specialty groups, and third-party administrators. I reach out to Self-Insureds. Oh, and those lawyers that handled Insurance defense claims as part of their broader business mix. I talked to them too.

I was partially effective with this reach, but keep in mind I was not skilled enough to effectively gauge their AIDA or my sales skills. I recall driving all the way to Southern Maine to talk to a Claims VP of a small carrier, only to find out they had little or no work in Southern New England and none in New York State.

My plane was losing altitude quickly as my checkbook was getting leaner and leaner. It was hard to let go of employees I trained in my work methods and company culture. I wasn't replacing revenue fast enough and had to lighten my load.

I waved goodbye to sub-contractors almost immediately, and my part-timers went back to their day jobs. Two employees went to law school. One chose to be a stay-at-home mom. My surveillance manager went to work in a non-competing position with his friend for a while, before changing careers entirely.

Since the remaining two employees and I had surveillance training, our plane was skimming above the treetops with surveillance jobs and the fraud cases, but full-time paychecks were not always the norm. I didn't cut wages, but the bonus plan was thrown out the bomb bay doors along with the annual conference training classes.

For a while, it seems that a scaled down version of ISI, and the lower altitude was less stressful on the two engines. Our third sputtering engine was getting stronger with cases from new clients. When I wasn't marketing, I was back on the street doing investigations and doing surveillance on weekends. We were leveling off and even climbing, but it was a grind.

We took on some work that was not particularly lucrative, but it did absorb overhead. That summer, I traveled to Eastern Massachusetts one night a week to help an SIU Director run off the remaining case files of his laid-off staff, as they outsourced new cases to the National competitor. It even made his job redundant. I was working him out of a job, but it seemed like we would survive to go into the fall of 2001.

One September morning, under crystal-clear blues skies, my first hire Jon and I were driving back from a weekend surveillance in Princeton, New Jersey. We were listening to Howard Stern when reports came into him that a plane had hit one of the twin towers. And then the second plane hit the other tower. Nobody knew what to think at first, but as videos of the crashes made their way onto network TV, Stern reported on what he saw.

We were on Route 1, heading towards New York City and, as we crested a rise, we saw smoke billowing from each tower towards Brooklyn. Where was Mike, my third hire? We couldn't get ahold of him. Finally, he got to a landline and called his wife

SECTION EIGHT: FLYING FORTRESS

to tell her that he was safe in Brooklyn, but that all the bridges were shut down. He would eventually get home that night.

Ourselves, we skirted the city. As we crossed the Tappan Zee Bridge over the Hudson and North of the city, we saw both towers had collapsed. Moreover, with that collapse went much of the work I built up over those six months. Insurance companies put the brakes on all spending.

Shortly after that, when the business paralysis that gripped the country began to loosen, we were able to resume operations.

The idea of the regional company (Bangor to Baltimore) evaporated when I went back on the street with only two employees. I was determined not to lay them off, but in the end, I could only keep one of them on. Luckily the second found a good job, thanks to the skills he learned from me and my glowing testimonial.

The following year, the remaining employee had accumulated four years of experience between ISI and the previous surveillance company, and created his own company, parachuting to safety over the English countryside.

I landed alone seven years, almost to the day, after taking off.

I owned my own business but was barely keeping out of the poorhouse. My revenues plummeted 80% from the high years to where I was scratching out about 26 billable hours a week by myself. The funny thing was, my overhead was pared down to the bone and my income improved. However, this was not my idea of a fun time. I had to stop blaming smarter, better-funded competitors.

I rebranded as Squire Investigations, determined to make it as a solo-generalist serving the legal community in Southern Connecticut.

I finally listened to my Chicago friend and took a page from his playbook!

I joined the National Association of Legal Investigators. There I found many Private Investigators, experts in their field, who were wholly dedicated to their craft and seemed to make a good living. I sat for and passed the rigorous testing to become a Certified Legal Investigator. Later, the association elected me their Regional Director.

I joined the Milford, Connecticut Chamber of Commerce where I met a business coach. He was offering a 12-week group class. I put the expense on an interest-free credit card and started learning about business and marketing. I took a day-long course put on by Jimmie Mesis, the former owner of PI Magazine, to learn affiliate marketing. I will mention more of Jimmie in *How To Boost Your Private Investigation Business Into Orbit: Make $1,000 Every Working Day!*

This is a story about almost crashing and burning. I am sharing this, so you understand I started my firm with few business and marketing skills. When faced with adversity, I didn't quit, but I also didn't learn everything I needed right away. I was stubbornly running faster on the hamster wheel, but not getting ahead.

Squire Investigations became the beginning of my metamorphosis from an investigator in business, to a business person providing investigative services.

That happened when I focused on learning how to market and sell those investigative services.

SECTION EIGHT: FLYING FORTRESS

CONCLUSION

Tony Russo is well-positioned with his Business clients and his Criminal Defense Lawyers. He understands that marketing is part of his business and works hard at it.

He has had some success, and some problems with the "associates" part of Russo & Associates and he has some crucial decisions to make about strategic growth and a possible a change to his end game.

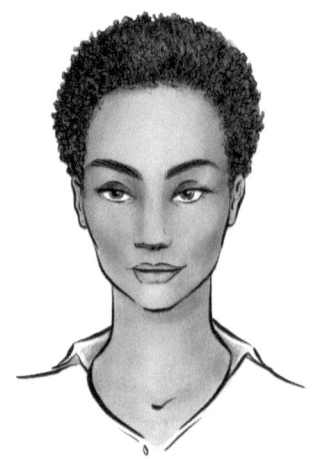

Beth Clark launched with a strong inbound marketing strategy and hit a home run right out of the box with her outbound marketing to upscale women in the greater Austin area. She moved gradually from a soft launch and added employees to fill specific needs as the business blossomed. She knew that she had to learn about business no differently than the new skill sets from her army training. She was open to change from the beginning and embraced it. Within a short period, she realized that she had both a specialized skill set and passion for OSINT.

Everything is going as planned, but she faces a decision of what to do with her OSINT side hustle. Does she stay in the B2C world, or pivot to B2B before she adds more employees? She had begun with the goal of building a business that her employees will run for her or one that she can sell to a competitor.

CONCLUSION

Truthfully, John didn't employ every strategy he learned, but the ones he did implement were tested and measured. Marketing less than 5 hours a week was born from the Squire Investigations rebranding and startup. He was determined not to make the same mistakes he made with ISI. He still had a few wonderful insurance customers from those days, but he learned. New skills, such as criminal defense and forensic genealogy. He learned everything he could about investigative interviewing and was much more adept at locating people, and he balanced this skill building with learning about sales and marketing.

Get out your planner, set the timer, and start putting your marketing plan together.

It doesn't have to be exactly perfect. You will test and measure as you go along. We started this book off with a simple adage. "The marketing you do is better than the marketing you should do, but don't."

I will finish it with another quote. An old homicide detective once told me, **"Ain't nothing to it, but to do it."**

Now go and do it.

BOOK THREE

HOW TO

BOOST

YOUR
PRIVATE INVESTIGATION
BUSINESS INTO ORBIT

MAKE $1,000 EVERY WORKING DAY!

INTRODUCTION

JOHN A. HODA

You are a licensed private investigator, and you own an investigations business. You may exceed expenses with your revenues, but you don't have a plan for taking your business to the next level.

Maybe you are tired of treading water with all the exertion needed just to stay afloat.

You might be planning to start your PI business but are unsure how to expand your business once you start making enough money to pay your bills.

For those slogging along or just starting out, we are talking about "boosting" your business.

I use an orbiting rocket for this book in the series. Overcoming gravity and the drag of the atmosphere is paramount for a successful launch, but the rocket scientists figured out they need a booster stage to take the payload into a sustainable orbit where only a tiny amount guidance and thruster energy, by comparison, is needed to give you those beautiful photos from space. I thought long and hard on this analogy both for internal resistance (gravity) and external forces on your business (atmospheric

INTRODUCTION

drag) and how to overcome them with a booster rocket (Ideas from this book).

The concept of making $1,000 every working day is the orbiting goal. How does $261,000 a year sound? The experts say 261 days is the average number of working days a year. That number does not include holidays and vacations. Let's assume you take all the holidays and two weeks of vacation. You would still be looking at around 240 days a year or $240,000. That is a lot of money for most people, but it also sounds a little daunting and may be unachievable. I am told that you eat an elephant one bite at a time. I have never eaten an elephant. It doesn't sound appealing, so let's change the analogy to, "Let's take it one day at a time."

Can you do this as a solo? Yes. Is it better to have some help? Yes. Want to own a business that runs without you in fulfillment or operations? I will give you an example of how that works. For that example, you will need to make more than $261K a year, but we will cross that bridge when we come to it if you choose to work every weekday every week.

Whether you are a solo practitioner or have a team working with you, it is possible to invoice $1,000 a day, every working day. "Whoa," you say, "if that is your top line, what is the bottom line after overhead? What about taxes?"

I agree. We need to define "make" right now.

"Make" means gross - How much you gross each working day.

"Make" is not net. It is not after you take out all your expenses apportioned for that day.

"Make" is not net after taxes. It is not after your expenses and your taxes apportioned for that day.

"Make" is the top line — revenue - even above the cost of goods sold (COGS).

Stop here if you think I misled you. If you are not interested in learning how to receive payments from clients and/or customers to the tune of almost a quarter-million a year, I will gladly refund your money for this book.

If you gross $1,000 a day, but it costs you $1,250 in overhead, then we are not talking about an orbiting rocket, but a sinking ship on its way to the bottom. So, we will be mindful of expenses from here on.

Part of the reason I focus on the top line is simple. You have a daily goal. You have to set up enough cases you can plan to execute $1,000 of invoices every working day. To have enough cases that you bill a grand every working day means you need to have enough cases in your pipeline. To have enough cases in your pipeline, you need a steady flow of clients and/or repeat customers. To have a steady flow of clients and/or repeat customers, you need a scalable and repeatable marketing program. Of course, all this is predicated on you providing a service that meets or exceeds customer expectations which you can deliver efficiently.

You invoice your time either hourly, on flat rates, by contract, or with a budget. Hourly is a simple calculation.

INTRODUCTION

For example, you bill $150 an hour for some work. Your other services have a weighted average. For example, you perform an asset check and charge a flat rate of $350, and it takes you two hours on average.

You make $175 an hour for that flat rate. In this example, we'll say you bill four hours to a file and do one asset check. You invoice $950 for the day. Oh, that was close.

If you can break your goal down to daily billing, it gets a lot simpler to work backwards from there.

I will tell you here. I did not hit a home run with my first business. If I did, that would be boring. I made mistakes, and I stubbornly continued to make those mistakes. It was not until the market changed like quicksand under my feet that I scrambled and learned how to run a business.

Until then, I managed a group of highly-trained employees. I focused on learning more about our tradecraft than the business of investigations. I stumbled and made false steps until I couldn't take my own gravity (resistance) any longer. Even then, I had to take baby steps before I could walk.

It is better to learn from my mistakes than spend time, money, and emotional attachment to chasing down the dream along the wrong path. These lessons were hard-earned, and I hope to point them out to you so you can avoid stepping on snakes when you are lost in the weeds.

If I say to you, "Do as I did to change your attitude and to begin implementing sound business advice," you would only get a narrow view of my path.

Instead, I have created two other characters with different backgrounds, goals, wants, need, and fears. Their companies meet utterly different customer segments. We'll watch them launch and learn how they market to those segments in the two previous books in this series. On this spectrum of investigation company business models, you will find advice to meet your specific needs and get ideas you may never have considered.

Now that they are further down the road, they are making money and doing well, but cannot continue to throw more time and energy at their success. They must grow, or they will slowly stagnate and possibly quit from burn-out.

INTRODUCTION

Meet Tony

Tony Russo lives in Queens with his wife as empty-nesters. As he was getting ready to retire from NYPD as a Detective Sergeant in charge of a squad of detectives in Mid-Town Manhattan, he realized he and his wife were living above their means and had to reign in expenses.

The Russo and Associates start-up was as much about freeing himself from the layers of bureaucracy at the Police Department as tightening their belts to pay off debt. Tony carefully ruminates on what he wanted his business to look like and decides on a Professional-to-Professional (P2P) mode (a term I coined), to provide services to small businesses, Attorneys, and CPAs that deal with businesses with repeat investigative needs.

It is very much a person-to-person approach, and Tony learns to show up regularly at meetings, seminars, conferences, leads groups, and other places where his target audience meets and drinks.

Unexpectedly, he finds he enjoys working in neighboring Nassau County for Criminal Defense attorneys with clients considered to be innocent of the charges. He is wildly successful in his first case, and his face is plastered across the newspaper headlines and on TV in Long Island.

He is busier than he wants to be, and he contemplates a different end to his second career.

Meet Beth

Beth Clark lives and works in Austin, TX. She is a two-tour army veteran who specialized as an Intelligence analyst in Afghanistan. She was working for an armed guard company when she caught the bug to start her own business.

She had the pre-requisite skills and experience to get her PI license and slowly launched her B2C Business-to-Consumer (B2C) company, Truth Be Told Investigations, Inc. with incredible results providing infidelity surveillance and background checks to consumers in the Greater Austin area.

Beth comes into this start-up with no preconceptions. She understands her WHY (the reason she wants to do this work): to provide quality service to regular people who need it, without the layers of bureaucracy she had to endure in the army or guard service.

She builds her business to sell so she can retire early and do adventure travel. She builds her business around Inbound marketing of attracting and keeping prospects on her website until she or her employees can close the deal.

Her outbound marketing of visiting businesses catering to upscale women in the area produces high-margin cases and an equally repeatable and scalable marketing method, which she expands by offering referral commissions to those hair stylists, aerobics instructors, and wellness professionals who point their clients her way.

She is at the cusp of expansion or exhaustion. In her present work, she discovers a real talent and passion for OSINT (open source intelligence) searches.

INTRODUCTION

Her upscale female clients hire the best lawyers in Austin to handle their divorces based upon the , and background checks Beth's company conducts. These high-powered law firms and their growing corporate client base are clamoring for Beth to do extensive Intelligence analysis.

She is at a crossroads where she has to decide between sitting in a sweltering surveillance van, peeing in a coffee can, on a hot, humid summer weekend evening to get video of Mr. Smith and Mrs. Jones committing adultery, or sitting at her desk in an air-conditioned office during regular work hours, churning out reports for grateful, high-paying clients.

Does she grow her B2C business to meet their growing demand?

Does she pivot into B2B and rebrand?

Does she split the baby in half and do both?

Meet John

I talk about my experience in the third person. Where Tony and Beth are modern days, my experience occurred in 2004.

John has just crash landed Independent Special Investigations. ISI was a B2B providing insurance fraud investigations for Property & Casualty Insurance companies in the Northeast.

Armed with a 1986 Oldsmobile, a 386 computer, and a borrowed surveillance camera. He took his Rolodex of contacts and went out on his own Labor Day weekend of 1997.

John is a former police officer, insurance fraud investigator, and claims manager who taught a cadre of hard-working employees in his expertise.

Things were going great. He was growing his staff and territory to meet his goal of being a super regional powerhouse, "From Bangor to Baltimore."

Then a significant disruption in the industry essentially commoditized his services.

He was fond of saying his company were artists and the industry was now hiring house painters. That attitude didn't help him change his mindset until it was too late.

Two national firms, using the latest technological advances (claims adjustors could check the status of their cases online in the earliest of dashboards), went to the highest levels in the claims departments and locked down nationwide two-year contracts.

INTRODUCTION

Local PIs who once had great relationships with their local claims departments and SIU (Special Investigation Units) were now like kids banned from their favorite candy stores. This was a harsh lesson in learning about users as opposed to the ultimate buyers of services.

John became a solo DBA as Squire Investigations after he parted ways with his team. Most were able to parachute to safety, but he had to lay off one employee. It was painful for John and the valued employees. He broke the unspoken agreement of happily ever after.

He began learning about Criminal Defense investigation and Forensic Genealogy. The former was a skill set he had never considered, and the latter was a new Bright Shiny Object.

John had pared down his expenses and, as a solo, was taking home more money than he did with all the overhead from ISI.

He still wasn't making $1,000 every working day and had no plan to do so. His wife was working, and the kids had been out of daycare for a decade. The pressure was not as high as when he first went out on his own.

He was still recovering from the sting of having to start over. He was going to learn from his mistakes but was not sure how to start the rebuilding process.

One thing was for sure: the call to create a company he could sell to employees was as strong as ever. He would learn the right way to grow a company.

JOHN A. HODA

OVERVIEW

This book introduces you to well thought-out business decisions (Strategy) and gives you the tools (Tactics) needed to boost your business to the next level.

Section One: Stagnate, Change, Grow, or Slowly Die (Page 345)
- Strategy
- Tony's story- Changing the ending
- Beth's Story- Pivot and Sell to Competitor
- John's Story- Pivot to B2C and then IMHF

Section Two: Just Do It. Increase Revenue. (Page 367)
- It Depends
- Raise rates
- Fire Customers
- Upsell and Affiliate Marketing

OVERVIEW

Section Three: Wearing Fewer Hats (Page 383)
- Jobs You Shed Depend On Your Customer Segmentation
- Tony
- Beth
- John

Section Four: Hiring (Page 399)
- Hiring Checklist

Section Five: Do As I Say And As I Do (Page 411)
- Training Checklist

Section Six: Huddling (Page 419)
- Taking A Page From The Great Game Of Business

Section Seven: Sharpening the Saw (Page 429)
- What Got You Here, Won't Get You There
- John: Action Coaching Business Coach
- Tony: Mastermind or Pick Four
- Beth: APPSUMO, Thrive, Hubspot

Section Eight: Booster Rocket Engine, Engage! (Page 441)
- Tony
- Beth
- John
- Endings are beginnings
- Conclusion

SECTION ONE: STAGNATE, CHANGE, GROW, OR SLOWLY DIE

SUCCESS IN THE LONG RUN

I will address a plan for a solo to make $1,000 every working day, but it requires meticulous crafting. I will submit it to you towards the end of the book after you taste all the different recipes. Then if you want to remain a solo, you will have a more full understanding of what that entails as a lifestyle business.

Success has its advantages. You have more work than you can handle. You are not visiting your post office box every morning to see if checks are there. You are not robbing Peter to pay Paul on your bills. Nobody is breathing down your neck or threatening you with collections.

As you grow your business, you could be breathing more relaxed, but you are breathing harder because you have more work in any given day and you still have to administrate it, invoice it, and account for it. These tasks are known as backroom operations.

Not to mention the marketing you need to enact, sooner rather than later.

Many investigators operate under the false impression that when things are going great, they don't have to market anymore. They can just work at what they do best, their investigations (Fulfillment). However, when the pipeline starts to dry up, they take on work they might not usually take on, or they take it on a deep discount just to pay the bills, and before you know it, they are racing to the bottom.

If you know better than to forego marketing, you keep the pipeline full, and now you have to hire help. Working seven days a week, week in and week out gets old. You don't even have time to hire help.

Now here is the fun part. You get so busy that you start making mistakes. You catch so many fish you are in danger of swamping the boat. You are getting the work done, barely, but are delayed on reporting the results.

You put off your regular, steady clients to take on new and promising better-paying work (which doesn't pan out) and now your best clients are no longer calling you, and you don't notice (or care) until your nets are empty.

You may start cutting corners or taking short cuts. For a while, nobody notices, until it blows up in your face.

Your best client sends you back the bill for the time and effort you spent unsuccessfully trying to find their client. Seems their paralegal called 411 (yes, old-fashion directory assistance) and connected with their client.

Are you going to tell the client you failed to note the only time you tried that same number, unearthed from your databases, you got a busy signal? You never tried the number again. You forgot in your haste.

You have to rebuild the trust you worked so hard to earn. You confess your own success is doing you in and you recommit to provide the service you promised. You rip up the bill. You are not happy with the quality of your work. You are better than that.

In desperation, you decide to hire. Your second mistake, it may be worse than the first. Depending on what you hire that person to do, you most likely abandon that job function to them. I pray, for your sake, it does not include handling money or clients directly.

At first, you breathe easier. You might even get your weekends back. You take that vacation your significant other has been bugging you about for months.

Things seem to be working okay. Your new hire (last name, Friday) handles the easy stuff and takes some of the load off your shoulders. You are even thinking about surprising Friday with a raise.

You come back to your office after a significant time away with only minimal email and text contact with Friday, to find they are quitting without notice, and have been sandbagging you and your clients about the work they were doing in your absence.

Friday feels justified because they were never properly trained. They were not told what the expectations were. They were never shown what satisfactory performance looks like.

Friday complains that payroll was always screwed up and you didn't pay them for all the overtime (and you didn't create an HR manual to clear up confusion on the subject).

Friday threatens to call the Department of Labor unless you honor the last pay sheet they submitted. Friday's files reflect less than 20 hours of work, yet you are being extorted for 80 hours of pay. The clients will be screaming - the same clients you almost lost once already.

The calm restorative relaxation from your vacation is now a faint memory as the acid churns in your stomach.

So you meet Friday in a Walmart parking lot half-way between your locations. Friday hands you shaky video and incomplete reports for only a portion of the work on the timesheet. Your equipment looks like it was dragged through the mud. Friday repeats the threat, and you reluctantly turn over the final check. You watch Friday burn rubber.

A month later, you get a call from the Department of Labor acting on Friday's overtime complaint.

You vow never to hire another person as long as you live, which is your next mistake and react to the crisis by suspending marketing and turning down new work.

You are now sliding down the slippery slope of your own success. This stagnation is the road to a slow death.

If you planned for growth, your early and hard-won success would not cause the demise of your business.

Instead, what if you plan for your growth instead of acting surprised and unprepared when it happens?

As you watched your numbers grow faster than you planned, you accelerated your hiring plans. Yes, it means more work at a time you can ill-afford it, but at least it is under your control, and you are reacting to the anticipated growth, rather than have the growth soon weigh on your shoulders.

Each evening after dinner, sit down and speed up your work on:

- A recruiting checklist
- A hiring checklist
- An HR protocol for getting employee documents filled out and getting them on the payroll before their start date: hire letters, I-9, W-9s, a real application form with language allowing you to pull credit reports DMV and fingerprint checks. Probationary language in both the application and new hire letter. I liked hiring a person at X pay rate and spelling out that, after 60 days of satisfactory performance,

they would receive X plus 10% as their pay. At the sixty-day mark, they would receive their first evaluation following a process that clearly defined satisfactory performance in their training sessions. We would either part company, or they would receive a bump.

- HR handbook for the little things like Holiday, Vacation, Sick Time, and Overtime. The stuff that keeps you out of trouble with the Department of Labor, if things go sideways with your employees: a boilerplate code of conduct, rules on tardiness, absenteeism, attire, maintenance of and an inventory for equipment, and so on.
- Benefits/Workers Compensation forms/Auto insurance coverages
- Training Plan and Checklist
- Employee evaluation process
- Annual performance reviews

The hiring process shows the applicant you are serious about the importance of their hire to the overall health of the company. The care you take in their selection, the commitment you make to their training, and their supervision pay off huge dividends.

Throwing warm bodies at a problem is a band-aid at best, and it can make the situation worse.

Ask them to fill out a multi-page application. Question it closely. Call the references and the prior employers. Pull the credit report and do the DMV check. Then send them a pre-interview questionnaire. Have them return it before setting up the time and place for the interview.

Once there, take the time to explain the job description, your expectations and show them the training curriculum and performance evaluation.

If the only questions you get are about pay, benefits, vacation time, and sick days, you may have gone deep into the process, but it was better to shake hands and part company.

If, on the other hand, they sound excited about the challenges they will encounter and the growth opportunities presented, you will have 60 days to kick their tires. You can test this vibe out with persons new to the business or persons that have been to the rodeo a few times. The veteran investigator can be enthusiastic about the opportunity to be treated well and will relish the opportunity to show off their skills to someone who will take the time to appreciate them. It also gives you a chance to watch for bad habits ingrained from their previous jobs.

So far, I have concentrated on finding a replacement for you or an addition to you in fulfillment.

What if we talk about your next hire being in operations?

Can the checkbook handle it?

Can you run the numbers to see if you can support it?

Counter-intuitive, you may say, but let's see how Tony, Beth, and John handle the growth.

Tony's Story: Sell

I didn't sign up for this, Tony says to himself. He has been running flat-out for weeks. The growth in his P2P business is steady, then explodes when the Nassau County District Attorney's office drops charges on a murder case Tony worked on. The former DA, now Criminal Defense attorney, Abe Schwartz, who helped Tony get started by introducing him around the Bar Association, told Tony he had an innocent client.

Tony performs an investigation that completely contradicts the State's probable cause for arrest. It forced the State's hand. The publicity results in Tony taking on more and more Criminal Defense cases, some for a premium and some for "Low Bono," as he jokingly refers to not-quite Pro Bono cases.

His carefully laid business and marketing plans didn't account for this growth.

Where he once had time to work his business cases at a crisp pace, the docket calls for Criminal Defense–and spending two to three weeks non-stop during trial–is kicking his ass.

He likes all the work. Correction, he loves the work, especially dissecting and exploiting the weaknesses in the Nassau County cases and finding reasonable doubt.

He didn't take on the NYPD by choice. Tony doesn't want to be staring at detectives from his old precinct days. This is different from managing the flotsam and jetsam of cases back in the Midtown squad room. Here, the system is failing the innocent while real criminals are on the street creating mayhem. The victims are not being served by the false arrests either.

He had planned to "keep it small and keep it all." This is supposed to be a second career. For gosh sakes, he already had a pension from his first job. The long hours are both exhilarating and exhausting. This is supposed to be his lifestyle job. He eases off the marketing, and his shadow does not grace the doorway of many of the meetings he once faithfully attended. Tony had planned to work this gig until his wife was ready to retire from her Board of Ed job.

Meanwhile, the Russos benefit from the upsurge in work. They are careful with their expenses after Tony did the math during his launch phase and saw that they were over-extended on credit again. Twice, they had remortgaged their house to consolidate debt.

Pulling the reigns in on their spending, combined with Tony's unplanned growth in revenues have the desired impact on their finances. He is paying off debt, supplementing his 401K, and they refinance the mortgage to a 15-year note. Tony plans to work long enough to guarantee a retirement where they can live well, but not extravagantly. The extra money also allows them an occasional treat. What if he could make more money and leverage his success? Would that speed up the clock to his full retirement? Would that allow him a better retirement plan?

About the time Tony is pondering the predicament of his success, he learns the judge got sick during lunch and didn't return to the bench. The trial is adjourned to the next week giving him some breathing room to reassess.

He had no further to look for an answer than his friend, the former DA. After switching sides of the aisle, Abe started as a solo and now has an office support staff, paralegals and a few hand-picked former DAs and associates fresh out of law school. Their practice mix is a mirror image of Tony's. Is that coincidence?

In the following scene, Abe and Tony pack up the exhibits and make the long walk out to their cars in Nassau County courthouse parking lot in Mineola, NY.

"Abe, what have you gotten me into?"

"What do you mean, this is a good case; we are going to win it." Abe retorts.

"Not the case, Abe. All of it. Some days, I don't know whether I'm coming or going."

Abe laughs. "Things could be worse Tony."

"Not that I'm not grateful for all you've done for me, Abe, but I think I may have bitten off more than I can chew. Like this weekend, instead of taking it easy like a retired detective should, I am billing out cases and working on my quarterly reports."

They get to their cars and talk as attorneys, and their investigators sometimes do, but this conversation takes a different tact.

"What's your plan, Tony. How did you see Russo & Associates growing?"

"Honestly Abe," Tony says, playing on the words, "I had planned to turn off the lights and lock the door when we got our retirement nest egg to where we wanted it. I was going to ride off into the sunset with a more secure retirement than if I had just taken my pension."

Abe shakes his head. "You're building value with your brand. It's a shame just to walk away from it. If you could snap your fingers and make it perfect for you, what would you do?"

"I would hire an admin to do my books and open and close the cases. I would hire an investigator to take over most, but not all, of the business cases, and I would train a young gun on how to do the Criminal Defense work. I would cherry pick the cases that are most interesting to me and still be the face of the company for marketing.

I'd be home most nights and weekends unless it's something hot or we are going to trial." The words flow out in a rush.

"What else?" Abe asks.

"I would eventually turn over the marketing and hire more investigators whom I would manage and occasionally ride along with, so I that don't forget what it's like to be a living, breathing real-life detective."

"And?" Abe prods again.

"I would sell it to them." Boom! There. Tony says it, and everything falls into place.

"Okay, doesn't that sound better than riding off into the sunset?" Abe waves and gets into his car.

Tony sits in his car on a sun-splashed day, admires the fall foliage and writes out the 5-year plan in his notebook. He looks at it and realizes he had a succession plan. Now, all he has to do is put it all together on the fly.

Beth's Story: Pivot / Sell to Competitor

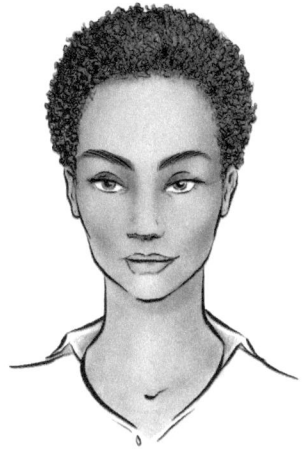

The pie chart on Beth's laptop said it all. First, there was the revenue from the inbound marketing on her website.

When a spouse suspects their betrothed of stepping out, he or she goes online to look for a private investigator. They enter keywords in the search bar of their favorite browser, and Truth Be Told Investigations, Inc. comes up first (after the paid ads). This was no accident.

The person's eye zeroes in on the deliberately worded, A/B tested cache phrases and then click on the link to the website and see testimonial after testimonial before the website fully loaded. The slider below the banner then parades more testimonials across the screen. This website is optimized for all display screens, especially cell phones. Then there are the video testimonials of women talking about choosing Beth Clarke. A live chat pop-up populates the home page with Beth's face and the number. If the person clicks away before they could leave the site, an offer for a free report comes up.

All the viewer has to do is give Beth their email address or phone number for the free report on "The Seven Signs Your Spouse is Cheating on You." That free report rotates with surveillance video of a couple kissing and groping in their car at a secluded part of a well-known park before the email/phone ask pops up.

A six email auto-responder gives the viewer more reasons to know, like, and trust Beth and Truth Be Told over the next several days - always with the pop up for the live chat. Beth and her employees, Mary and Pat, field the phone calls and move the callers through the sales funnel to click on the retainer agreement and add their credit card or Paypal to become a customer.

Using her army training to plan the surveillance like recon missions results in superior results, garnering more testimonials and referrals. Beth prices the surveillances economically with 4, 6, and 8-hour flat rates. No drive time, no mileage. Video is uploaded to a secure, password-protected cloud server.

This slice represents the most extensive time commitment to sell, administrate, and investigate, but it also represents the smallest slice of revenue.

The next slice is twice the size and represents her outbound marketing of upscale women who frequent businesses that cater to them. Beth went to these service-related businesses and made her pitch. She gave free surveillances to some of the workers who had their suspicions that their significant others might be getting something extra on the side.

Even with a cut going to the business people that referred new clients, Beth still makes twice the money on these custom-made longer-tail investigations. She can charge more using multiple investigators per surveillance and other technologies allowed under state law. Because most of the woman are referred, her consultation time yields a higher conversion of prospects to customers. The almost identical number of assignments yield double the revenue as the inbound cases.

But what pops off the chart is the amount of money per hour spent on the Open Source Intelligence (OSINT) up-sells or assignments. Half the revenue in the past 12 months came from OSINT - twice as much income as the outbound-marketed surveillance, and four times as much as inbound consumer-based surveillances. The most astonishing facet of this new-found business is that it is all organic. Word of mouth referrals, and getting into some well-heeled law firms and plush corporate board rooms.

She was marketing B2C and was making most of her money B2B with no end in sight. The OSINT has gone from a side hustle to paying hobby, to part-time and now threatening to go full-time. Beth is not sure how to proceed. Her business plan accounted for the growth of the surveillance business with an administrative assistant, Pat, and two more surveillance operatives working weekends to take the pressure off of Beth and Mary Chambers, her first hire, but nowhere did they plan for this cash cow.

SECTION ONE: STAGNATE, CHANGE, GROW, OR SLOWLY DIE

John's Story: Pivot to B2C and then IMHF

John looked at his PI license differently now that he was a solo with Squire Investigations. He had to get a license 7 years earlier, when he started Independent Special Investigations, LLC. His goal then was to service the Property & Casualty Insurance industry, doing what he had done most of his career at the Police Department.

He was growing ISI to become a regional supplier of insurance fraud investigations from "Bangor to Baltimore." In the middle of that growth, two national firms seized competitive advantage and left John and many other local firms in their dust.

That PI license now came in handy for his phoenix to rise from the ashes.

He had a vague idea of what private investigators did, from talking to them when he made surveillance assignments back his days in SIU (Special Investigations Units). He began attending his local PI association more regularly and paying attention. He joined the National Association of Legal Investigators in 2004 and offered to teach a course at their annual conference in Indianapolis on Investigative Interviewing. It was eye-opening to see how many different specialists and experts were in attendance.

Most of the attendees were solo operators like him, but some worked with associates, and a handful owned large full-service firms. If money or people were involved in disputes, there was usually an attorney involved, and they needed a private investigator to get the facts to prevail in court.

He learned about a Los Angeles lawyer that specialized in Cable Piracy law. If a bar or lounge was showing a heavyweight fight without paying the cable operator for the rights to show it, they were stealing the feed.

The TV show "Cheaters" was offering franchises around the country. He had success with the piracy cases and luckily didn't pay a franchise fee for the Cheaters cases. Callers thought they would get their cases on the TV show for free.

He became one of the go-to PIs for other PIs around the country. He volunteered at the local courthouse, doing indigent intakes for the Public Defenders office when two investigators went out on sick leave and maternity leave. He tried his hand at skip-tracing.

John began cobbling together billable hours as a generalist. Lucky for him, Connecticut is a small state, and he still held his New York license as well. If customers wanted to pay him to go to NYC or Long Island, he could whistle a happy tune while he drove down and back.

He built an SEO-rich website and started receiving calls from the full spectrum of consumers, professionals, and businesses that needed his services.

He still had some clients from the ISI days, and those loyal clients formed the basis of his new business.

A local Criminal Defense attorney gave him a shot on a couple of small interview-intensive cases. She was then appointed by the court to handle the defense of a young man accused of murder. John began working that case at the state-appointed rate, which was less than 22% of his standard rate. He used these types of cases as "loss leaders" to get law firms to try him out, before trusting him with their larger, full-pay cases.

During this time, another lawyer hired him to find a missing heir. He gave John three weeks and a small budget. John exhausted both the time and money and when he asked for more of both, he was told no. But then the lawyer said, "Why don't you find her yourself?"

"Who will pay me?" John asked.

"You find her and convince her to give you a percentage of her inheritance in exchange for telling her where the estate is."

"Is that legal?" John asked.

He replied, "I will release you from the estate, and you are free to speculate on this case. It is called Missing Heir Research, and yes, it is legal and very lucrative."

John began learning Forensic Genealogy along with Criminal Defense investigation. His bag started filling up with missing heir and murder cases—an odd mix for sure.

He created a second DBA, Hoda Genealogy. John never found that heir, and it is still an open file on his desk. He started going to local Probate courts on Friday afternoons after he had met his billing goals for the week. He researched on nights and weekends. Over time, he had some successes and was able to do searches all day Friday. Then it became two days a week.

In April of 2008, John made as much from finding and signing heirs to one estate as the total of all his billable cases in 2007. He had a dozen other cases of variously projected payouts in the pipeline.

The murder case, mentioned earlier, went to trial in April. It was a three-week slugfest and, in the end, the young man was found not guilty in the first week of May 2008. John waited until after the celebration to tell the attorney he was moving on.

John decided to slowly disengage from Squire Investigations, to devote more time to Hoda Genealogy with a plan to go national. If it could work in Connecticut, he reasoned, why wouldn't his methods work around the country.

On Labor Day, 11 years to the day from his startup with ISI, John relaunched as International Missing Heir Finders, LLC.

Where Are You And Where Do You Want To Be?

An Expert can charge a premium for their time. What does it take for you to turn your specialties into expertise?

$500 an hour contracts are not unheard of.

$5,000 non-refundable retainers just to look at a serious problem is another.

Higher education, certifications, and a killer curriculum vitae may be in order. Who decides if you are an expert? Most of us do ponder what does it take to be an expert in court. A judge decides. What is that criteria? Who are court-admitted experts in your field?

Is it worth finding out you can take your specialty and elevate it to an area of expertise?

Appearing regularly on an Investigations reality TV series is another plus.

Anything with Forensic in your credentials is a plus.

Another excellent example of Expertise that does not have to be court-admissible is Background investigations for C-suite hires and mergers and acquisitions.

Bug sweeps and forensic examination of a cell phone, computer, and smart machines are two more examples.

An Expert PI company at the highest level of need for well-funded corporations, governmental agencies, or wealthy individuals brings together celebrity investigators and a vast network of contacts to the client. Think Bo Deitl, Kroll & Associates, and The Mintz Group.

What can you do in your little bustling burg to be that PI? Hint-Marketing and Public Relations are the keys. A colleague of mine is experimenting with billboards. The message is mixed, but it's better than the thousands of dollars PIs wasted on yellow page ads–those were the business listings in the back of paper phone books, for you youngins' :)

How do you get the word out that, for anything investigative in your zip code, people should come to you first?

Join your local Chamber of Commerce and show up regularly.

Join your State PI association and, after you make voluntary contributions to setting up meetings or conferences, throw your hat in the ring to get elected to a seat on the board. Here, you get to know who is good and who is not for your referral network.

Join a national Organization and make sure you spell out exactly what your skills sets are and the towns or cities where your car drives to regularly.

Offer to write articles for the association newsletter of your target audience in your state.

What webinars in your area of expertise will translate into continuing education credits for professionals in your bailiwick?

All of this builds credibility and, with a decent level of sales savvy, you can command a higher compensation because you are the expert in your area's large city.

A specialist crossing business segmentations by a skill set.

A stable surveillance company can cross business segmentation either B2B, P2P, or B2C. Can you create two-tier pricing that adds value to the B2B segment, such as two-car surveillance or a pre-surveillance and background check package?

How about Investigative Interviewing? Trial attorneys need written statements, Insurance companies need recorded statements, and Criminal Defense attorneys need both. Family Law and Unfair Employment Attorneys, ditto.

What do you do better than anyone else? Can you charge a

premium because you are the best in your area? Can you train a staff up to your standards?

A Specialist with deep penetration in P2P, such as working exclusively for the niche of trial attorneys, or B2B such as insurance arson investigations (not an arson expert who can testify to Origin and Cause).

A Generalist working in a hard-to-reach geographical area. Aruba or Gig Harbor are just two examples. Showing up at International conferences and having a kick-ass SEO optimized website are two pre-requisites to become Magnum in Hawaii.

A Generalist competing on price, usually in the B2C world. Razor-thin profit margins have to be offset by volume and a lean fulfillment process. Be prepared to be a manager that has to fill in for employees who call-off sick.

Solo Generalist/Specialist with a few associates or part-timers. You have a steady amount of work coming in the door that pays the bills, and the workflow can be adjusted for busy or slack time.

Solo Generalist. Either your working your ass off or you have another source of income such as a pension or the means of pooling expenses with the other people in your personal life.

Sub-contractor or part-timer by choice for now. Maybe you are finishing school or working at another job and want to change your status sometime sooner than later.

SECTION TWO: JUST DO IT. INCREASE REVENUE.

$1,000 DAYS

Bill 4 hours at $250 per hour and you invoice $1,000.

Bill 6 hours at $170 per hour and you invoice $1,020.

Bill 8 hours at $125 per hour and you invoice $1,000.

Bill 10 hours at $100 per hour and you invoice $1,000.

Bill 14 hours at $75.00 per hour and you invoice $1,050.

First, how many $1,000-days do you need to make a living?

Jo needs to net $6,000 a month, after taxes of $3,000 a month, and $4,500 a month in businesses expenses, or $162,000 a year. Jo needs 162 days to cover costs. 172 days, if Jo wants to fund a $10,000 SEP IRA. That allows Jo to take five weeks of vacation (25 days), 12 holidays and every Wednesday (52), for 261 total work days a year. Jo doesn't work the weekends at all!

It seems far-fetched, doesn't it? The math is sound. It hinges on two premises: Jo is billing $1,000 every workday, but how much Jo charges per hour makes those billing days reasonable (6@ $170 per) or miserable (14@ $75 per). The obvious answer is that

Jo doesn't have to be miserable charging $75 per hour for services rendered. Jo just needs to staff up.

"But," you say, "what about marketing time, administrative time, non-billable travel time, and time spent on bookkeeping and accounting?"

On the 6-hour billing day, it is possible. On the 14-hour billing day, without help, it quickly becomes overwhelming.

I only have concentrated on the revenue side of the equation, and that is where I will stay. I am not here, in this book of the series, to tell you to clip coupons or forego an occasional meal. How you tighten your belt, both in your personal expenses and business expenses, places less pressure on your billing days. But that doesn't help you make $1,000 every working day.

Raise Rates. Just Do It.

All the arguments against raising rates are internal resistance or the gravity that weighs you down.

"But," you say, "my customers will leave me."

Not if you frame the increases like this:

- Announce a 10% increase for the New Year at Thanksgiving (or some other holiday to holiday period) and tell them they should get assignments to you before the price increase takes effect.
- The following year, round up to hourly rates to the next number ending with a zero. For example: $115 becomes $120.
- Add a new feature to each of your flat rates to justify the increase. Tell your customers how that new feature helped a client, with a testimonial from that client. A $299 flat rate with this new and improved feature is now a $350 flat rate.

- Rush assignments and holidays are premium times. Clients understand the concept of overtime. (Although I went to a bowling alley last night, a Friday night, to interview witnesses on an Indigent court-appointed case at $35 an hour. It is necessarily a favor for an old client. All the witnesses I needed to talk to were there, and none of them were favorable to his client.)

I have raised rates several times. I had to have this advice pounded in my hard head, not once, but twice.

I didn't lose any good customers. I lost the burners and the grinders. I didn't go out of business by raising rates. I began to get paid for the real value I gave to my clients.

This advice fits here, and it may be the only time in this book of the series that I offer marketing advice.

Six weeks before your planned vacation of more than a week, you contact your top clients and tell them of your plans. They will ask where you are going and for how long. Your call acts as a tickle for them to get off their patoot and send you over that file that has been sitting there on their desk collecting dust.

But Don't Stop There

Go into your database of clients (CRM) or assignment log of who gave you work last year, but haven't called this year. Leave messages with them telling them of your upcoming vacation plans.

It is a non-threatening call, and it is a great way to re-establish contact. It results in more work from people that are again your clients.

The added benefit of this call is that your clients will respect you more. They will value you for the professional that you are.

You are giving them the courtesy of telling them how to avoid the emergency assignment later on. They will respect you for being able to take a vacation. They see you are organized and trying to lead a balanced life. This is part of why you can charge what you do.

It's a subtle reminder your time is valuable.

One-Time Customers

"What are your rates?" "How much do you charge an hour." You get asked almost immediately. You haltingly, and with a catch in your voice, answer with your customer-friendly per-hour rate. You hope they don't nickel and dime you.

Don't do that. Don't do that ever again.

According to one of my closest mentors, Jimmie Mesis, former owner of PI Magazine, the answer is two very simple words:

"It depends."

That is the ledge for you to start asking questions about the case.

"What have you already done?"

"When do you need it by?

"Is there anything more I need to know about."

"What is the outcome you are looking for?"

But here is where the magic comes in.

You ask, "What have you set aside for the matter?" The other way to phrase it differently is, "What is your budget?"

In response to either answer, you sigh and say, "Tell you what, I will be able to do at least X,Y, and Z first for (slightly less than the amount they named), and we'll see where that gets us." If you priced it right, you have a budget for far much more per hour than if you quoted your hourly rate and did all the steps. You can get authorization for more money if the next steps bring them closer to their goals.

If they come back really low, tell them you will not be able to do it for that amount, but you have somebody who may be willing to do it for that price. However, there is no guarantee of success. Go back over their needs, overcome the price objection with your offer again, and ask, "That sounds reasonable to me, what do you think?"

Retainers

I take retainers from everybody except for in-state attorneys and regulars.

On complicated cases where putting together a couple of flat rates isn't even a suggestion, I tell them I work on refundable retainers of $5,000. I can send them the retainer agreement, and when I receive the funds, I start putting together the case. It could be as much as 40 hours of work on a homicide case or 20 hours of work to try and find heirs in Slovenia ($125-$250 per hour). I have a real incentive to be super-efficient with my time. The takeaway for you is this:

Divide the number of hours you think the case should take into $5,000. That answer should be more than your hourly rate. Don't be greedy, but it should be more. Two things happen here. First, you get paid up front and don't have to chase the money. Second, you are working the case for a premium, and you didn't sell yourself short (again). Send them a report with your results with the little bit of left-over money or apply the money to the next retainer. They will be happy with your results if you stay within budget, hopefully–definitely, with a return of some money.

Stop Discounting

Always round up, not down, when you figure out what your budget will be. Always think 1.1 to 1.25 times your average rate. You can handle surprises on the street much better that way.

Give a volume discount when you get the volume.

Suppose I have three interviews lined up with witnesses at the same location. I have a flat rate for signed statements. I invoice for 2.5 statements. My client is happy, and I am ecstatic. I didn't have to drive to and from three separate statements.

Clients sometimes promise a lot of volume, when they haven't paid you for the first and only case that you have. Politely, tell them the price will change when the volume comes in. Period.

Don't discount for taking ApplePay, PayPal, or charge cards. You have set up systems for your clients to pay you conveniently. That is their benefit.

Stop Giving Stuff Away For Free

Except for When You Will Make A Ton Of Money By Rewarding Great Customers, Or In A Targeted Marketing Campaign.

Framing the conversation around this issue is not tricky. If you need to clinch the deal, throwing in extras is not the way to close. Continue to talk about their need and your value. They will respect you more for holding your ground. You are worth every penny they will pay you. This begs the question: how much do you need their business? Part of getting to making $1,000 every working day is the ability to be selective. That you have so much in the pipeline, you can afford to be picky.

Mary is frantic. She calls you up and says they can't find their client who has to be served for a deposition the Tuesday after an upcoming holiday weekend. It's late Friday afternoon. You say hold on. You just happen to be in your favorite low-cost database.

A) You pull up the client's new cell phone, and you get the client on the phone while Mary is listening on the other line. You tell the client that Mary, from their law firm, will call in a few minutes. Mary is ecstatic. You tell Mary you love working for them and the reasons why. You just pulled a rabbit out of a hat and best of all;

you tell her because you value their business so much, you are happy to do this one for free.

B) You pull up the client's new cell phone, call the client, and make the connection. It took you five minutes. You call Mary back and tell her the client is waiting for her call, and you will be sending the bill over Saturday morning for your usual LOCATE flat rate she is accustomed to. Mary is grateful.

You decide which is more important to you. I personally like doing magic - it's more fun. I can make money mostly every working day.

Fire Customers

	Fast paying	Slow paying
High paying	H+F	H+S
Low paying	L+F	L+S

You can, and you should, fire customers.

The first to go are the low-paying and slow-paying clients. You are better off using that time to market and up-sell your high-paying and fast-paying clients.

"But, but," you sputter, "how do I turn away that work? It's steady. It fills up my work days."

Think about your goal of making $1,000 every working day.

You are dragging an anchor under your sailboat.

Plan a date to politely start telling them that you are jammed up with your other cases. You may try to rehabilitate them by saying you need them to send you $X with the assignments from now on. They then become good-paying-fast-paying clients. If they balk, cut loose that anchor before it snags on the bottom.

I did this with an insurance company that only paid for 4-hour time blocks of surveillance with no drive time or mileage. I made money with their work by hiring part-timers from the local Criminal Justice graduate program. Their cameras were not expensive, and neither was the video download programs. We made report templates and, like the organized chaos of Lucy and Ethel on the chocolate drop assembly line, we handled their work, but at an emotional cost.

The claim representatives would pay when they felt like it and nit-picked constantly. They made up 20% of my revenue, but when you subtracted out all of the overhead and my time, the aggravation was not worth it. Firing them was liberating. It freed me up to use that administrative time to find better clients, and I did.

Next to go are the low-paying fast-paying client. That is a harder sell, I know.

This is the predicament Beth Clark has with her inbound marketing of infidelity investigations surveillance. They pay the bills, they absorb overhead, and they keep people on the payroll, but they chew up her time. Time she could spend with high-paying clients that pay on time, or those she has to send an occasional reminder to.

By offering flat rate blocks of time with no extras, she has packaged a service to be a commodity. There is nothing wrong with commoditizing a service. If you can scale it, it can be profitable. This why it is so tempting for Beth to keep offering this service. She figured out how to do inbound marketing while her competitors were writing on the cave walls. This repeatable and scalable business does offer her great value if she could move out of operations and fulfillment, or sell this lucrative piece.

It took me a while to get around to asking you this question: **What is your time worth?**

This may be the reason for most of your resistance and the gravity that holds you down. If you are going to settle for grinding out hours, and spending hours administrating those hours to barely keep your head above water, you have to ask yourself why.

I find a witness that says my quadriplegic client had the green light while the police throw their hands up in the air about who was at fault.

I go to the crime scene and realize it was impossible for the State's star witness to see the client commit the murder. After I confronted her, she tells me she was making it up based on cues from the detectives.

What is my time worth to the disabled person, or the defendant, both facing a lifetime of misery? What was the result worth to the attorney paying my bill?

What is my time worth to the business customer who has a problem if my results solve their problem? It might be worth X to them. If they went with the cheaper and less-effective competitor they might pay less for per hour, they run the higher risk of still having to pay X.

These are the questions you have to ask yourself, and even ask the client when they hem and haw at your quote. Don't underestimate your value to the client. They can do a good enough job of that for you. Part of your sales technique is to help them realize why you and your company are the best fit. You are worth it.

Understand that a gourmet restaurant and McDonald's both serve food. Don't confuse the different customers' expectations. But that does bring me to the next heading. "Do you want fries with that shake?"

Up-sell and Affiliate Marketing

I still do not do enough up-selling.

Straightforward example: I am asked by a client to go to an accident scene and find security cameras that may have captured the events on video.

I go there twice if the accident happened after hours. During the daytime, I visit the business establishments (when the owners would be most likely be there) to talk them into sharing their video feeds.

Then, I go to the scene again on the same day of the week, at the same time of day as the accident, to canvas for witnesses. My clients are happy with my results.

But what if I suggested that we ask, under the Freedom of Information Act, for the 911 caller audio tapes and the body cams or dashboard cams of the responding officer?

That up-sell gives value for which I can charge more, and we might also identify additional witnesses not listed on the police report, which can be a further up-sell.

Do you know how many of those 911 callers tipped the scale in favor of my attorney's client? I am learning to make that up-sell at the time of the assignment.

Always lock down the original assignment first, then talk about the value add.

"I normally charge X for this, but since I am already (in the data) (at the scene) (over by the courthouse) (whatever your upsell is), I can do it for 85% of Y. Makes sense to me, what do you think?"

Here is the fun part. In my assignment log, I note the up-sell in with a check mark in the up-sell column and then type in the dollar amount in the money field right next to it. Every quarter,

I total the up-sell dollars. Can you do this on the road to making $1,000 every working day?

Look at every service you provide. How can you up-sell them?

"Do you want a background check with that shake?"

"Do you want an asset check with that shake?"

"Would you like me to run a search for Y while I am in the data with that shake?"

If the kid at the McDonald's register can do that, why can't you?

If the server at the fancy restaurant can ask, "We have a special on Harvey Wall Bangers, can I start you out with one?" Why can't you?

> There was a time when I charged clients $3.00 a page for transcription. My business, at the time, was very report-heavy and all my people dictated reports. I paid less than $1.75 a page to an overnight transcription firm. I was able to take my family of four to a warm weather vacation every February from charging that extra $1.25. Charles Dickens didn't have anything on me! I didn't have a single B2B client complain about my transcription costs. It was part of the territory. However, in the P2P world, my clients want more flat rates instead of itemized bills, and I adjusted.

Affiliate Marketing

You can't be an expert in everything. When your clients call you for an assignment that is way beyond your skill sets, you tell them you can't help them, sorry.

Wrong!

You instead connect them to your good friend Ryan or Terry, who have the expertise and the proven track record. They can do the job, and for the referral, Terry or Ryan will send you a percentage of the fee as a referral fee. What is 20% of $5,000? You just made your $1,000 for that working day by taking a phone call and making a phone call. Of course, you have worked hard to earn the trust of your client and spent considerable time culling a group of experts to surround yourself with.

USABugSweeps.com is a great example. This is where I formally introduce you to my friend and mentor of two decades. Jimmie Mesis is recognized as an expert in the field of residential and business Technical Surveillance Countermeasures (TSCM) bug sweeps. He has been associated with the field of TSCM for more than 35 years and conducts several hundred sweeps every year throughout the United States and abroad. He has a referral program for PIs around the world. What a great marketing idea.

Here are other experts for example

- Accident re-constructionist
- Forensic computer and cell phone recovery for data extraction or recovery from digital devices
- Handwriting experts
- Recovering data from security cameras
- Skip Tracing
- Arson Investigator

- Forensic Genealogist
- Forensic (Fill in the blank)

This list is by no means exhaustive. The idea is merely to have your clients come to you for all their needs. If you have targeted your audience carefully, your specialization will align with their needs. Experts or other sources are just a phone call away for you. Or you could have your clients call your competitors. Your choice.

*A client needed to locate their ex-wife in St. Maarten, this past January. I jokingly offered to go, but then I did the next best thing. I went into my INTELLENET directory and emailed three investigators on the Dutch side of that Caribbean island. Two got back to me quickly and took the time to talk it over with me. I forwarded both of their contacts to the client, who ended up choosing one. I didn't take a fee from either of them, but I charged the client for an hour, which he happily paid. I now know two good PIs for everything St. Maarten.

Hint: Going to national conferences or super regional conferences like FALI, TALI and CALI or the SuperConference Jimmie Mesis puts on every other year is a great way to learn about the latest technologies from vendors wanting to do a free demo for you, meeting folks from all over the world, and learning from experts. I come back from EVERY conference with something that will make me money immediately, and it always offsets the cost of being away from my billing days and the expenses associated with the travel.

I budget for two conferences a year. I recommend you do at least one.

SECTION TWO: JUST DO IT. INCREASE REVENUE

SECTION THREE: WEARING FEWER HATS

EMBRACE YOURSELF–REPLACE YOURSELF

The job functions you shed depends on your customer segmentation. Your labor intensity and the degree of specialization of your service plays a factor, as well. Some assignments are more burdensome on your administrative shoulders than others.

It has been my experience that Professional Investigators let go and sometimes actually drop the ball on the wrong functions first. When most PIs get busy, they stop marketing and then hire someone to help with the investigations (Fulfillment) when in reality it is much better to hire a part-time bookkeeper to do the books. (You still control the checkbook.)

Do you think I wake up on a beautiful Saturday morning looking forward to sitting with my bookkeeper, doing the books and reconciling the credits cards with QuickBooks? Not really, but it does allow me to spend time during the week wearing other hats.

In B2C and B2B, an administrative assistant can be trained to take in cases from the inbound marketing and callers. Your AA can open cases, assign investigators, maintain a diary on the cases to make sure none get dropped or delayed, put the reports together, and send you the reports for invoicing (again, no one entity in your operation handles every process altogether).

You think the time you are no longer spending on keystroking accounts payable and maintaining the assignment log among other administrative chores can be spent on investigations.

Wrong!

That time is better-spent marketing. Then you go on to hiring and training people to do fulfillment. You have to fill the pipeline to have others handle fulfillment.

The goal of making $1,000 every working day is met by having enough cases in the pipeline to plan your $1,000 working day for the week ahead, or maybe even into the following week, on your scheduled appointments.

This is where resistance and drag intersect to keep you for propelling into orbit. You want to hold on to investigations because that is what you like and that is what you are better at.

The first thing PIs who own their businesses give up is Marketing, and that is not to be given up but has to be expanded if you wish to maintain and grow. There is no such thing as lifetime customers. Customers come and go. How do you replace customers that leave if you are no longer marketing? How do you plan to grow if you are not marketing to more prospects, and better-paying prospects?

I would rather investigate. I would instead canvas a crime scene in the Projects on that sun-splashed Saturday morn, then work on the client newsletter. So it took me a long time to appreciate the value of marketing.

You have to then add investigators, to where you have so many investigators that you hire an investigations supervisor and get off the street and out of fulfillment. This is where most PIs stop. They don't hire the investigations supervisor, and they don't hire a full-time marketing person. Yes, hiring to handle bookkeeping and administrative services make the load much lighter. Replacing some investigative time with some combination of sub-contractors, part-timers, and full-timers help the bottom line, and you can pick and choose your cases, and the ones that you want to ride along on for supervisory or quality control reasons.

Your internal resistance and the drag of carrying a load of a team now keeps you from getting into space. Part of your resistance is the mistaken belief that when you or somebody along with you increases the marketing effort, you are paying for unnecessary overhead.

How could anybody be productive 40 hours a week marketing your little company? It goes back to the original misconception that if you do good work, you will always be busy. Many PIs fail to grasp the obvious. X number of hours marketing or working on marketing functions produces a multiple of X in billable hours of investigation. Marketing types will say you can exponentially increase your yield by constantly tweaking your message.

For example, one year, I set out to increase my billable hours to 35 hours a week for myself and a new part-timer. Doesn't sound like much, but when you are billing an average of $150 an hour, you are making $1,050 every working day.

Marketing less than 5 hours a week, I was able to achieve that goal consistently. Imagine a 7-to-1 ratio of billable hours to marketing hours. Here is the rub: you didn't form your investigations company to become a full-time marketer, and the thought of having to hire and manage a full-time marketer places you way outside your comfort zone. It goes back to your root assumptions that you want to grow your investigative skill sets and not your marketing skills.

At 2pm next Thursday, you have two webinars going off at the same time. One is "Better Background Checks," and the other is "How 2 A/B test your CTA (Call to Actions)." Which one is going to capture your eyeballs? I thought so.

Which one will have a more significant impact on your bottom line? You know the answer.

This false ceiling of mindset keeps the owner in fulfillment and marketing is done on a catch-as-catch-can basis. This is the bane of most small business owners and not just PI firms.

Stay With Me On This

You then hire a part-time marketer to expand your pipeline even further to where you could promote from within your probationary investigations supervisor.

You are now managing a bookkeeper, an administrative assistant, a part-time marketer, and an investigations supervisor. You outsource IT and the managing of your website, but you still can add content, if you wish.

You still plan the marketing and do the quality control of the investigations, and you still oversee field training. The billings have to absorb all that overhead from the people that don't bill files. You have to watch the right numbers (metrics) and make sure you are strategically aligned with them.

If you have done your planning right, you can go out on the cases you want to work with your staff and still take that trip to Paris you have wanted to do for years.

You then promote from within a Director of Administration, Marketing and Operations.

That is how you build a business that runs without you but remember, you always oversee the checkbook.

That is a good exercise, and for many people, it is something worth aspiring to.

However, more practically, I want to return to the proposition of making $1,000 every working day. We will apply these ideas to each Customer Segmentation below towards making sure you are meeting your goal.

The weekend after completing the five-year plan, Tony does his invoicing and looks at the quarterlies. He compares how much he made this quarter to the previous quarter. He compares his billable hours from Criminal Defense to Business Investigations. He compares them to the previous quarter by segment. Then he made the same comparisons to the same quarter last year. Criminal Defense was not even in the same quarter in his first year. He compares flat rates to hourly cases to budgets and retainers. He saw which upsells were working and which ones weren't.

He is growing exponentially—in layperson terminology: by leaps and bounds. He could easily afford a part-time administrative assistant who could do light bookkeeping. That position could grow into full-time as he added more investigators. He had been tracking his Admin and BK time and saw that it averaged 15 hours a week. Before he even launched Russo & Associates, he started tracking his time, and it was an ingrained habit. After getting the admin up and running, he would devote five of those hours to more marketing, five to recruiting and hiring associates and he would give himself five hours off and plan to do something for himself on these precious days. He has been sprinting

SECTION THREE: WEARING FEWER HATS

work-wise for months now, and it is time to get back in the gym three days a week.

One of the people from his Chamber of Commerce meetings wants to spend more time at home with their kids and left their job as an executive assistant. Tony pitches the job to them and aside from two hours every other Saturday at Tony's office for bookkeeping, they can work remotely. They shake hands on it.

Two detectives from Tony's old squad are looking to work part-time in retirement. They are happier than tall dogs in a meat store to work with him as associates.

That Associate thing on the website and business cards is now going to pay off, he thinks.

In short order, they get their PI licenses, Insurances and become "1099" sub-contractors. They are free to refuse cases. They are free to work the cases the way they want, when they want, and how they want to. They are free to work for other PIs, after signing non-competes and non-disclosure agreements with Tony. Abe and Tony's accountant makes sure they are genuinely sub-contractors. Tony nets 60% after expenses on their 20 hours a week each, which gave him more breathing room, even with the increased emphasis on marketing.

One morning after a client arraignment, Abe pulls Tony aside. "Tony, I want you to meet somebody." He said.

Abe motions to the man who walks over to them with an uneven gait.

Tony shakes hands with the man who is half his age. The grip is strong, and the eyes are clear, and they don't look away. As Tony takes him in, he sees an over-developed upper body and the tell-tale sign of a prosthesis where a lower right leg had been.

Abe doesn't miss a beat. "Joe was on a foot beat in Brooklyn when an uninsured and unlicensed drunk lost control of his car and pinned Joe up against a wall."

"Abe tells me you are good people and that you were "real police" when you were on the job," Joe says.

"He's been handling some of my process serving while he finishes his rehab and is now ready for some steady work," Abe adds.

"How do you feel about Abe and I working for criminal defendants?" Tony asks point blank.

Joe shrugs. "I miss the work, but not the BS. I never got a chance to go after my gold shield. I was slated for a plain-clothes detail until this happened." He pointed to where the pants cuff touches the right shoe. "I figure this would be the best way to use my brains. We both know that the cops don't always get it perfect. I've watched you guys from the gallery a few times, and I liked what I saw."

"Before you decide Joe, why don't you ride with me a few days and if you like it, we can do a 60-day probationary period. Whaddya think?"

"I'd like that." The smile was wide and grateful.

SECTION THREE: WEARING FEWER HATS

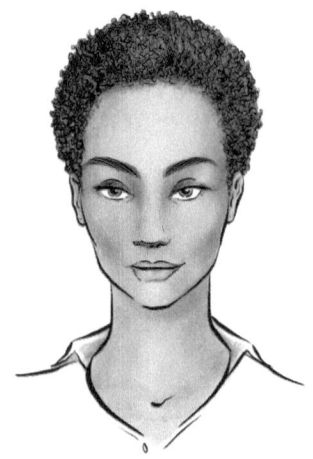

Beth decides to split her operations. Mary Chambers consistently steers business away or into the 4- and 6-hour blocks. However, she is the perfect trainer and field supervisor for the newly hired surveillance operatives. In very short order, they had to hire even a few more. Beth gave Mary more responsibility with the surveillance teams while diverting Mary's marketing calls to Pat, the administrative assistant, who converts better on the inbound calls and for more 6- and 8-hour blocks.

Pat is full-time and will soon be overseeing a burgeoning business that grew out of online dating.

Background checks on prospective spouses have increased. Beth and Pat create a template for them, just in time to capitalize on a marketing stream generated from Internet Dating.

Truth Be Told Investigations, Inc is getting assignments from all over the country to do backgrounds on the persons that the well-to-do prospect are going to meet for their first date after connecting on an internet dating site.

Where online access to criminal records is blocked in individual states and the subject does not leave any social media footprints, the clients are advised that when Jack or Jill lived in that other state, they can not report without hiring a field investigator to access the records and do the background in person.

Beth devotes a landing page just for Internet Dating background checks, offers a free report in exchange for the prospect's email and streams voice testimonials from clients who were adequately warned. The thankfulness just gushes over the phone.

Beth can hire a full-time background checker who also handles inbound calls, as well.

Beth continues to market to the upscale woman's market in the Greater Austin, TX area now that she is not pulling surveillance shifts. She rotates different operatives with her on the marketing visits and finds one operative to be particularly adept at learning how to make the pitch.

Sam took marketing courses in college and understood what Beth is trying to do. Beth rides along with Sam as Sam markets to businesses catering to upscale women in the surrounding counties. With a growing population, the area is now supporting over 2 million people. Sam quickly goes to half-time as a marketer and half-time doing surveillance.

Although Beth is not on the street anymore, she and Mary randomly show up at surveillance sites to check on their people, especially on the one-car surveillances.

When an operative was fired for falsifying time sheets, word got around that somebody is watching the watchers.

That is not to say that Beth is resting on her laurels. She continues to grow her OSINT business, and with help from Pat and the full-time background checker, it can stand alone.

She finds it very elusive training them to her level of expertise. Much of their work is routinized, and her case management system allows them to collaborate real-time and more importantly, for them to work remotely.

She looks hard at this business and realizes that she needs to tap into other intelligence professionals if she wants to grow it.

What was it? She has grown out of her Truth Be Told brand for this lucrative side business.

SECTION THREE: WEARING FEWER HATS

She needs to rebrand if she wants to position her new business effectively in the market place. She has to learn how to market this B2B market without leaning on the law firms that handle TBT clients Family Law and Divorce cases.

How can she replicate and scale this organic growth?

Barely four years after leaving the Armed Guard business, Beth is at the crossroads again. Her goal was to build Truth Be Told to be sold, but what about this new bright shiny object that her proof of concept shows to be a cash cow?

The offer stuns her and changes everything. Her old employer sees the value of her company and how when combined with the acquisition of a security firm would create a B2C and B2B powerhouse.

Where Beth had not wanted to dilute her brand with doing corporate and insurance surveillance, her former employer is ideally positioned to capitalize on her people's advance surveillance skills and a support infrastructure to go with it.

The deal will be paid out over three years. This year's revenue will be matched up front, and half of each of the next two years' revenues will be paid to her monthly with a guaranteed monthly minimum.

Beth will receive two-plus years of revenue spread out over three years. Business valuations for her business say this is a premium offer and she should take it.

She can bank the payouts and accelerate her plans to retire early to go on adventure travel trips, while she bootstraps her way into the OSINT B2B world.

Her former employer's contacts with the Banking, Energy, and growing Corporate headquarters scene of Austin is her toehold into that B2B where her new buyer has nurtured contacts for years. It is very gratifying to see how her hard work and professionalism is appreciated. Her buyer is making out well. She has built a turnkey operation that will open the doors on a B2C world for them with her proven inbound marketing plan.

There are a lot of tears and hugs at the year-end holiday party for Truth Be Told Investigations, when Beth tells her staff about the changes that will take place in the next couple of weeks. She has to cancel her travel plans between Christmas and New Years to finish the valuation for sale and to complete her business plan for Clark Intelligence Solutions, LLC.

SECTION THREE: WEARING FEWER HATS

John expanded his new company, International Missing Heir Finders, LLC into New York, New Jersey, Massachusetts, and Rhode Island. He hired two people to visit probate courts in those surrounding states on a weekly schedule, to look for files where people had died without a will, and where the possibility of missing heirs existed.

He had competitive advantage in CT and hired a full-time genealogist to carry much of the load while he handled the sales (signing heirs to contracts) and he oversaw the attorneys until the cases paid off.

John's fledgling company scored big on a case where ten cousins kinda-sorta forgot they had two half-aunts and a half-uncle with whom they had grown up, and John discovered. IMHF signed them up, and the courts agreed that those ten cousins were not entitled to a dime. John's heirs would take the whole estate.

Finally, when the money came in from that estate, John could roll out a national expansion. He hired a marketing rep and marketing company to help him with the rollout. He hired a full-time Administrative Assistant and implemented a custom-made Case Management System.

A dozen reality-TV producers pursued him, and one followed John around for two days just before Christmas around Columbia, South Carolina, and Milford, CT to create a "sizzle reel" that they shopped to the Oprah, Discovery and TLC channel.

John hoped to have local genealogists scout out cases in the rural counties around the country as his experience was beginning to show that his firm were guppies swimming in the shark pool of most urban areas. John wanted to follow the "Tracer" model of other forensic genealogists and pay the tracers 10% of what he received after his attorneys took their fees.

International Missing Heir Finders attended the genealogy conferences around the country and made its pitch. The marketing rep cold-called genealogists who lived near the county seats in those rural counties. More urban counties were going online with probate filings, and more searching was done online.

One Sunday morning, John found an estate in Memphis, Tennessee. It looked strange with only a niece coming forward. In their research, they found that she was actually a "niece-in-law" and was not entitled to a penny.

They found and signed up 34 of 35 cousins. They also hired per diem sub-contractors for target-rich areas which did not appear to be shark-infested. Missing heir research is a highly competitive business. John learned quickly where not to swim. The infrastructure was completed with the hire of another desk genealogist.

The goal was to fill the pipeline with so many cases. The far-and-few-between large pay-outs would be buttressed by a steady stream of smaller and mid-size cases. He planned to grow the business to effectuate an employee buy-out in 2017 with a gradual three-year payout to 2020.

SECTION FOUR: HIRING

TAKE THE BLINDFOLD OFF

Unless you plan to boost your business by commanding an expert's compensation or have a highly-specialized team of associates, you will need to hire full time or part-time personnel. You will have to offset their costs and the increase in overhead with even more billable hours. The time to recruit, hire, train, supervise, evaluate, and fire (don't think you are immune from bad hires) takes away from other time you spend wearing your other hats, including fulfillment. So you will have to have them shoulder part of your load as well.

Hire slow and fire fast. The recruiting and hiring function is crucial when building a business. A wrong hire compounds the time needed to correct the situation and make a proper hire, usually at a time when the time is short supply and high demand.

SECTION FOUR: HIRING

Doing an autopsy on a lousy hire usually reveals:

- What the prior employers couldn't tell you. Ask, "Who else can I talk to who worked with you but no longer works there?"
- What references gloss over on work history. They feign ignorance of parts of their friend's life. Ask, "Can I interview your best friend?" If the applicant balks, ask why.
- Other past employers not listed on the resume and skipped over on the application.
- You, yes you, glossed over the red flags staring you in the face on the pre-interview questionnaire and during the oral interview.
- Glaring discrepancy between what was thought to be job-specific experience and performance, especially after you train them to perform satisfactorily.
- Tardiness, absenteeism, lateness on work and report completion.
- A relapse in alcohol or drug addiction that now explains the previous gaps in employment. To anyone who has recruited and hired employees, it only takes one or two Dr. Jekyll and Mr. Hyde experiences to see what this behavior looks like. Unfortunately, it happens too often in Small Businesses as the applicant thinks they can fool a small business owner who does not have formalized hiring practice.
- They could hide in a larger organization, but now the spotlight is glaring on them in your small business. Ensure the oral interview includes questions on projects and team involvement. This employee is going to be working on YOUR project and YOUR Team now.
- You didn't train them well, and they could not overcome your lousy training. That one hurts.
- You run your business like Spanky's clubhouse and have demotivated a person that held real promise. Every day is a

Chinese fire drill at your office. They quit and tell you why they are quitting. They pull no punches. That hurts worse.

- The lack of process and procedure place an undue burden on performance.
- There is no consistency in their supervision.
- A non-existent performance appraisal process is compounded by always catching them underperforming. Sometimes praise has to be muttered as part of the appraisal process.

Beth came from the Army, Tony from NYPD, and John was once a manager with multi-national insurance and financial giant AIG. Previously only John had the flexibility of selecting staff, but all three were experienced in supervision and performance appraisal.

Take responsibility for a bad hire. The sooner you see you failed to make the best possible choice you could or provide them with a workplace where they had a chance to succeed, the sooner you can fix the problem, because it IS your problem to fix. Here are some tools that you can use.

New Hire Checklist
Employment Application

- Personal information
- Employment Desired
- Education
- Employment History
- Additional Information
- proof of citizenship
- can you perform all essential functions of a job
- Any accommodations or workplace modifications needed?

- Authorizations for Credit, Driver's history and Criminal Background.

Pre-Interview Questionnaire

- What is the number one reason you want this job?
- How can you make a difference at our company?
- What are the three most important things you think our company does every day?
- If you've ever been fired, tell us what happened:
- What makes for satisfying work experience?
- Tell us something you are excited about?
- Where do you see your career five years from now?

Interview Questionnaire

- What brings you here today?
- Tell me about yourself?
- What events from your childhood shaped who you are today?
- Tell me three or four things of which you are most proud.
- What is the most important thing to you about any job?
- What were the most significant contributions in your current and previous jobs?
- What are your natural strengths?
- What do you like doing best?
- What are some of your natural weaknesses?
- What do you like doing the least?
- Tell me about some of the most important projects you have ever worked on? At least one that worked out and one that didn't (job by job)
- What was your most exciting work experience in the past five years?

- What was your worst work experience in the past five years? How did you contribute to this scenario?
- Who is the best (investigator) you have ever met
- What is the greatest challenge that you've had to overcome in your work career?
- What is the most significant opportunity that you "blew" in your work career?
- Please describe something that felt unfair at your previous place of employment?
- Tell me about a time when you had a conflict with (a boss, subordinate, co-workers). How did you resolve it?

Receipt Of Hire Letter Acceptance

- Hire Letter; may reference the position contract (below)
    - Appointment
    - Remuneration
    - Performance Reviews
    - Probationary period
- Signed Employment Application
- W-4 for tax withholding
- I-9 copies for permanent file
- Employee Handbook Signature Page
- Equipment inventory sign off
- Non-Compete Agreement
- Business cards
- Sign up and passwords for databases
- Association memberships
- Workers Compensation addition and correct job classification

SECTION FOUR: HIRING

- Errors and Omission addition to policy
- Timesheet sample

Employee Handbook

- Welcome page
- Acknowledgment Page
- Equal Opportunity
- Employment Classification: Full time, Part time, Temporary, 1099
- Confidentiality Clause
- Personal Information
- Attendance
- Work Hours
- Overtime–Overtime work is only performed when approved in advance by your supervisor. You are expected to work mandatory overtime when requested to do so, and you will receive time and one-half regular pay for the time exceeding forty (40) hours in the given work week.
- Lunch period
- Safety and accident rules
- Use of company property - person use exclusion
- Use of company computers
- Substance Abuse Policy
- Sexual Harassment
- Performance & Salary Reviews
- Payroll
- Holidays
- Vacation
- Sick Leave

- Maternity Leave
- Funeral Leave
- Jury Duty
- Time off for school conferences
- Time off for voting
- Military Service
- Group Insurance
- Continuation of Medical/ COBRA Insurance
- Workers Compensation
- Educational Assistance
- Layoff and Recall
- Termination of employment

Position Contract

Can be used instead of an employment application.

- Job Title
- Location
- Reports to:
- Pay Rate
- Performance Review Date:
- Type of Position: FT, PT Contractor, Intern
- Results to be achieved by this position (Expected outcomes and Performance Measures)
- Standards for this position (standards of Excellence)
- Work requirements for this position (Duties, Responsibilities, Accountabilities)
- Success Factors
- Analytical thinking

- Business knowledge
- Communications/ Listening
- Company Knowledge
- Critical Thinking
- Customer Focus
- Decision Making
- Leadership
- Organization
- People Development
- Resilience/Flexibility
- Results Orientation
- Team Building
- Teamwork
- Functional Excellence
- Company Values
- Experience needed for a position
- Other/special requirements for this position

Policies and Procedures

See Employee Handbook

TAKE THE BLINDFOLD OFF

SECTION FIVE:
DO AS I SAY AND AS I DO

TRAINING TO COMPETENCY

It starts with the textbooks such as these examples:

- *Fundamentals of Criminal Investigation* by Charles O'Hara, Gregory O'Hara
- *Uncovering Reasonable Doubt: The Component Method* by Brandon A. Perron
- *Casualty, Fire and Marine Investigation Checklists-9th* by Ken Brownlee and Pat Magarik
- *Memory-Enhancing Techniques for Investigative Interviewing: The Cognitive Interview* by Ronald P Fisher and R. Edward Geiselman
- *Tracing Missing Heirs* by Ralph D Thomas
- *Code of Professional Conduct (2006 ed.)* by Kitty Hailey, CLI
- *Techniques of Legal Investigations* by Anthony M. Golec

These are just a few on my bookshelf. What's on your bookshelf or e-reader?

Subscriptions:

- *PI Magazine* by Publishers Nicole Cusanelli and Jim Nanos

- *Data2Know* by Cynthia Hetherington, The Hetherington Group

Next, come the Checklists.

Have they been written down and given to each trainee?

Examples:

- Statement guides
- Surveillance preparations and protocols
- Scene Diagrams, Photos, and Measurements
- Location steps
- Skip-tracing steps
- Background steps

If it is a repetitive task, create a workflow process. Learn it yourself, discuss best practices with peers, minimize mistakes by rigid analysis and continuous self-improvement.

Continue your education with seminars, webinars, and classes.

Have the trainee ride with you to observe best practices. Don't throw them out there on their own with a wave. "Just do A, B, and C and bring back 1, 2, and 3." They will go to the store for lettuce and sometimes come back with cabbage.

Allow the trainee enough situations to create a replicable pattern. One-and-done is a recipe for disaster. Think about the repair garage owner training a new mechanic on how to install brakes. Don't you want the owner over the mechanic's shoulder as they work on brakes for the first time, and maybe the second time, and even the third?

Observe the trainee undertake the interview, the surveillance, or investigation under your direct supervision to reinforce the training. You may have to jump in to assist, but the frequency and depth should decrease over time. You have to allow minor, correctable mistake-making. They are still painting by numbers and will go outside the lines. It won't be a DaVinci the first time they pick up the paintbrush. It wasn't for you either, when you first started.

Offer feedback and continue to seek out situations where you can ride along to cement the learning and minimize bad habits from forming.

Can you distill the textbooks and checklists into training modules for your employees? The caseload is not only there to be worked through. It offers you a plethora of chances to build the foundation of the employee's investigative skills.

Replicable satisfactory performance is the goal.

What I see most times, with other PI firms, is that training is transactional and not transformative. The "what we do" gets passed on, but the foundational "why we do it" does not. You can fiddle with your smartphone or talk about how your team blew the lead on your ride-along, or you can plan the windshield time to reinforce the teaching from similar cases. Explain why you do things that way and not the wrong way. You are teaching the skill, but you are also teaching critical thinking. At some point, that trainee will be an employee out on their own.

Do you want them to be able to react quickly and think on their feet?

Example: A personal injury attorney asks you to secure an affidavit of no insurance from the owner/operator of a striking vehicle. Knowing why you are doing that task helps you deal with that person when they would rather slam the door in your face.

The second issue I see is not teaching time management and prioritization skills. These skills turn lead runners into investigators who can handle their cases from start to finish.

Is there a fear that the employee may learn how to handle their caseload? Is it the mindset that lower paid lead runners are easily replaceable parts in the machine, whereas skilled investigators will leave to go out on their own and compete with you? Why are you creating your drag? How can you boost yourself into orbit if you are carrying that mindset of resistance?

Edit reports with tracking in Word so the employee can see your editorial comments and learn from them. It might be faster at first to fix their mistakes, but you will always get stuck fixing their mistakes.

Performance appraisals done at the end of the year seem more like you are ambushing the employee so that you can justify a misery raise. What a demotivating exercise!

What if, on each and every case report, you gave them a reply that included measurement of:

T	Timeliness
S	Executing the investigative plan with substantive work in a logical manner
O	Meet or exceed the investigative objective.
B	Bonus points for getting the facts to justify an up-sell

They could agree or argue, based on their understanding of the unique circumstances that you may not be aware of right then and there, which is more helpful than defending a vague memory a year later.

What if the company bonus pool was tied into revenue growth and quality standards for each and every file handled by each and every employee?

What if the employee was given this data and asked to participate in their own performance appraisal? Hint- Honest employees are tougher on themselves than you would be. Those appraisal criteria are lifted right from their Position Contract:

- Results to be achieved (Expected outcomes and Performance Measures)
- Standards for this position (standards of Excellence)
- Work requirements for this position (Duties, Responsibilities, Accountabilities)

Bring your employees to conferences and seminars on the topics they are training in. Have them watch webinars and buy the guides or checklists they need for their work bag. Have them assist you in your training presentations. Allow them their time on the floor as the trainer.

How do you keep up their momentum of learning? That is your golden ticket.

"Enquiring minds want to know."

You can't train curiosity. You can only encourage it.

People ask me, "John, what are your proudest achievements in your career?"

I could talk about the cases that have appeared in the headlines or on TV. I could talk about the money I have made and the comforts that I have enjoyed.

Instead, this is what I tell them: "I am most proud of the investigators I have trained in my methods, and how they have blossomed in their own careers I have inspired aspiring investigators and hopefully passed on a legacy that will long outlive me and that they can pass on to further generations of investigators."

Do you want to be able to say that as well?

Will following hiring and training protocols also bring you closer to your financial goals?

SECTION SIX: HUDDLING

GIVE YOUR EMPLOYEES A STAKE IN THE OUTCOME

Be sure to stay to the end of this section. It holds the key to how to structure a buy-out.

The Milford, Connecticut Cracker Barrel had a beautiful round table in the back dining area reserved for the huddle.

Monday was an office day for International Missing Heir Finders, LLC, and a breakfast meeting started promptly at 8 am to kick off the week.

Only the occasional tour bus made it noisy, but otherwise, Dot, the usual server, was happy to greet them. Food was ordered and delivered. A light banter of the weekend's activity swirled about. The plates were cleared, and the meeting began.

Dot didn't mind. She was guaranteed to receive a 50% tip on the bill while she refilled coffee and hot water.

On that day, Claire led with a ten-minute presentation and handout on the latest Genealogical nugget she had unearthed. She is a Certified Genealogist and delighted in looking for obscure places to find the familial connections most important to the lifeblood of the company.

SECTION SIX: HUDDLING

Each employee would take turns sharing their latest discoveries.

The senior genealogist showed the assembled group the company's website which displayed reworked landing pages that helped heirs in their decisions to sign contracts with IMHF.

The executive assistant had worked with the Case Management company to figure out how to filter data by State and Tracer to show where they were getting quality cases for jacketing and the ponds where they were getting no bites. She and the marketing rep worked closely together.

A glass of water sat next to the table setting for the remote marketing rep who Skyped in. The marketer brought up the spreadsheet appearing on everyone's laptop, showing where tracers were being courted, added or dropped. Links to courts going online every day were also sent to the group.

The New York and New Jersey tracer, John regaled everyone with the latest Celebrity estate coming out of Manhattan. Like Los Angeles, it was the final resting place for many of the rich and famous. He often found good cases that hopefully the sharks had not gobbled up.

John, the owner, gave a recap on the highs and lows of courtroom battles on their cases from the previous week and which cases were on this week's docket.

He talked about the successes and failures in signing up heirs. The spreadsheet had every heir accounted for, and his batting average was there for everyone to see.

Where he found that heirs were contacted by other missing heir research firms that competitor data was on display as well, the group began to understand why they were guppies in some of the shark tanks around the country. Finding success around the country was proving more elusive than what was initially thought.

John ended with the financial numbers tallied from the previous week, compiled for him every Saturday by the bookkeeper.

Except for everyone's salary, all the company's numbers were available in the report. The critical numbers to the success of the company appeared in the cash flow snapshot. The health of the company was there for everybody to see and comment on.

Every number measuring everything the company did was transparent to every employee.

Did John just make this huddle stuff up? It was pretty radical.

Are you sharing all the numbers? Showing what was behind the magic curtain? Operations talking to Marketing, talking to Administration, talking about Legal, and employees talking directly to Ownership?

This is a model where everyone in a company from the janitor to the CEO has input in how to improve the company's performance and how that performance impacted on its financials, where everybody had a stake in the outcome.

Flashback to the previous September.

John A. Hoda and Jack Stack had a good laugh when they met for the first time over dinner and talked about how a missing heir research company and a dirty, greasy mid-western remanufacturing company of automobile and truck parks had so much in common.

When John toured the plant the next morning with others from around the country, he talked to a guy up to his elbows tearing down a diesel truck engine. The guy talked about how he was going to school at night to finish his degree in Business, how he sat on the factory's safety committee, and what his per hour labor charge-out would be if an engine was not worth remanufacturing and he spent too much time on diagnosing that issue.

SECTION SIX: HUDDLING

He showed precisely how is productivity affected the bottom line of the company. He had a higher degree of financial literacy and an understanding of the numbers than John.

John became a fanboy of Jack and went out to Springfield, MO, and St. Louis a couple of times as a practitioner in the Great Game of Business, GGOB for short–Open Book Management, to give it a generic name. Jack wrote both *The Great Game of Business* and *A Stake in the Outcome* with Bo Burlingham, then the editor of *Inc. Magazine*.

To borrow from the dust jacket of *A Stake in the Outcome*:

> "The pioneer of "open book management" Stack and twelve other managers began their journey in 1982 when they purchased their factory from its struggling parent company. Springfield Remanufacturing Company grew 15 percent a year while adding a thousand new jobs and the company's stock price rocketed from 10 cents a share to $81.60 per share in 2002 at the time of the book's publication." Bolded on the back flap: "In a successful ownership culture, every employee had to take the fate of the company as personally as an individual owner would."

Back to the Cracker Barrel.

The employees were well on track to become the eventual owners of the company. No equity had been apportioned yet. The company had not reached its mature state yet and was still growing.

This was the end goal that John had begun with when he started IMHF.

The date of transfer was not determined yet. When that day came:

Over three years, John would receive 50% of the company's revenue

(25% in the first year, 15% in the second year, 10% in the third year).

The goal for the company was to have revenues of eight figures to the left of the decimal point. That was a brass ring worth reaching for.

The employees did not have to be saddled with a loan to buy the company and with long-term exposure to financial literacy and the methods of sharing best practices, were better positioned to remain successful. When the time came, they would continue to be practitioners in the Great Game of Business.

I see the biggest hurdle to get over is opening the books. You can no longer use the company's checkbook as your personal piggy bank. What you take out of the business weekly or monthly should be commensurate with the risk you took, your capitalization, the value of your original ideas, and your sweat.

Of course, you don't share how much Sally makes with Harry or what Harry makes with Larry. It's also little harder to justify your new Mercedes that year when you just canceled the company bonus plan.

Change has to start at the top and how you treat the people most responsible for mining the gold becomes glaringly apparent when you open the books.

Getting your people to engage their minds, not only in their job function but also in how they can continuously improve their processes is part of the fun. Watching them keep a sharper pencil on the line items reduces waste and unnecessary cost.

A team approach to growing the business takes a lot of the burden from your shoulders. It is harder to stop a team than just one player.

Hint: You are not the only one with great ideas.

If part of your "Boost" plan includes full-time employees, you owe it to yourself to read either book. I found *The Great Game of Business* to be as inspirational as it was informative.

If hiring employees is new to you, I definitely recommend it to you. You have a blank slate to work with. Why not follow a game plan tested a thousand times over?

If opening the books scares you off, the huddle can still work with all the other measurables of your business without bringing up financials. The good folks at GGOB have other publications and workbooks that can assist you to build a business around your greatest assets."

GIVE YOUR EMPLOYEES A STAKE IN THE OUTCOME

SECTION SEVEN: SHARPENING THE SAW

WHAT GOT YOU HERE, WON'T GET YOU THERE.

Sad, but true. If you are coming at your business from a technician's viewpoint, the business of your craft has to be learned. If you are the refugee of a corporate or large organization with management skills, you still have to learn marketing. If you have marketing skills, you still have to learn strategic planning. What got you launched will not get you into orbit. You need to learn new skills. Most Private Investigation companies peak at the level of the owner's core set of competencies.

Action Coaching Business Coach

In 2004, John began attending a morning leads group with his local chamber of commerce. One morning, an Action Coaching Business Coach gave a short presentation on the math behind growing profits. At the end of the session, which was very informative, he mentioned he had a 12-week "boot camp" group class that would meet every other Wednesday for the Summer. John joined the class. It was an eclectic bunch. One attendee was looking to launch an Internet business, where he would match up clients with master mechanics who could give them a second opinion for a set fee on whether or not they needed a costly repair. There was a pest control company owner, a Landlord lawyer looking to become THE LANDLORD LAWYER in CT, an HVAC guy looking to boost his small company into Orbit (which he did). John couldn't remember what the last group member did, only that he always had excuses why the training wouldn't work with his business. He also never did his homework. Yes, there was homework. John was being taught about business in the practical sense, and the teachings were just as applicable to each member of the group.

John repeated the Action Coaching course at no additional charge when the course was revamped a year later, at the time he was about to launch IMHF. Both courses formed the basis for his financial literacy and some foundational training in how to approach and execute marketing campaigns.

When combined with the reading and training with the *Great Game of Business* (GGOB), John moved from having a team-based and project-based management strength to a more strategic view. He was prepared to market his new missing heir research firm and to teach his staff that their productivity had a direct impact on the company's financials.

His growth as an owner came at a time when he still attended conferences in Genealogy, both as a student and an exhibitor. The investment in learning what he needed to know paid off as he was able to ramp up IMHF to have a National footprint.

Pick Four and Mastermind Group

A fellow attendee of Tony's Chamber of Commerce leads group suggested forming a Pick Four Group.

This was the brainchild of Marketing Guru Seth Godin, who unabashedly gushes about being a disciple of the legendary Zig Ziglar.

Cassette tapes and workbooks from Zig's classes were the Holy Grail for marketers.

Godin distilled the **Pick Four** from Zig's teachings into a thirteen-week workbook where the user planned and executed four goals a quarter, hence the name Pick Four. The group members would meet for an hour after every other Tuesday's meeting to discuss in their allotted 15 minutes, what they had done on each goal in the past two weeks and what they planned to do in the next two weeks.

Weak goals or excuses were exposed pretty quickly, and suggestions on how to overcome the blocks or obstacles were suggested.

Tony was happy to receive the advice. Three decades of detective work didn't prepare him for all the facets of running a business. He was able to offer suggestions as it related to training and supervising from all those years of overseeing a detective squad in Mid-town Manhattan.

The group ran for a year, and at the end, they looked at what they had accomplished. Paying attention to goals on a daily, weekly, and bi-monthly basis allowed them to distill large goals into manageable tasks.

Tony found his next level to be a Mastermind Group. These

business owners came from different sectors of the economy, but all had an interest in Marketing. They met in person on the third Saturday of each month and rotated to each member's office. Tony was able to use Abe's conference room for the day that it was his turn. They all had uploaded their presentation materials in Google docs, and everyone had a screaming fast internet connection that allowed for real-time collaboration.

Each member had to give an hour-long presentation broken up into three 20-minute segments that allowed for feedback from the others. The first session was on what was working well, the second was on what was not, and the third was something new such as an app or Podcast or free e-book that could be shared with a group.

Tony held his own with these other heavyweight business owners. Who didn't want to hear from a former NYPD detective sergeant who was growing a PI business?

Hearing what worked with five other group members was great, but the learning hit home with the lessons from what wasn't working. The feedback was brutally honest and not much different from the autopsies on his squad's cases that resulted in acquittals or the DA refusing to sign an arrest warrant.

Tony couldn't keep up with all the actionable tips each member brought to the group. This executive-level mindset helped him get out of seeing everything through the eyes of a hard-boiled detective.

He was not on the street as much but was spending more time marketing and growing his business. Joe was working out great under Tony's tutoring.

Tony saw how college interns were a great source of quality hires with the other mastermind members. It wouldn't be long before they started taking work in the City, except for Staten Island, with their own interns who would be graduating soon from John Jay

College. The internships acted like a mini-probation period. The successful interns would be offered full-time jobs upon graduation.

Sub-contractors continued to supply part-time over-flow with two new full-time hires on the business Investigations side of Russo & Associates. Tony's skills as a supervisor were paying off, and he still worked the occasional case alongside his new people.

All of this growth was made possible by working his action steps from his Pick Four goals and then by aligning with the Mastermind Group.

APPSUMO- Thrive- Hubspot

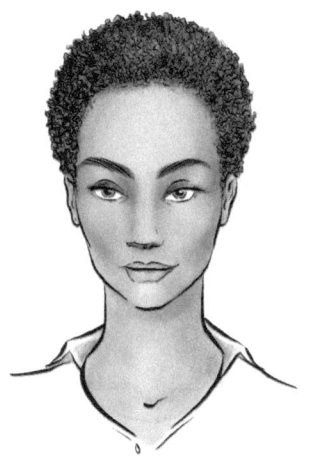

Beth is excited about the design for her new company, Clark Intelligence Services.

She is vetting former military and civilian contractor intelligence professionals. She is using Basecamp to keep all the data under one cloud-based platform.

Her team is 100% remote. They use 24 Sessions to talk and show off their new toys. These platforms are integrated with Hubspot, their CRM.

Her new Administrative Assistant comes from Big Pharma and acts as their librarian. Tracey takes care of vetting all the tools and is continuously growing the drop-down menus for each remote employee and sweats the details of connecting all the platforms through another app named Zapier.

Her continuing education was propelled by her friendship with the APPSUMO people in Austin, Texas. They provided Beth with a first peek at some of their deals. APPSUMO is a leader in proving lifetime access to apps for online businesses, but they have been growing their learning-based products to teach customer skills such as project management and hiring practices. Their greatest strength for the licensed private investigation company is their suite of e-mail list building tools.

The CIS, LLC WordPress website is running on Thrive Themes, and Beth is a subscriber to Thrive University which has become her one-stop resource for all her online business training. They have a lean no-BS approach to explaining why some content converts and some don't. The video training is short, well-produced and speaks directly to growing revenues. They speak to regular business folks without falling back on language only techies can understand.

Hubspot has created a best practices library of resources related to Inbound Marketing.

After her morning workout routine, Beth spends the first 75 minutes of each working day with her online training modules, webinars, and classes, then take a short aerobic break while her favorite coffee brews, before opening her dashboard at precisely 9 am Central. She often muses to herself. You can take the girl out of the army, but not the army out of the girl.

SUMMARY

What got you to where you are, won't get you to where you need to be.

Orbiting requires a boost, and that boost requires surrounding yourself with like-minded business people, using the tools of whatever method you choose to grow your skill sets. Give yourself permission to spend time on self-improvement.

Most PIs stop at the edge of their comfort level and retreat each time they get burnt. Making X and wanting to make 2 or 3X every working day is many times thwarted by risk aversion.

"Everything is okay. I don't want to take a chance on growth."

This translates into, "I am comfortable with the discomfort I feel now and am afraid of growing pains."

Part of that fear of failure comes from fear of the unknown.

Using a Business Coach or getting yourself into a Pick Four or Mastermind Group gives you access to people who have walked your path and have cleared out the thorns and snakes.

Companies that supply you with free or almost-free content do so to entice you to use their products or services, but the advice can be precisely what you need as you overcome drag and resistance.

SECTION EIGHT: BOOSTER ROCKET ENGINE, ENGAGE!

THE RESULTS

After payroll and overhead, Tony is making $1,000 every working day. He has a part-time admin that does much of the bookkeeping.

Tony signs off on payroll electronically and writes out most of the accounts payable checks.

Each employee has a company credit card with a $500 limit for gas, police reports, and court documents.

Joe and two full-time Criminal Defense Investigators (once interns) work along with two more investigators that handle Tony's original business plan, working with Business attorneys and CPAs in Eastern Long Island, which includes home-town Queens.

SECTION EIGHT: BOOSTER ROCKET ENGINE, ENGAGE

The two original subcontractors still help Tony with overflow. His profit margin hovers around 50%. He is down to working four days a week.

The time is evenly split between marketing, ride-alongs, and ownership. He has embraced the open-book management mantra and starts the week with a Monday morning huddle, much to the chagrin of the sub-contractors, who join in for the camaraderie and the free breakfast.

Joe is marketing to the Criminal Defense lawyers in their neck of the woods, while Tony continues to be the face of the company for Business clients. They grossed over a half million last year with a 10% increase projected for this year.

Tony rolled out a bonus plan tied to quality goals for each employee and net revenues. They already had a first-quarter "Bucket" pay-out, and everybody was pretty happy.

Then Tony's wife was diagnosed with breast cancer. They were able to treat it non-invasively, but it gave them both pause.

What were they working towards now? She was already pension-eligible from her Board of Ed job.

It was decided that by year's end, Tony would sell the business to his employees following a regular buyout plan. Joe would become the face of the company, and a significant rebrand was in the offing.

The Russos would travel and spend more time with their kids and grandchildren. The first payment would eliminate all of their real estate and car debt. The following years' payments would prop up an even healthier retirement nest egg. They could wait until the full retirement age for Social Security.

What started as a way to buff up his NYPD pension turned into a company he could sell to his employees.

Tony wouldn't miss the street. He had put his time in over the years between NYPD and Russo & Associates. He was pleased that he grew into a business person and was able to train his employees in his methods.

What started as a paying hobby ended up allowing him financial freedom from having to work with an excellent kicker at the end.

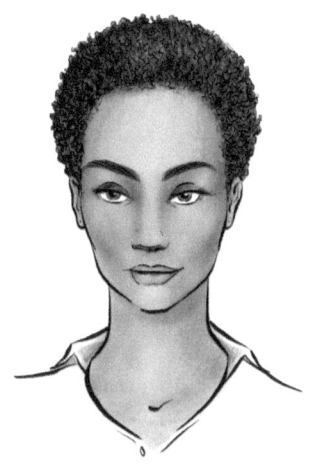

"I can live here," Beth thinks. She is resting on the beach of Phuket in Thailand after surfing Monsoon fueled waves for most of the morning. The water is blue she has never seen before. She had finished her fall and winter marketing at the major conferences with a booth for Clark Intelligence Solutions. She is supplying OSINT (Open Source Intelligence) to major corporations, large law firms, and businesses willing to pay her fees for in-depth reports that gave them actionable answers.

She sees that 3/4 of her business came from outside of Austin, Texas, and a healthy 10% of that work was international. After only two years of business in the B2B world, she has a full-time marketing team qualifying prospects at a dizzying pace.

The conferences also allow her to meet intell pros from all over the world. She has a way of convincing them to work with her. Maybe it has to do with a cutting-edge remote set up, surrounding them with the best tools to work with, and supplying them with a mission-critical sense of camaraderie.

She took a massive leap of faith at the beginning of the year to change from an LLC to a corporation, an employee-run company where she is the majority stockholder.

SECTION EIGHT: BOOSTER ROCKET ENGINE, ENGAGE

The lawyers and accountants were skeptical at first, but once it became employee owned and they saw the company's explosive growth the suits are now her most prominent evangelists. Everybody is thinking like an owner, and they have the tiger by the tail.

Her huddle is held online at midday to accommodate her employees in all four US time zones. They all laughed at her sleepy midnight demeanor from the night before, but she is amazed to see how well things work when they make decisions without running them by her first.

They are tough on each other in a good-natured way, when they add their critical numbers to the huddle board for Tracey to tabulate.

Beth's return flight is scheduled in two days, but a bunch of expats is heading down to the barrier reef in Australia for a snorkeling excursion. She hitches a ride with them. She will look at the dashboard after lunch.

What started as soft-launch to jettison herself from an Armored Guard service job into the B2C work of infidelity surveillances brought her to this dream life. She had a plan and no resistance to learning how to market and run it using best practices and taking full advantage of the Internet. She didn't stop there and took advantage of a growth opportunity which began as a weekend hobby, now turned into a gold mine.

Unfortunately, John had to close down International Missing Heir Finders, LLC. His youngest employee, who was listening politely during the huddles was now telling him the truth that John had been avoiding.

"You have to walk away while you still have some money on the table." The New York and New Jersey tracer said. "If you keep playing hands with this deck stacked against you, you will have nothing left."

He and John were stuck in bumper to bumper traffic coming back to Milford, Connecticut after racing to each surrogate court in four New York boroughs before closing time.

That afternoon, John had gotten bad news on two estates that were supposed to pay out that week. One became delayed when the judge gave yet another extension to the false heirs in the case to force IMHF to produce more evidence.

"This is how the good 'ole boys do it in Tennessee," John fumed to his lawyer.

The other case was worse. At the last minute, a federal tax lien was placed on the estate.

It seemed the decedent, an accountant herself, had not filed federal taxes for many years and the bulk of the estate would be eaten up by the lien. $175,000 net after the lawyer just evaporated, and they still had to pay him his 20K.

"You know what you are saying," John replied to his tracer.

"Yep."

SECTION EIGHT: BOOSTER ROCKET ENGINE, ENGAGE

They rode in silence for nearly twenty minutes before the tracer finally added, "We will survive, you have to think about yourself instead of finding a way to keep us working. If you said that you were going to keep trying to play, I'd say you were a gambling addict."

"You know I will have to lay you off," John said.

No employer likes to say those words ever, let alone a father to a son. It took much courage for John's son to deliver the bad news, but John had his listening ears on.

John had worked with a business coach from the Great Game of Business to create a dashboard for all the cases in the pipeline. The numbers were hard to tease out, but by going back to the beginning, they were able to create a living breathing document that told them some things in specific terms, and other things they could make reasonable assumptions on.

John no longer had competitive advantage in Connecticut, that much was for sure. The internet opened the doors where before they had to dig the files out of each probate court.

Searching for other jurisdictions around the country, where they could compete fairly against the entrenched missing heir competitors, proved difficult.

Most of the major metro areas, where the people with money resided, were shark tanks and IMHF were the guppies.

I have mentioned this phrase several times. I want to be fuzzy on purpose. I will not disparage a competitor's tactics without proof beyond a reasonable doubt. Yes, I am using a degree of evidence used in criminal cases.

As more courts went online, cases were made available to anybody with Internet access.

The market was flooded by competitors racing to the bottom

with lower and lower sign-up percentages. IMHF's thirty percent sign-up could not compete against others asking for nine percent.

John had been courted by a TV production company who filmed him in action finding and signing heirs. The "sizzle reel" failed to attract any Reality TV network. The instant fame and celebrity could not be mined for marketing gold.

In Connecticut, the cases closed in 11 months, from the time John found and signed heirs. The average time around the country was 22 months. The amount of money in the estate remained stable or increased before the final accounting was distributed.

Around the country, the original amount of the estate was drained by as much as 40% by the time all the payouts took place. Legal costs were triple for out of state attorneys.

The dashboard showed the numbers. The volatility of the market with its high-highs and low-lows could be assessed, and the assessment was not promising. That these two cases went bad were not entirely unexpected, but hastened the cash drain.

John met with each employee individually in the days leading to the next huddle at the Cracker Barrel.

At the huddle, John's eldest employee spoke up and said, "We could see the numbers as clearly as you. We were surprised that you didn't pull the plug sooner. We appreciate that you kept trying to find ways to keep it going. We all decided that we would keep doing our best until it was time to stop."

In the end, there was no finger-pointing or acrimony, and in December of 2011, International Missing Heir Finders held its last Holiday Party. It a meteoric rise and fall, for sure.

The unproven assumption that the early successes could be replicated around the country should have been proved (proof of concept) before making a significant investment of time, money, and personnel. IMHF could not break out of the atmosphere because of the drag of the external forces of the market and fell back to earth.

John would not be brutally honest with you if he told you that the lure of making a boatload of money was not a factor in going national.

Laying a six-figure check on the dinner table for the family to see, made payable to the company, was his way of validating to himself. To them, he was using his brains to the best of his ability. He thought he found a way to make the most money for his work-time.

Part of it was the timing of being at the right place at the right time with a curiosity of how to harvest the cases faster than his competitors.

Part of it was the drive to create a company he could sell to his employees, which had been his original goal with Independent Special Investigations, LLC.

Part of it came from a need to retire early and do something else in his second career, What AARP called an "Encore Career."

Did he not slow down at caution signals? Did he cruise through a few stop signs while humming a jaunty tune? Yes, he did, and yes, he was handed another character-building experience.

Endings Are Beginnings

With the money left on the table from IMHF, I was able to launch Elm City Detectives with the idea that I would turn off the lights and shut the door behind me when I was ready to ride off into the sunset for that encore career. I was working for Personal Injury Attorneys and Criminal Defense attorneys and began specializing in Exoneration cases. My son went to work with the soon-to-be owner of a Surveillance company in New York as his operations manager.

THE RESULTS

When that company was abruptly sold out from underneath them, and his position became redundant, we begin talking about forming Hoda Investigations, LLC, a P2P company serving Connecticut Trial Attorneys and Family Attorneys.

I work with my son, and we have a replicable and scalable marketing plan. We bill on the high end, even for the Northeast, and offer desirable flat rates to our clients. Our customers appreciate the value we bring to every case. I do my own bookkeeping and meet with my accountant quarterly to make sure that we are on target for our federal and state tax estimates. ·

We are proof that a solo with a part-timer or two most-timers can make the $1,000 every working day. It requires a full pipeline of cases lined up at least 10 working days out, and a replicable and scalable marketing plan that gets worked on at least 5 hours a week. Getting testimonials and referrals are our lifeblood, and we make sure to mark our territory at all the lawyer events.

I'm sitting in my favorite Starbucks on a Saturday afternoon as I finish this rough draft. My son, John, is doing much of the heavy lifting these days, but the old guy still goes out with the young gun every so often on a few select Innocence cases.

Our dashboard is a flip chart in the office where we measure how much we bill each week, how that compares with our goal and the variance. Besides an assignment log kept in Google Sheets, we show a color-coded stick count of how many and what type of cases we receive each week on the flip chart. We track the number of cold calls, contacts, appointments, and first-time customers. It's not crude, it's just not pretty, and it stares us in the face every working day. We do a cash flow snapshot twice a month. Cash is king. I haven't run out in 84 quarters, and I am not about to break that streak.

It has become a lifestyle business, one that my son will eventually take over. We are working on the succession plan. He has met

SECTION EIGHT: BOOSTER ROCKET ENGINE, ENGAGE

with and has worked for most of the customers. By the time this book is published, the website will be refreshed to really focus on the testimonials so crucial to a P2P company.

Twenty-one years ago, when I started my journey, I didn't know I would teach my son the business and pass on my skills and the company to him. Maybe there is a reason for everything.

Would I have liked to build ISI, or IMHF, to sell to my employees? The answer is yes, but I would never have learned the lessons that are so valuable to me and hopefully to you.

If I never ventured out of the insurance fraud investigation, I would never have learned about Criminal Defense or Forensic Genealogy. If everything went perfectly from the beginning, I would never have felt enough pain to change and grow.

CONCLUSION

Boosting your business to make $1,000 every working day is neither simple nor easy. The journey on your own path will begin at a different place, but some advice can apply to everyone along the way.

- Add planning time to your workday. Schedule it no differently than field appointments.

- Give, but don't abandon, some of your "job function" hats to other people to wear and automate as many repetitive functions as you can.

- Increase marketing time. Don't get lured into working cases all the time at the expense of growing your pipeline.

- The sooner you can share or shed the "fulfillment" portion of your time, the sooner you can start gaining altitude in your boost phase.

- Test and measure your marketing campaigns until you have a replicable and scalable method to attract your target audience. This can be as little as 5 hours a week and doesn't have to look like Mt. Everest to you. It is one step at a time, just like your boost plans.

SECTION EIGHT: BOOSTER ROCKET ENGINE, ENGAGE

- Fill your work pipeline out at least 7-10 working days. Plan the work and work the plan.
- Raise rates, create new offerings, and fire your worst customers.
- Be the go-to PI either for your territory or for your specialty.
- Refer cases to other PIs for a referral commission. Tout the services of your affiliates on your website.
- If you are not a world-renown expert or highly sought specialist, determine what you can do to upgrade your skill sets to be able to charge more for your time
- For most Private Investigations owners, going deeper into a market–and not wider–allows for better focus and immunity from competition.
- Track your progress. "That what gets measured, gets done," says Peter Drucker, Management Guru.
- Find a coach or others to help you elevate your game. This lowers the fear-based self-imposed obstacles in your path. Accountability is an essential component of your motivation.
- Build HR systems to recruit, hire, train, supervise, and appraise the people you need to boost your business into orbit. Using the checklists here are just the beginning.
- Creating a three-ring binder, literally or digitally, is an essential step if you plan to off-load any of your job functions to employees.
- "You gotta wanna." The good folks at the Great Game of Business coined this phrase.

Now, take out a clean sheet of paper, sit down with your favorite beverage, and get started.

"Ain't nothing to it, but to do it," an old homicide detective once told me.

CONCLUSION

NEED MORE HELP?

If you are launching your business soon and have questions or you are having trouble getting your company off the ground, I am available for a FREE 30-minute consultation. Please go to the contact form at www.ThePICoach.com and schedule a phone call with me. It may be an easy fix.

Also

I only coach PIs and limit my time to just eight individual sessions a week so that I can concentrate on helping each client reach their goals and achieve a life/work balance. Schedule a time today.

*To all my teachers, mentors and coaches:
You all helped shape my character, drive, and desire
to achieve success in whatever I attempted.*

ABOUT JOHN A. HODA, CLI, CFE

John A. Hoda is a licensed private investigator, blogger, and podcaster. He coaches other PIs how to be successful at **ThePICoach.com**

He graduated in 1975 with a B.S. in Criminology from Indiana University of Pennsylvania.

He is a former police officer, insurance fraud investigator, and has run several PI businesses over three decades.

He has written numerous articles for PI Magazine and is the creator of the DVD: *The Ultimate Guide to Taking Statements*. His cases have headlined in the Philadelphia Inquirer and the New Haven Register. He sat on the board of the National Association of Legal Investigators and the CT Assoc of Licensed Private Investigators. He is a Certified Legal Investigator and a Certified Fraud Examiner.

SECTION EIGHT: BOOSTER ROCKET ENGINE, ENGAGE

John also writes fiction and has been a lifetime athlete playing club soccer and playing/coaching semi-professional football.

His podcast audience at My Favorite Detective Stories is growing every day. John interviews past and present investigators about their specialties and teases out what it takes to make for a successful investigation. The entire podcast catalog can be found at **JohnHoda.com**

OTHER BOOKS BY JOHN A. HODA

Get your FREE *Mugshots: My Favorite Detective Stories* downloaded in your favorite format right to your inbox by going to **JohnHoda.com**.

Come ride around the country with veteran investigator John A. Hoda as he searches for the truth. He has selected great stories from a forty-plus year career and keeps serving them up like free refills at the all-night diner.

Non-Fiction

How to Launch Your Private Investigation Business: 90 days to Lift Off!

How to Market Your Private Investigation Business: Less Than 5 Hours a Week, Really!

How to Boost Your Private Investigation Business: Make $1,000 every Working Day!

SECTION EIGHT: BOOSTER ROCKET ENGINE, ENGAGE

Fiction

Odessa on the Delaware: Introducing Marsha O'Shea

A Crime Thriller with a mystery twist set in Philadelphia pitting a Russian mob enforcer against a homeless Marine Corp veteran. FBI Agent Marsha O'Shea is drawn into the case with a secret pushing her to follow the clues, only to uncover a greater secret that may get her killed in the final showdown.

Phantasy Baseball: It's About A Second Chance.

A thirty-nine-year-old little league coach discovers he has a magical pitch and gets a one in a million chance to try out for his beloved Philadelphia Phillies. He is unprepared for the roller-coaster magic-carpet ride in the Big Leagues.

ACKNOWLEDGMENTS

Rekka Jay for Cover Design, Illustrations, Editing, Formatting, Layout, Patience and Forgiveness.

My advanced copy readers who saved my butt countless times: Luis Reyes, Ron Getner, Rich Robertson, Brandon Perron, Cynthia Hetherington, Brian Ritucci, Jayne McElfresh, Lisa Garcia, Kate Minchin, Burt Hodge, Tony Raymond, Paul Rubin

The **Written Word-Milford Writers Group** for their support and encouragement.

Thanks to all.

www.ingramcontent.com/pod-product-compliance
Lightning Source LLC
Chambersburg PA
CBHW022102290426
44112CB00008B/524